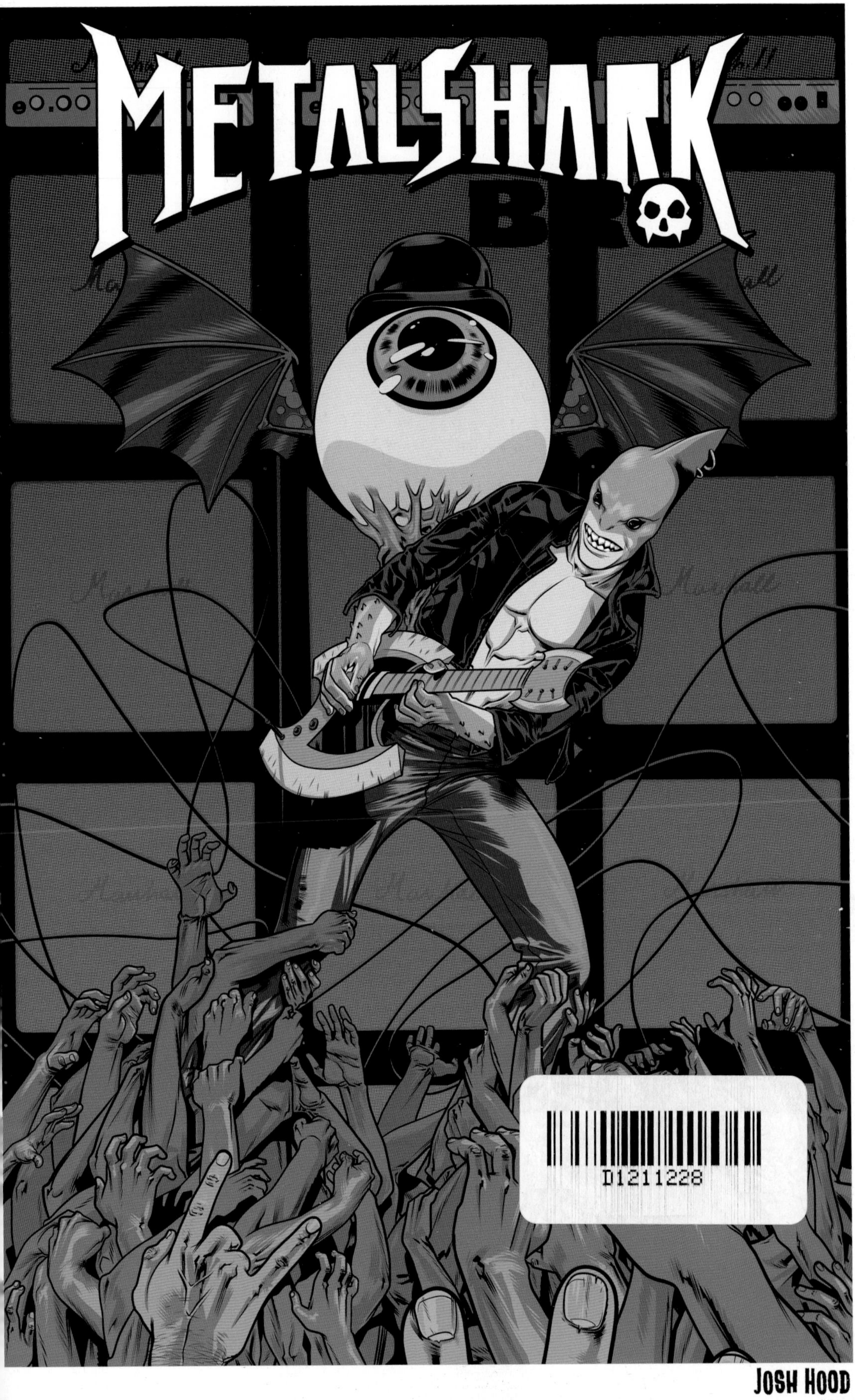
METALSHARK BRO

JOSH HOOD

METALSHARK BRO

CREATED BY BOB FRANTZ, KEVIN CUFFE, AND WALTER OSTLIE

ARTIST   - WALTER OSTLIE

WRITERS   - BOB FRANTZ AND KEVIN CUFFE

EDITOR &
LETTERER   - CHAS! PANGBURN

SOCIALS -
@WALTEROSTLIE - TWITCH, YOUTUBE, INSTAGRAM, TWITTER - WALTEROSTLIE@GMAIL.COM
@KEVIN_CUFFE - TWITTER
@BFRANTZ19 - TWITTER - METALSHARKBRO@GMAIL.COM
@CHASEXCLAMATION - TWITTER

ADDITIONAL TRADE PRODUCTION - JOEL RODRIGUEZ

SCOUT COMICS

Brendan Deneen, *CEO*
James Pruett, *CCO*
Tennessee Edwards, *CSO*
James Haick III, *President*

Don Handfield, *CMO*
David Byrne, *Co-Publisher*
Charlie Stickney, *Co-Publish*
Joel Rodriguez, *Head of Desi*

FB/TW/IG:
@Scoutcomics

LEARN MORE AT:
www.scoutcomics.com

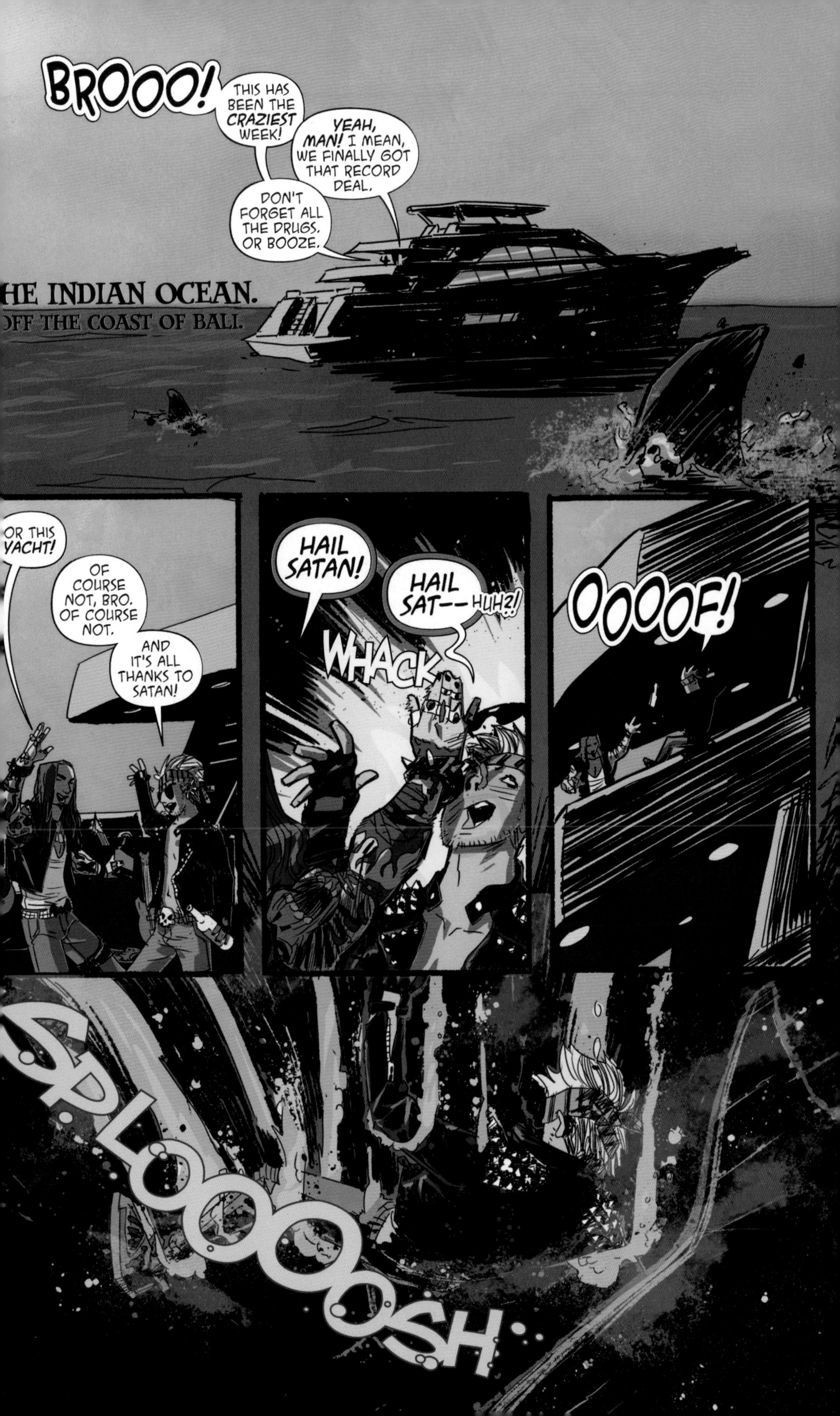
BROOO!
THIS HAS BEEN THE *CRAZIEST* WEEK!
YEAH, MAN! I MEAN, WE FINALLY GOT THAT RECORD DEAL.
DON'T FORGET ALL THE DRUGS, OR BOOZE.
HE INDIAN OCEAN.
OFF THE COAST OF BALI.
OR THIS *YACHT!*
OF COURSE NOT, BRO. OF COURSE NOT.
AND IT'S ALL THANKS TO SATAN!
HAIL SATAN!
HAIL SAT-- HUH?!
WHACK
OOOOF!
SPLOOOOSH

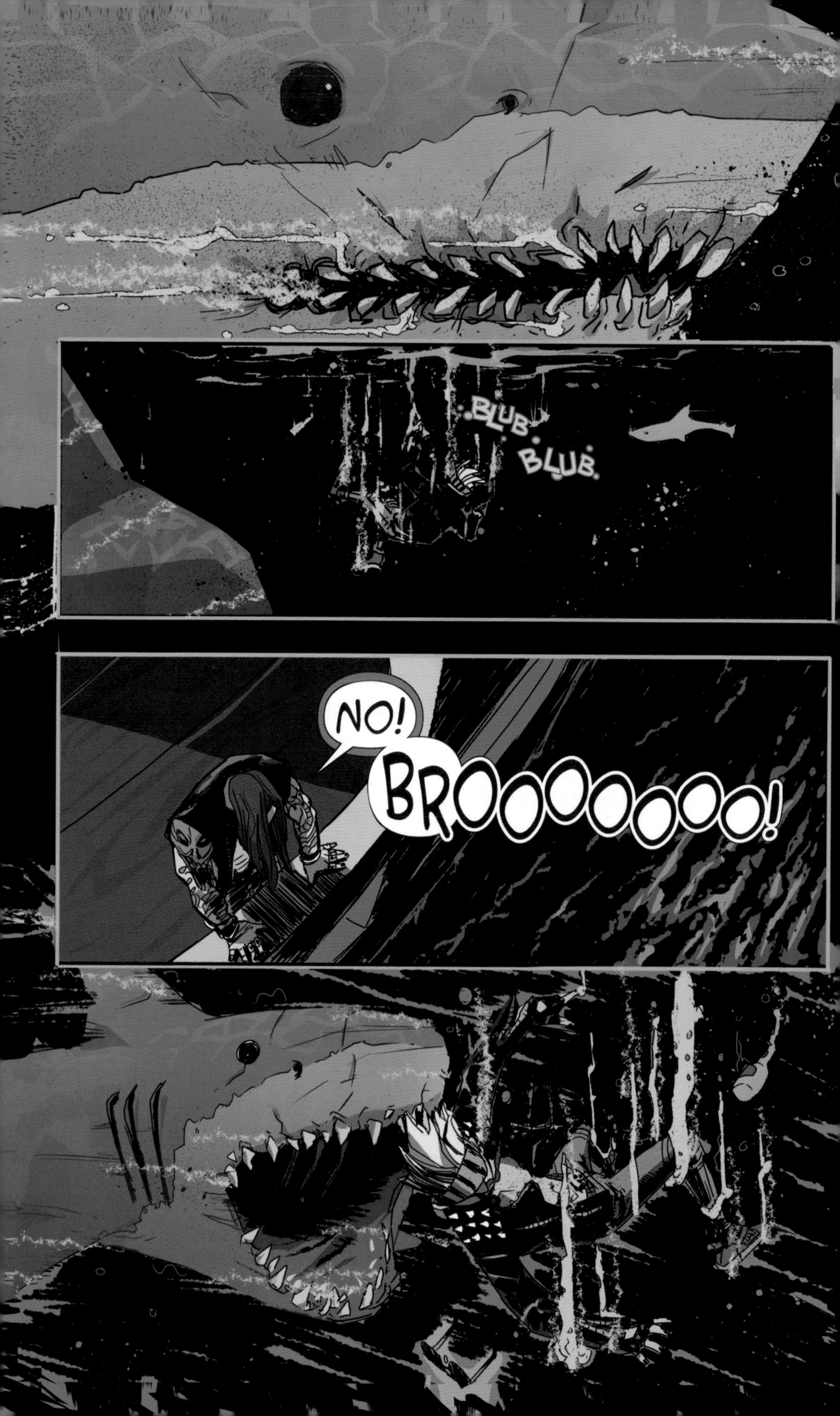
BLUB. BLUB.
NO!
BROOOOOOOO!

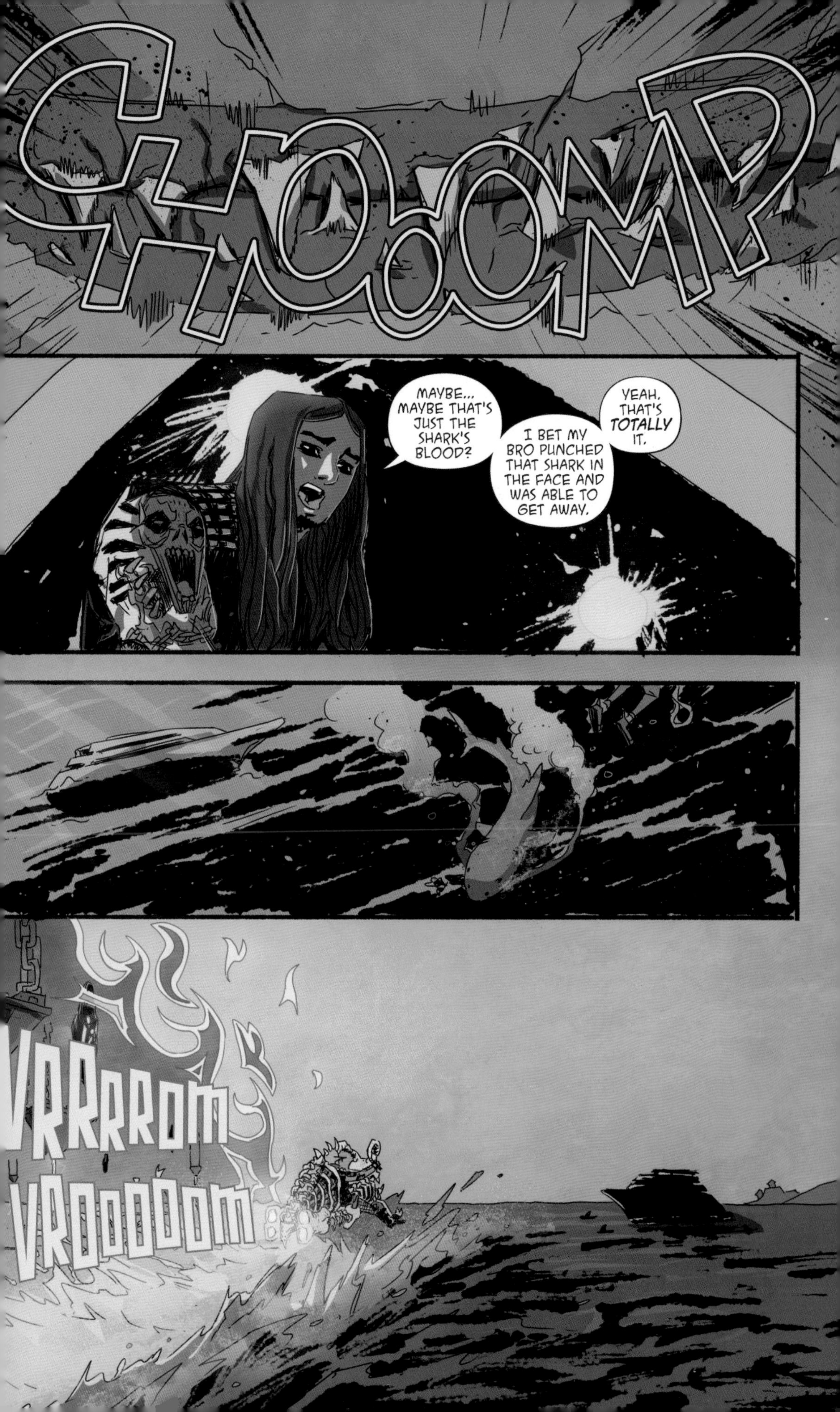
CHOMP
CHOOOMP
MAYBE... MAYBE THAT'S JUST THE SHARK'S BLOOD?
I BET MY BRO PUNCHED THAT SHARK IN THE FACE AND WAS ABLE TO GET AWAY.
YEAH, THAT'S *TOTALLY* IT.
VRRRROM
VROOOOOM

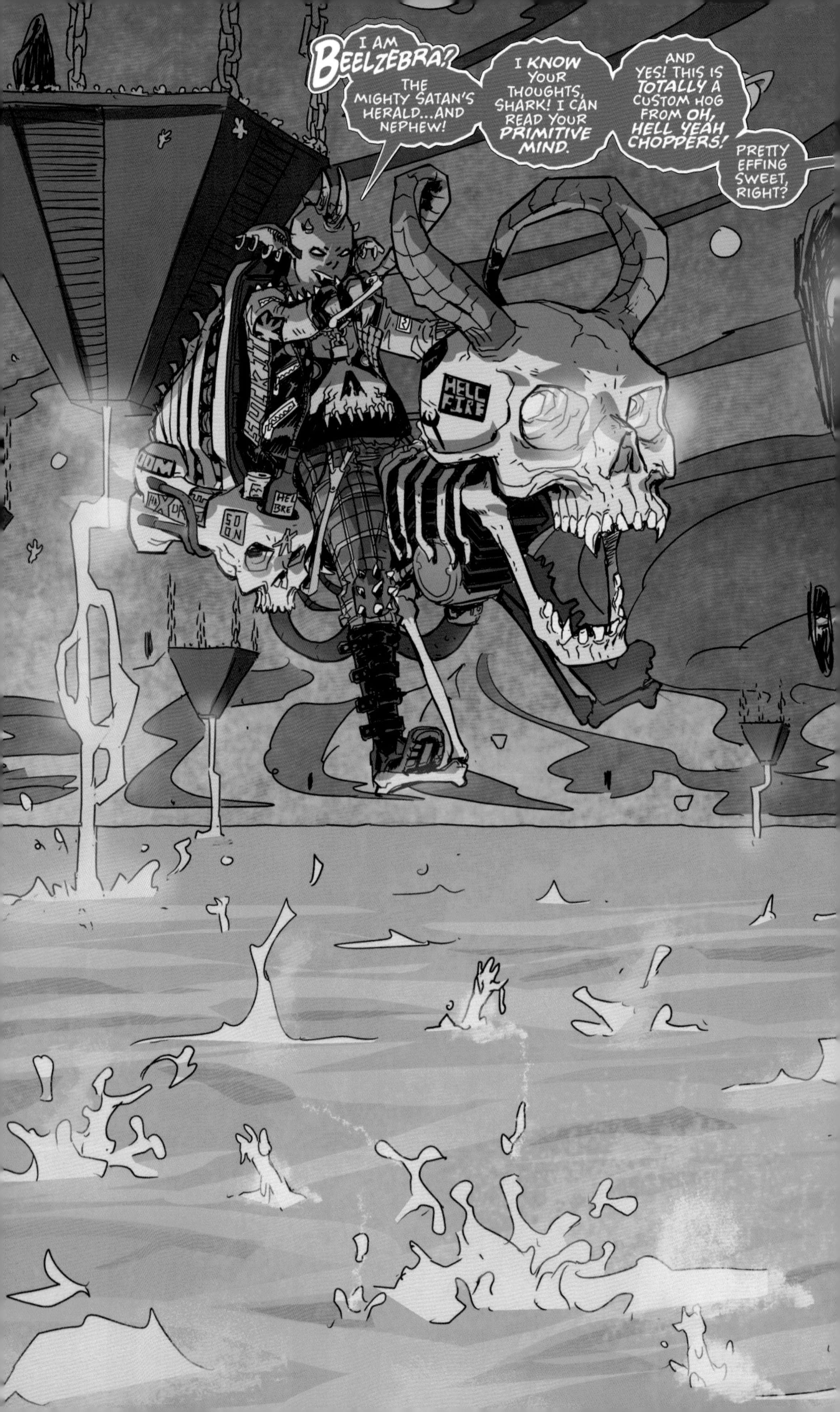
I AM BEELZEBRA?
THE MIGHTY SATAN'S HERALD...AND NEPHEW!
I KNOW YOUR THOUGHTS, SHARK! I CAN READ YOUR PRIMITIVE MIND.
AND YES! THIS IS TOTALLY A CUSTOM HOG FROM OH, HELL YEAH CHOPPERS!
PRETTY EFFING SWEET, RIGHT?
HELL FIRE

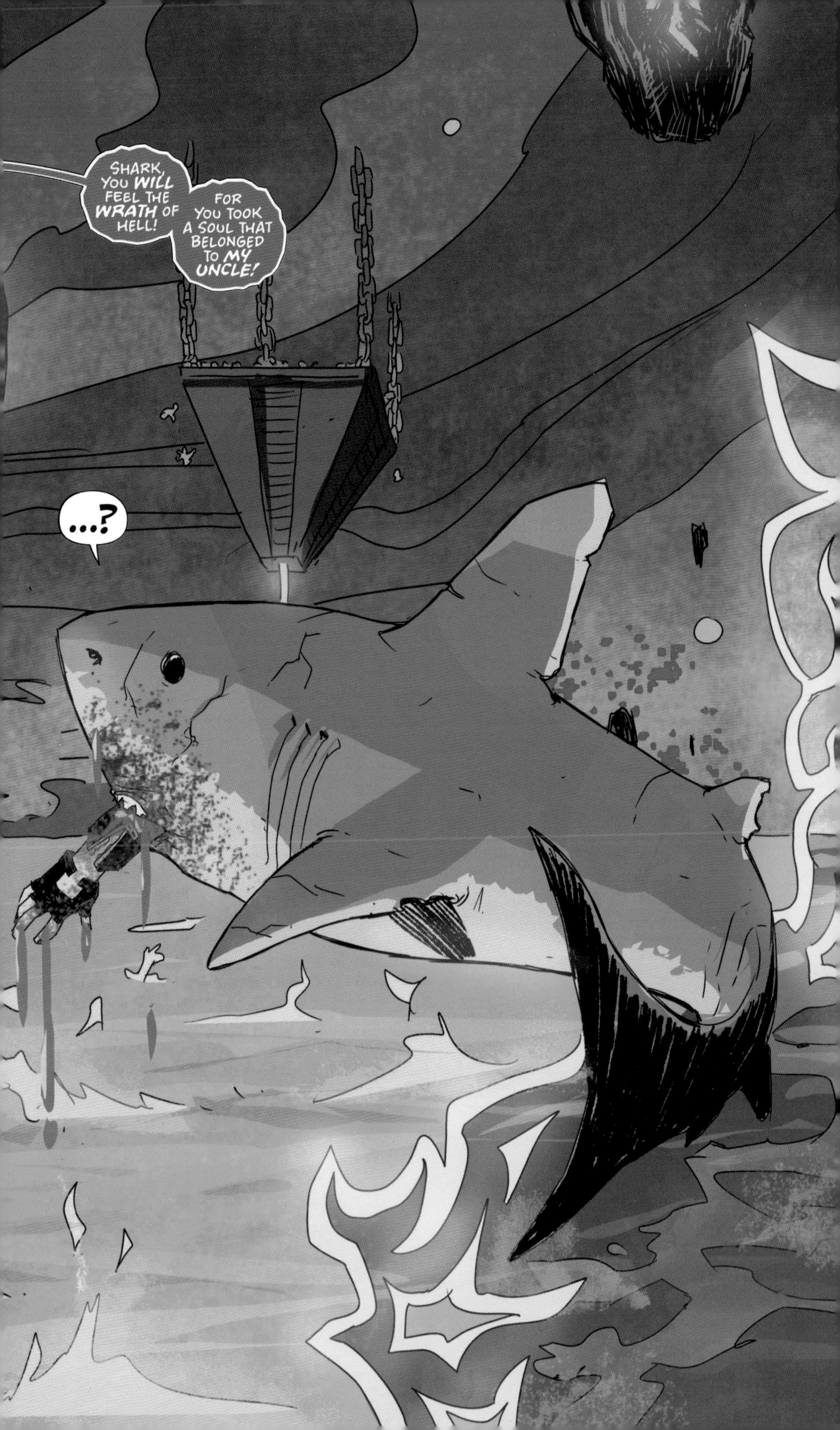
SHARK, YOU WILL FEEL THE WRATH OF HELL!
FOR YOU TOOK A SOUL THAT BELONGED TO MY UNCLE!
...?

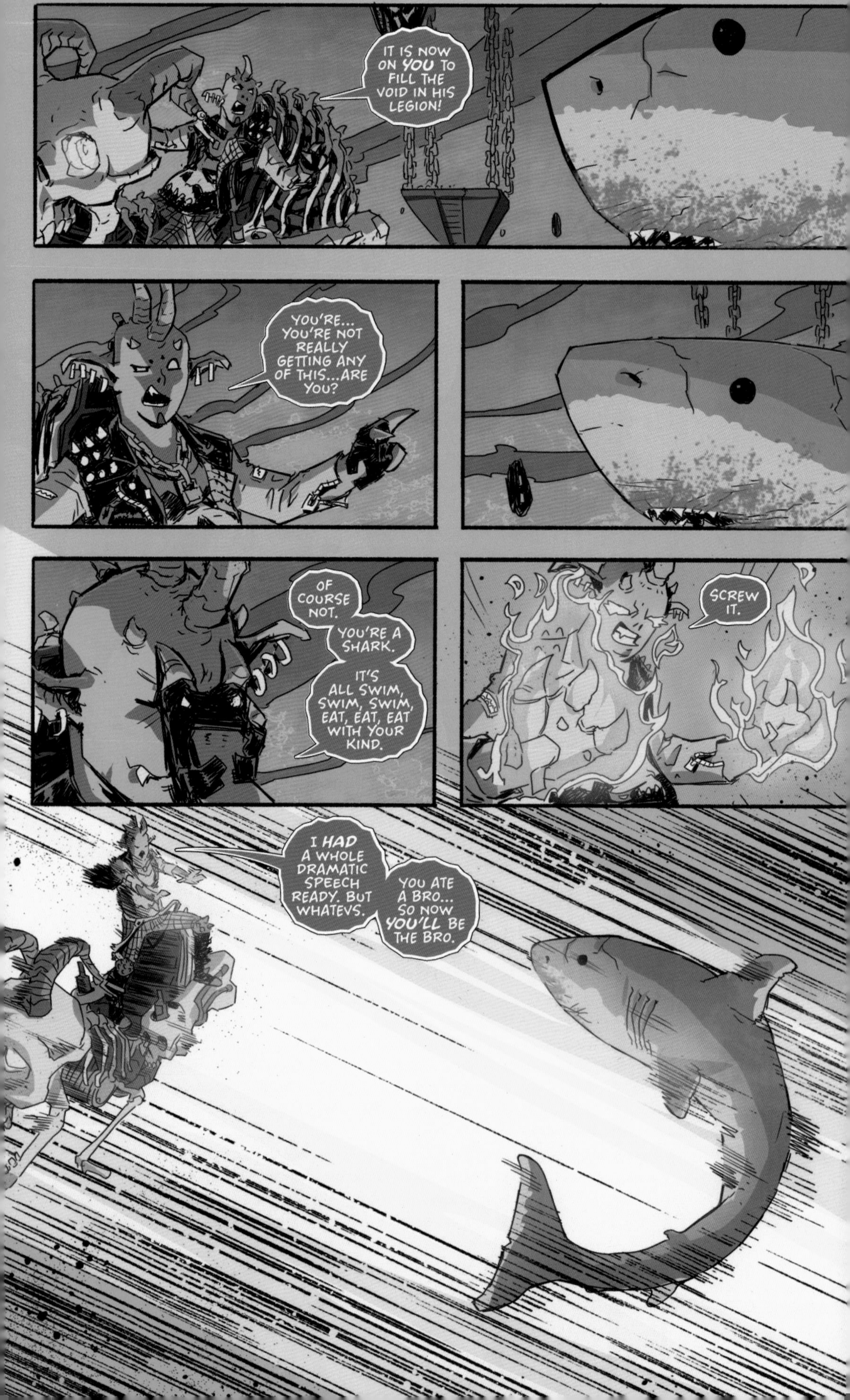

IT IS NOW ON *YOU* TO FILL THE VOID IN HIS LEGION!
YOU'RE... YOU'RE NOT REALLY GETTING ANY OF THIS...ARE YOU?
OF COURSE NOT.
YOU'RE A SHARK.
IT'S ALL SWIM, SWIM, SWIM, EAT, EAT, EAT WITH YOUR KIND.
SCREW IT.
I *HAD* A WHOLE DRAMATIC SPEECH READY. BUT WHATEVS.
YOU ATE A BRO... SO NOW *YOU'LL* BE THE BRO.

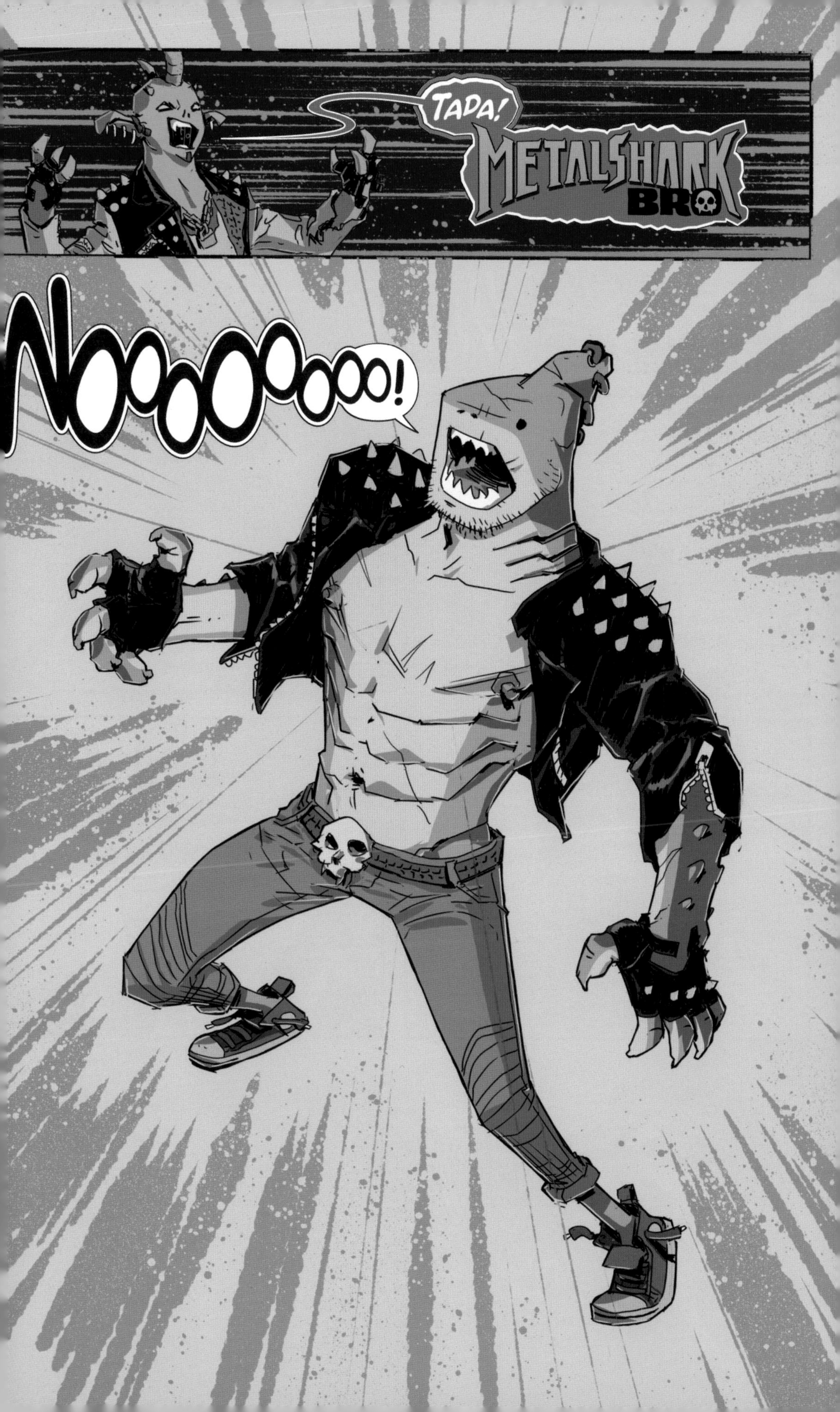
TADA!
METALSHARK BRO
NOOOOOOOO!

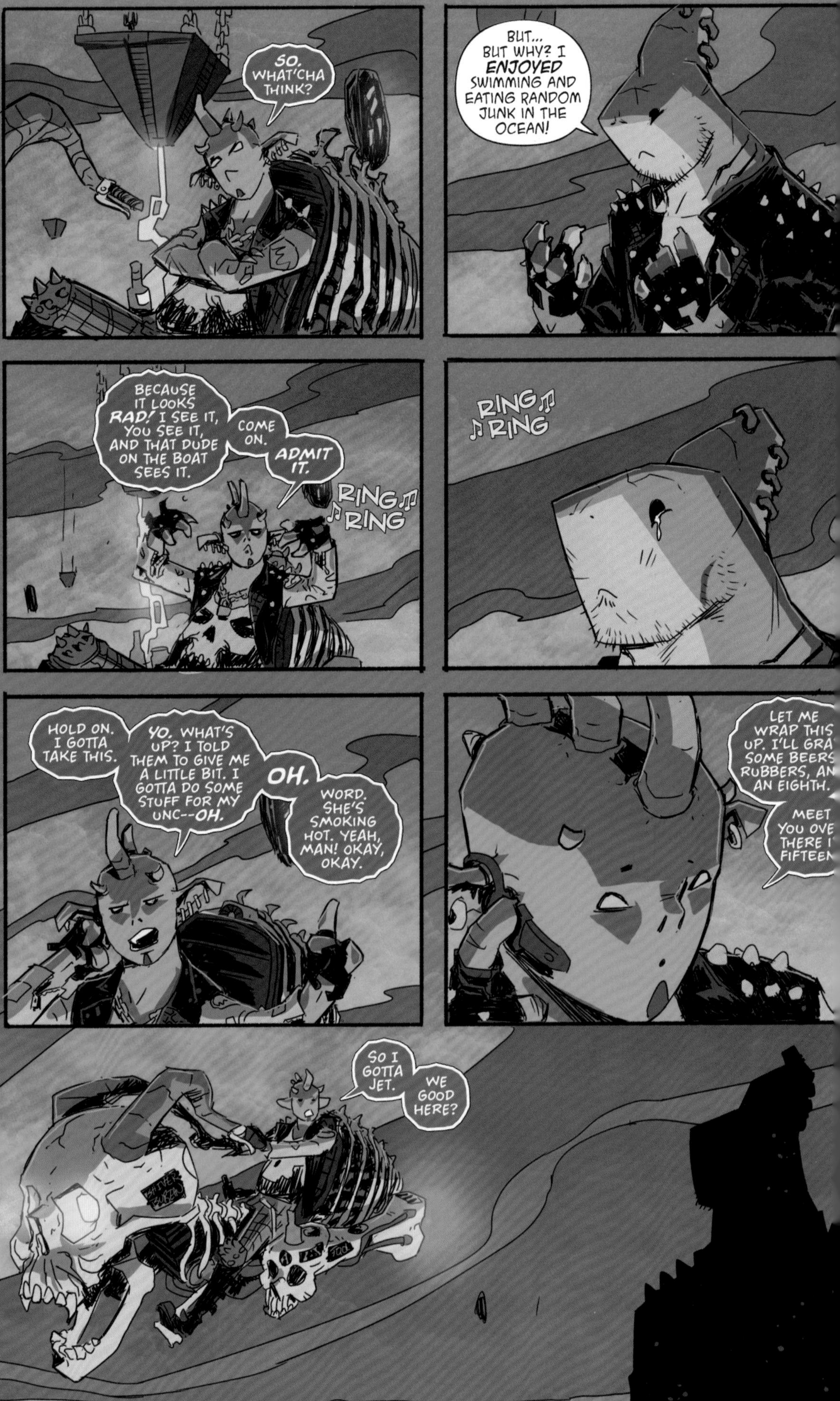

SO, WHAT'CHA THINK?
BUT... BUT WHY? I ENJOYED SWIMMING AND EATING RANDOM JUNK IN THE OCEAN!
BECAUSE IT LOOKS RAD! I SEE IT, YOU SEE IT, AND THAT DUDE ON THE BOAT SEES IT.
COME ON.
ADMIT IT.
RING RING
RING RING
HOLD ON. I GOTTA TAKE THIS.
YO. WHAT'S UP? I TOLD THEM TO GIVE ME A LITTLE BIT. I GOTTA DO SOME STUFF FOR MY UNC--OH.
OH.
WORD. SHE'S SMOKING HOT. YEAH, MAN! OKAY, OKAY.
LET ME WRAP THIS UP. I'LL GRA SOME BEERS RUBBERS, AN AN EIGHTH.
MEET YOU OVE THERE I FIFTEEN
SO I GOTTA JET.
WE GOOD HERE?

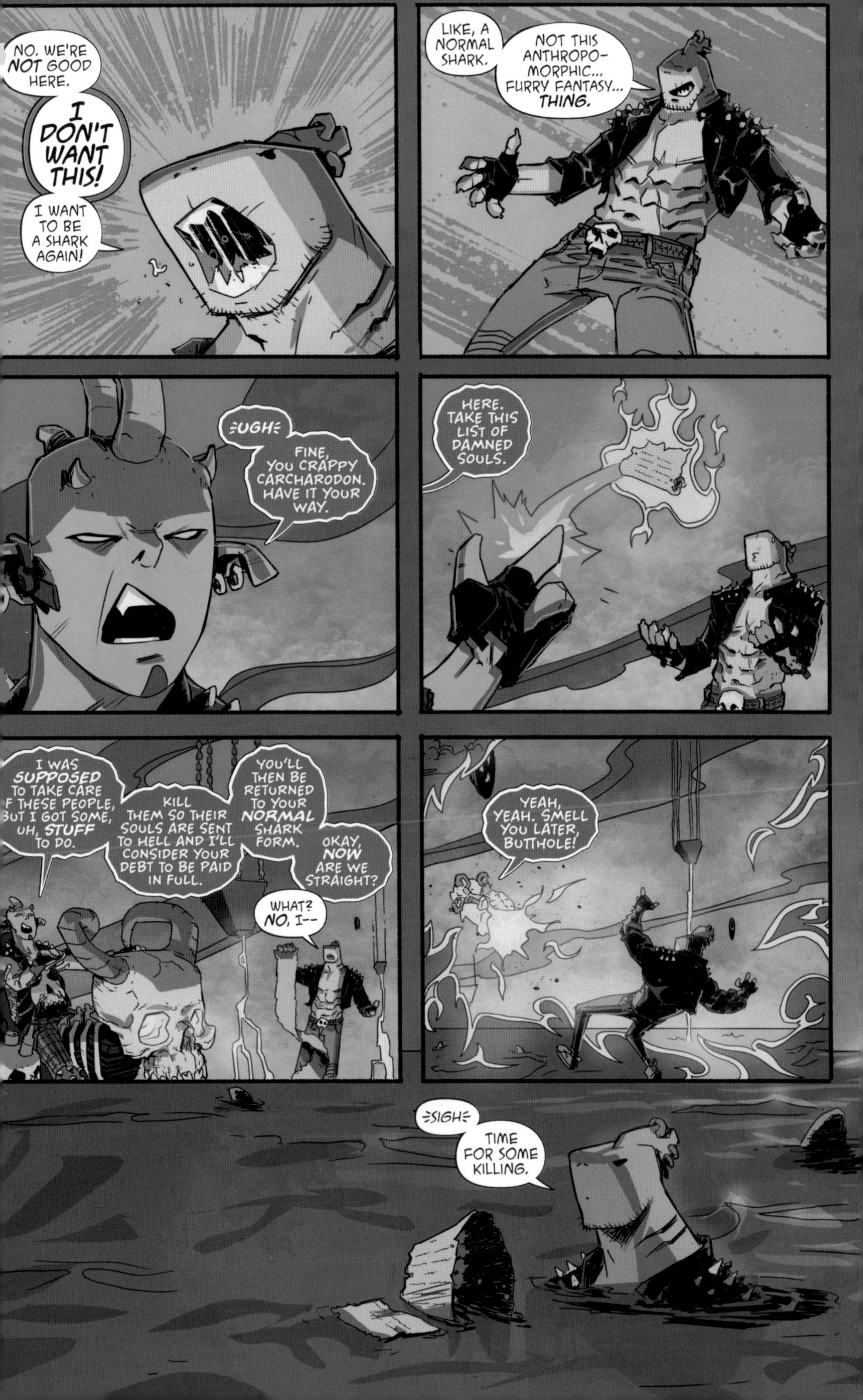
NO, WE'RE NOT GOOD HERE.
I DON'T WANT THIS!
I WANT TO BE A SHARK AGAIN!
LIKE, A NORMAL SHARK.
NOT THIS ANTHROPO-MORPHIC... FURRY FANTASY... THING.
UGH
FINE, YOU CRAPPY CARCHARODON. HAVE IT YOUR WAY.
HERE. TAKE THIS LIST OF DAMNED SOULS.
I WAS SUPPOSED TO TAKE CARE OF THESE PEOPLE, BUT I GOT SOME, UH, STUFF TO DO.
KILL THEM SO THEIR SOULS ARE SENT TO HELL AND I'LL CONSIDER YOUR DEBT TO BE PAID IN FULL.
YOU'LL THEN BE RETURNED TO YOUR NORMAL SHARK FORM.
OKAY, NOW ARE WE STRAIGHT?
WHAT? NO, I--
YEAH, YEAH. SMELL YOU LATER, BUTTHOLE!
SIGH
TIME FOR SOME KILLING.

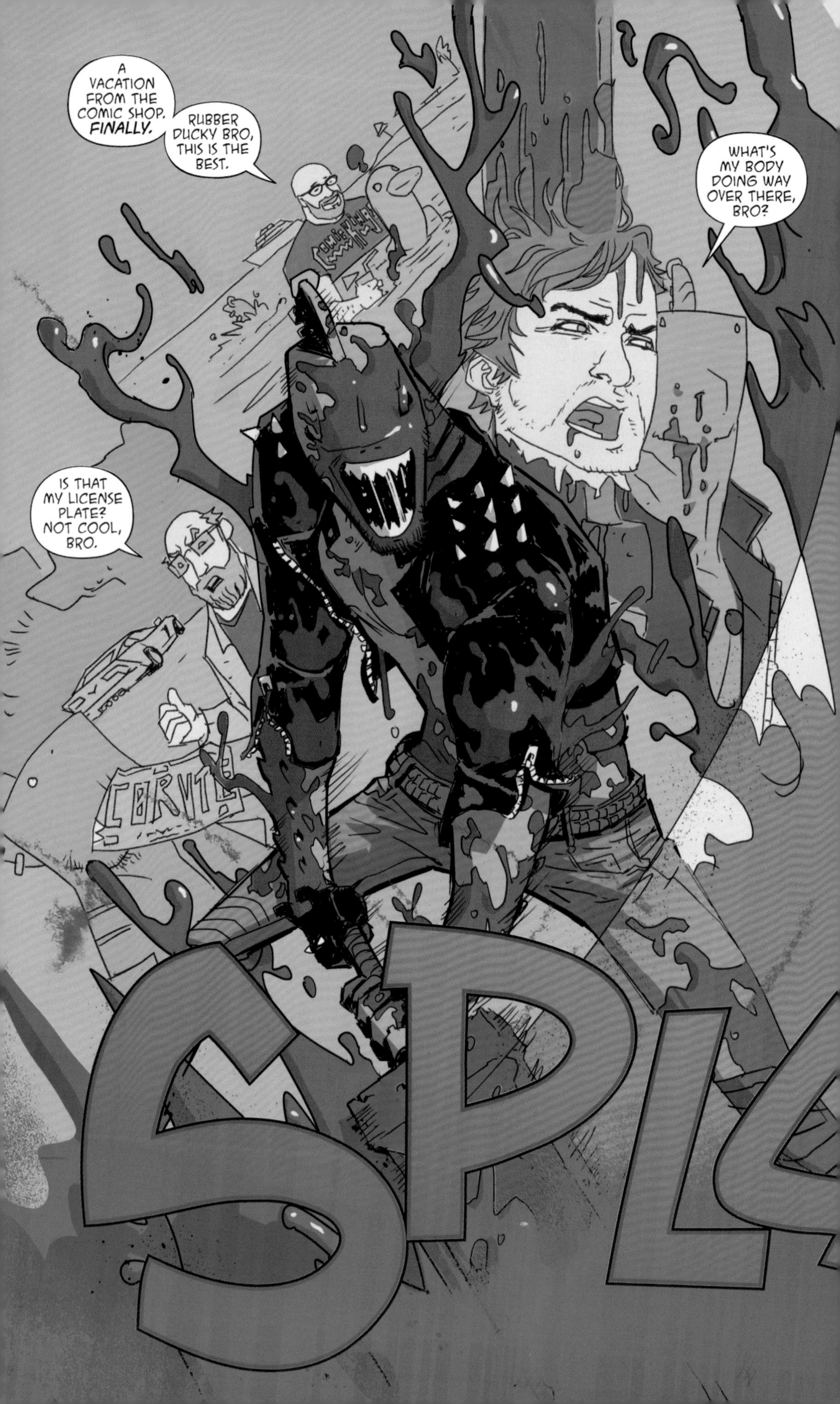
A VACATION FROM THE COMIC SHOP. *FINALLY.*
RUBBER DUCKY BRO, THIS IS THE BEST.
WHAT'S MY BODY DOING WAY OVER THERE, BRO?
IS THAT MY LICENSE PLATE? NOT COOL, BRO.
CORVTE
SPLA

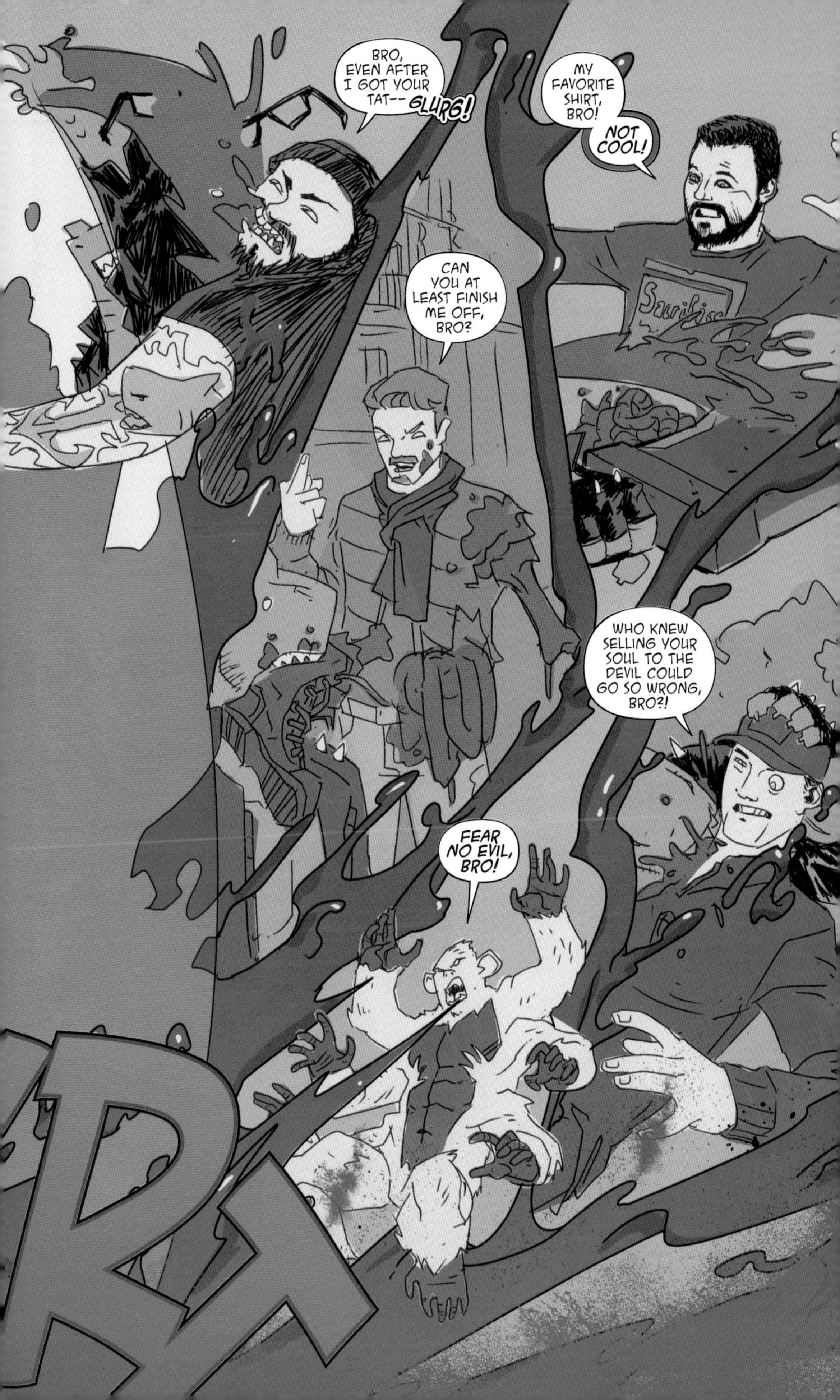
BRO, EVEN AFTER I GOT YOUR TAT-- GLURG!
MY FAVORITE SHIRT, BRO!
NOT COOL!
CAN YOU AT LEAST FINISH ME OFF, BRO?
WHO KNEW SELLING YOUR SOUL TO THE DEVIL COULD GO SO WRONG, BRO?!
FEAR NO EVIL, BRO!

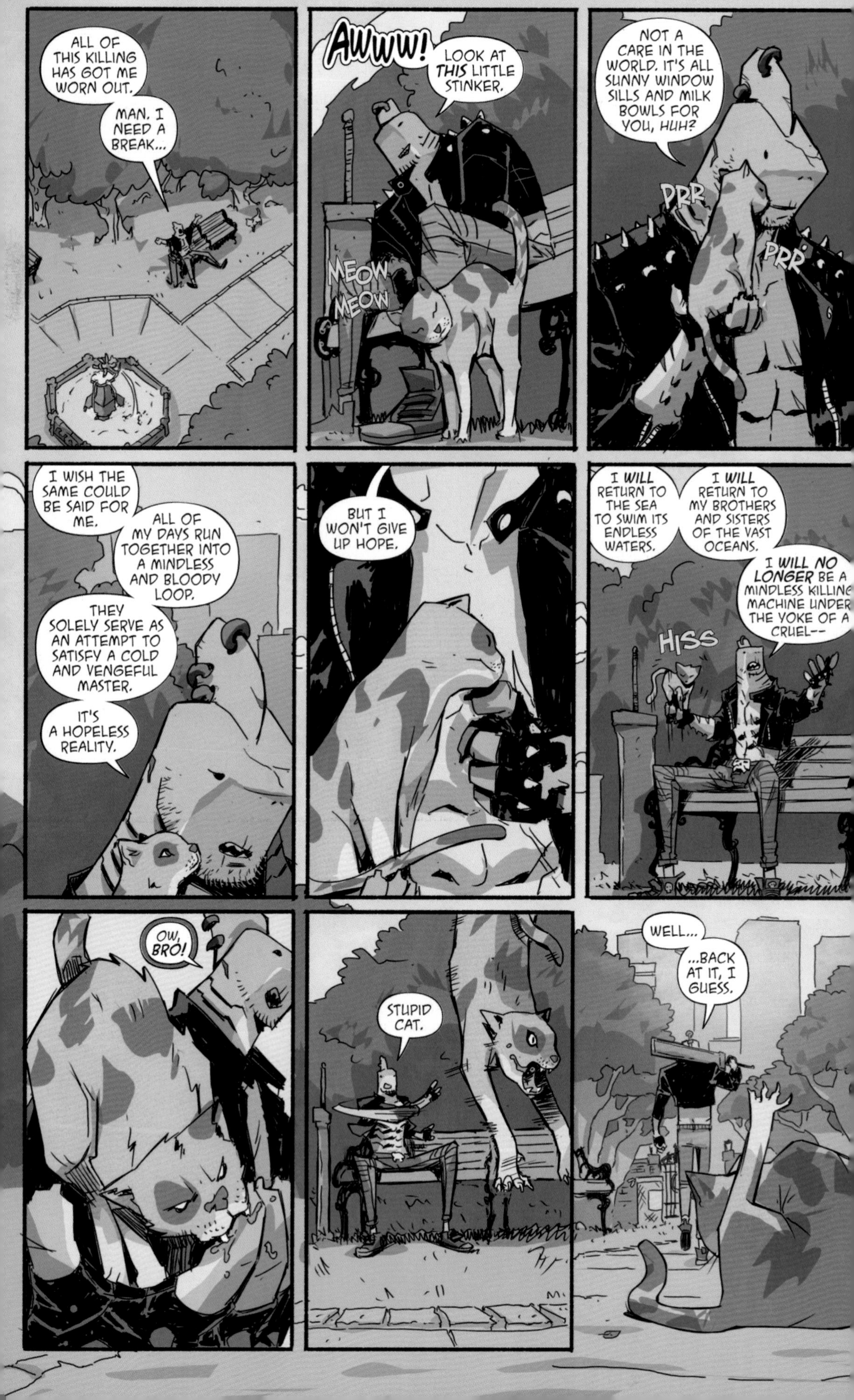
ALL OF THIS KILLING HAS GOT ME WORN OUT.
MAN. I NEED A BREAK...
AWWW!
LOOK AT THIS LITTLE STINKER.
MEOW MEOW
NOT A CARE IN THE WORLD. IT'S ALL SUNNY WINDOW SILLS AND MILK BOWLS FOR YOU, HUH?
PRR
PRR
I WISH THE SAME COULD BE SAID FOR ME.
ALL OF MY DAYS RUN TOGETHER INTO A MINDLESS AND BLOODY LOOP.
THEY SOLELY SERVE AS AN ATTEMPT TO SATISFY A COLD AND VENGEFUL MASTER.
IT'S A HOPELESS REALITY.
BUT I WON'T GIVE UP HOPE.
I WILL RETURN TO THE SEA TO SWIM ITS ENDLESS WATERS.
I WILL RETURN TO MY BROTHERS AND SISTERS OF THE VAST OCEANS.
I WILL NO LONGER BE A MINDLESS KILLING MACHINE UNDER THE YOKE OF A CRUEL--
HISS
OW, BRO!
STUPID CAT.
WELL...
...BACK AT IT, I GUESS.

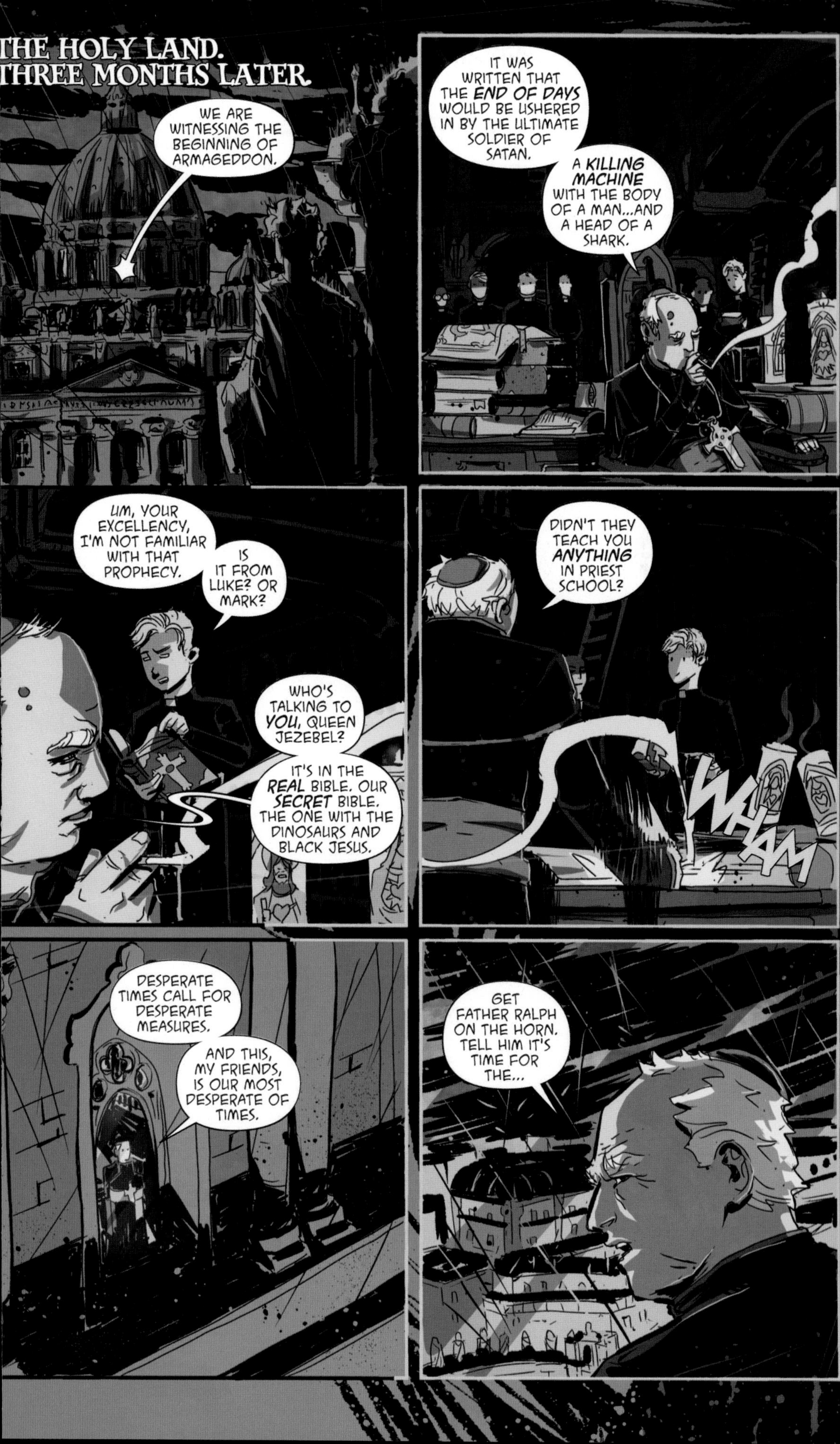
THE HOLY LAND. THREE MONTHS LATER.
WE ARE WITNESSING THE BEGINNING OF ARMAGEDDON.
IT WAS WRITTEN THAT THE END OF DAYS WOULD BE USHERED IN BY THE ULTIMATE SOLDIER OF SATAN.
A KILLING MACHINE WITH THE BODY OF A MAN...AND A HEAD OF A SHARK.
UM, YOUR EXCELLENCY, I'M NOT FAMILIAR WITH THAT PROPHECY.
IS IT FROM LUKE? OR MARK?
WHO'S TALKING TO YOU, QUEEN JEZEBEL?
IT'S IN THE REAL BIBLE. OUR SECRET BIBLE. THE ONE WITH THE DINOSAURS AND BLACK JESUS.
DIDN'T THEY TEACH YOU ANYTHING IN PRIEST SCHOOL?
WHAM
DESPERATE TIMES CALL FOR DESPERATE MEASURES.
AND THIS, MY FRIENDS, IS OUR MOST DESPERATE OF TIMES.
GET FATHER RALPH ON THE HORN. TELL HIM IT'S TIME FOR THE...

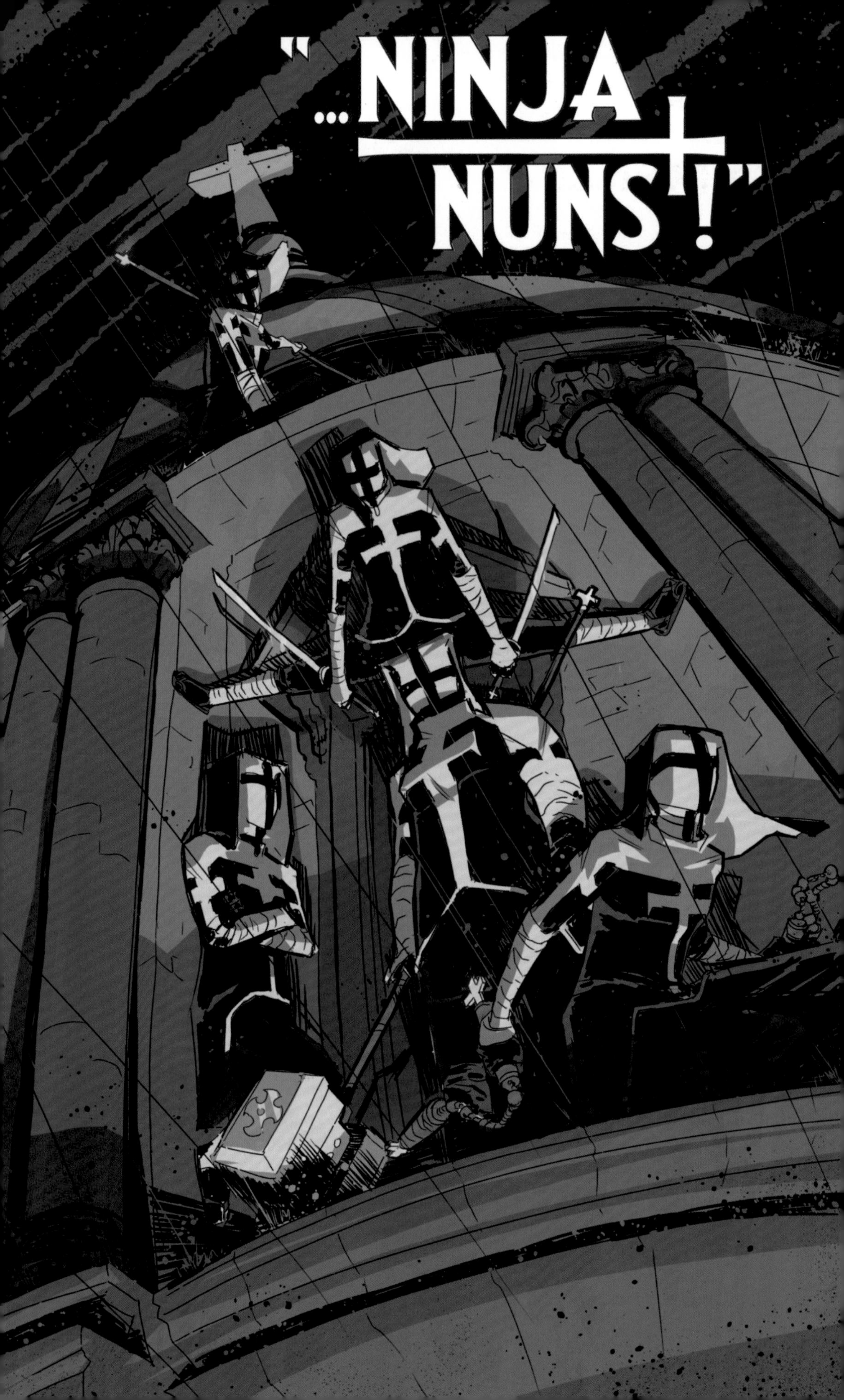
"...NINJA NUNS!"

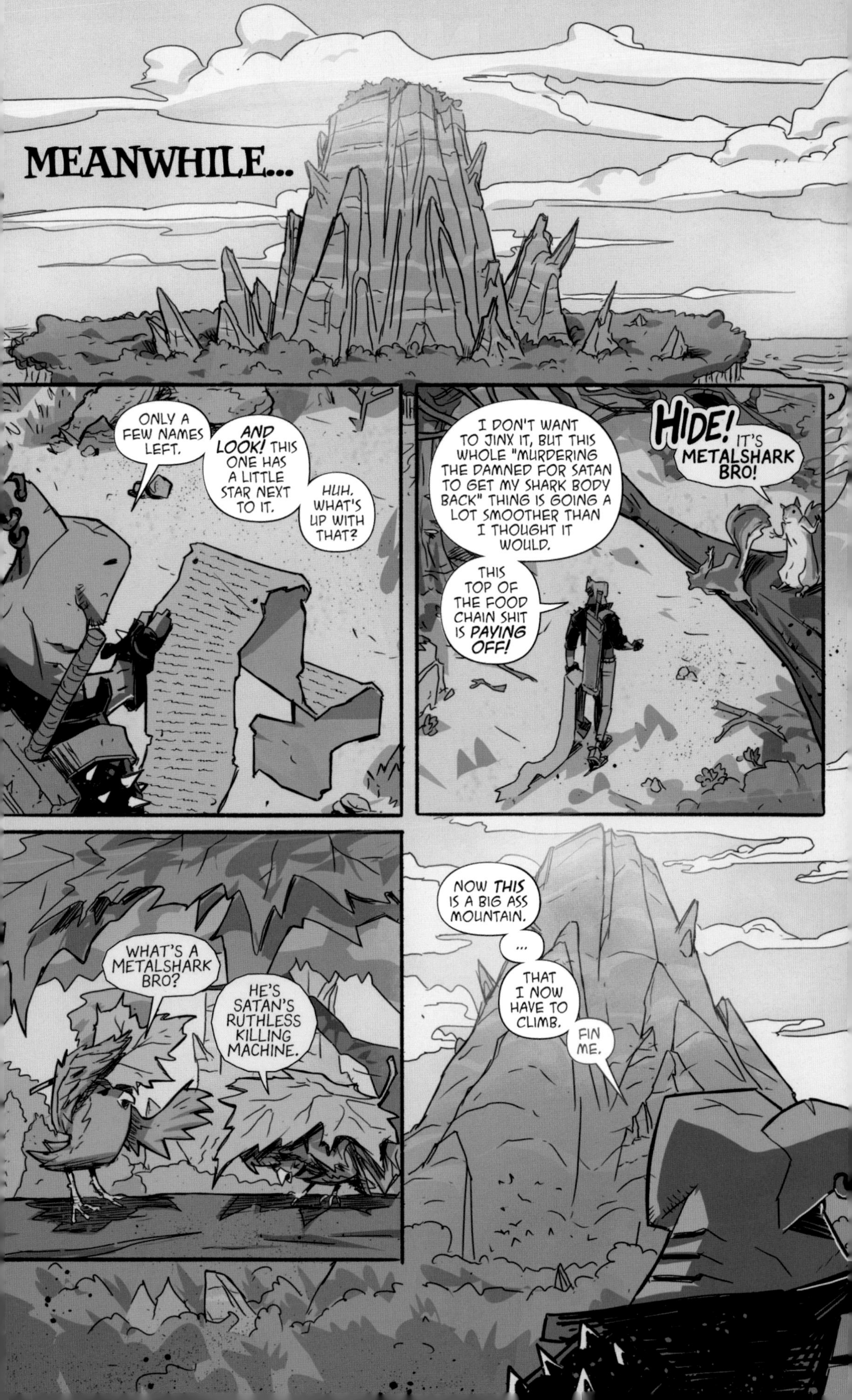
MEANWHILE...
ONLY A FEW NAMES LEFT.
AND LOOK! THIS ONE HAS A LITTLE STAR NEXT TO IT.
HUH. WHAT'S UP WITH THAT?
I DON'T WANT TO JINX IT, BUT THIS WHOLE "MURDERING THE DAMNED FOR SATAN TO GET MY SHARK BODY BACK" THING IS GOING A LOT SMOOTHER THAN I THOUGHT IT WOULD.
THIS TOP OF THE FOOD CHAIN SHIT IS PAYING OFF!
HIDE! IT'S METALSHARK BRO!
WHAT'S A METALSHARK BRO?
HE'S SATAN'S RUTHLESS KILLING MACHINE.
NOW THIS IS A BIG ASS MOUNTAIN.
...
THAT I NOW HAVE TO CLIMB.
FIN ME.

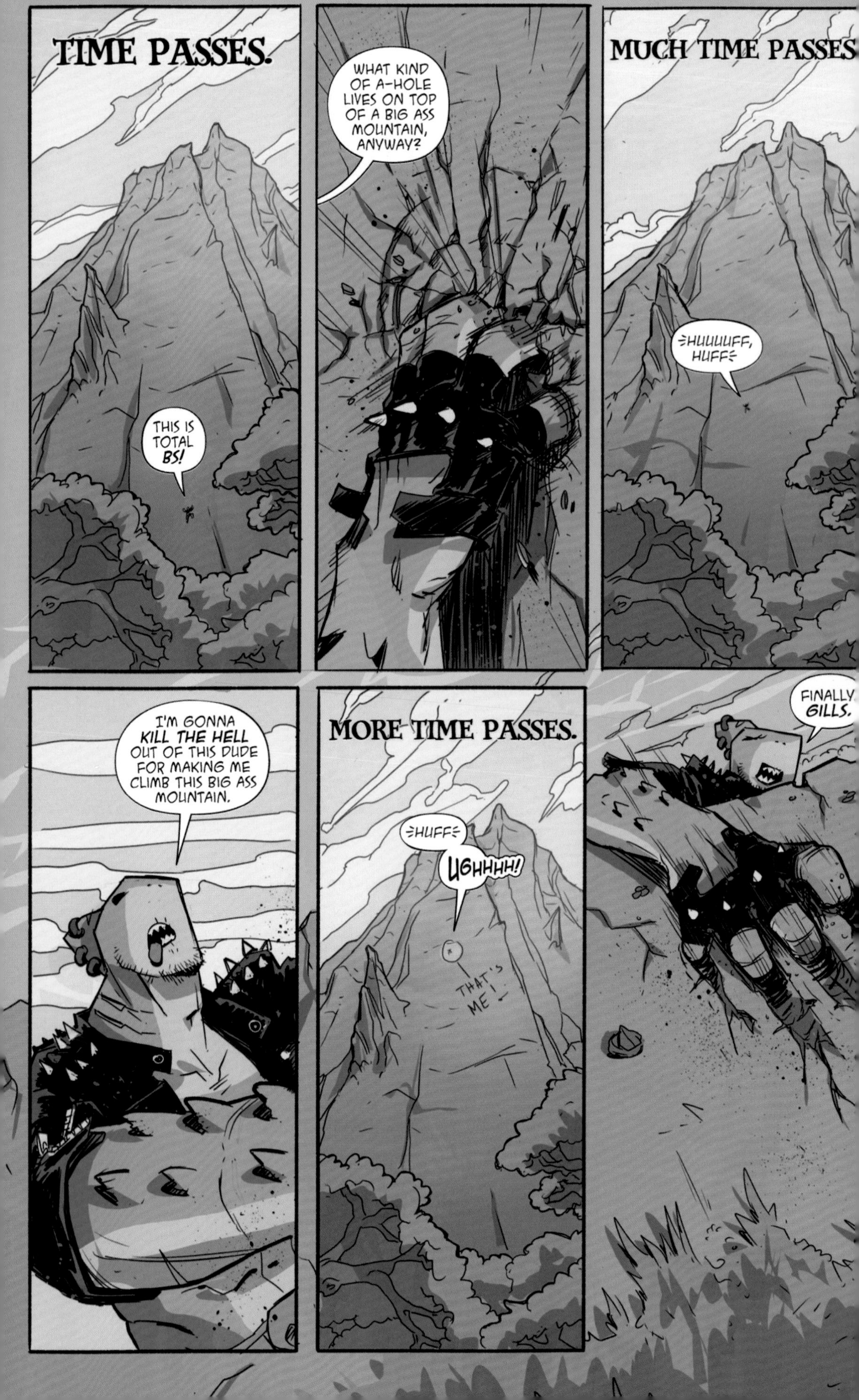
TIME PASSES.
THIS IS TOTAL BS!
WHAT KIND OF A-HOLE LIVES ON TOP OF A BIG ASS MOUNTAIN, ANYWAY?
MUCH TIME PASSES
HUUUUFF, HUFF
I'M GONNA KILL THE HELL OUT OF THIS DUDE FOR MAKING ME CLIMB THIS BIG ASS MOUNTAIN.
MORE TIME PASSES.
HUFF
UGHHHH!
THAT'S ME!
FINALLY. GILLS.

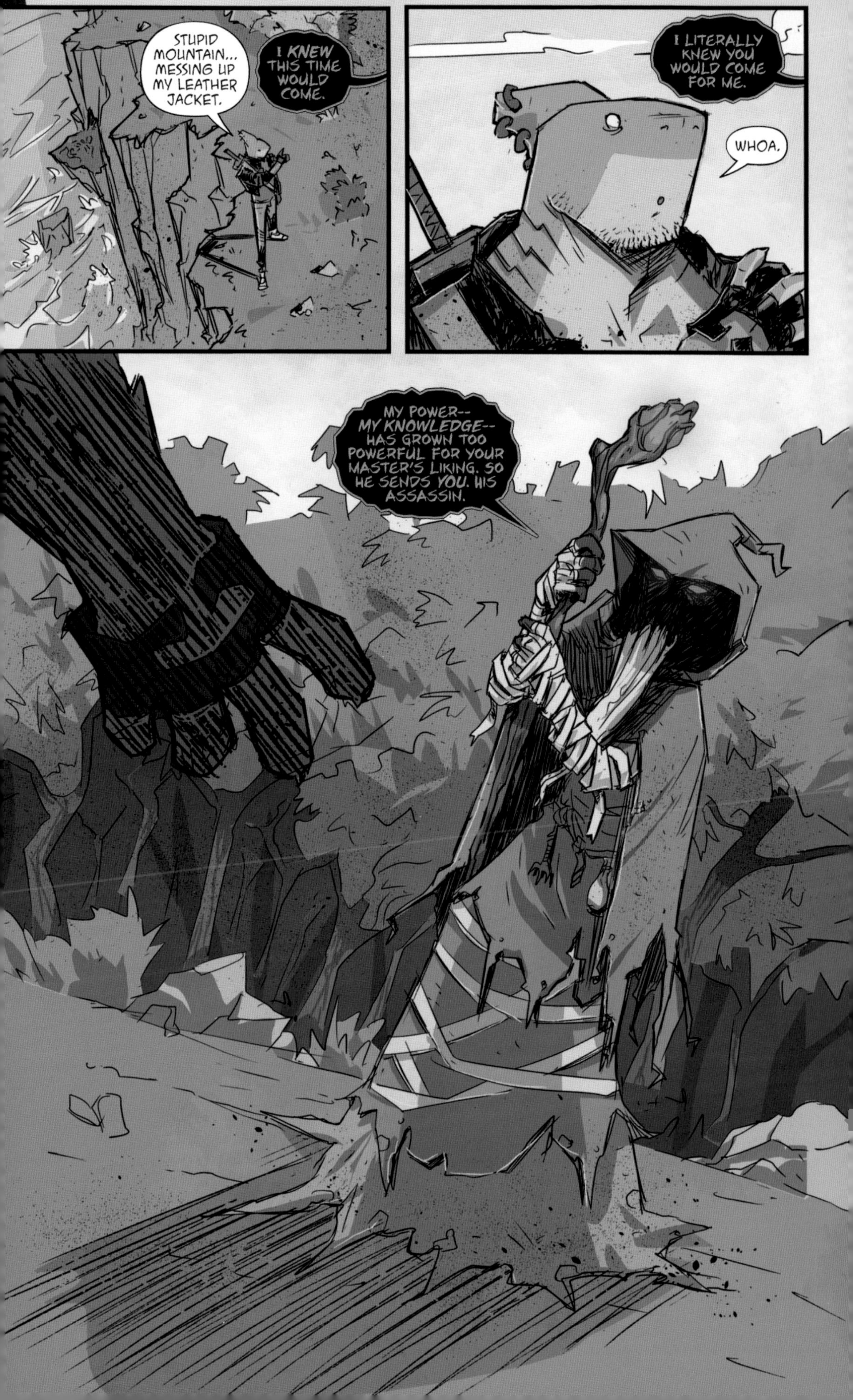
STUPID MOUNTAIN... MESSING UP MY LEATHER JACKET.
I KNEW THIS TIME WOULD COME.
I LITERALLY KNEW YOU WOULD COME FOR ME.
WHOA.
MY POWER-- MY KNOWLEDGE-- HAS GROWN TOO POWERFUL FOR YOUR MASTER'S LIKING. SO HE SENDS YOU. HIS ASSASSIN.

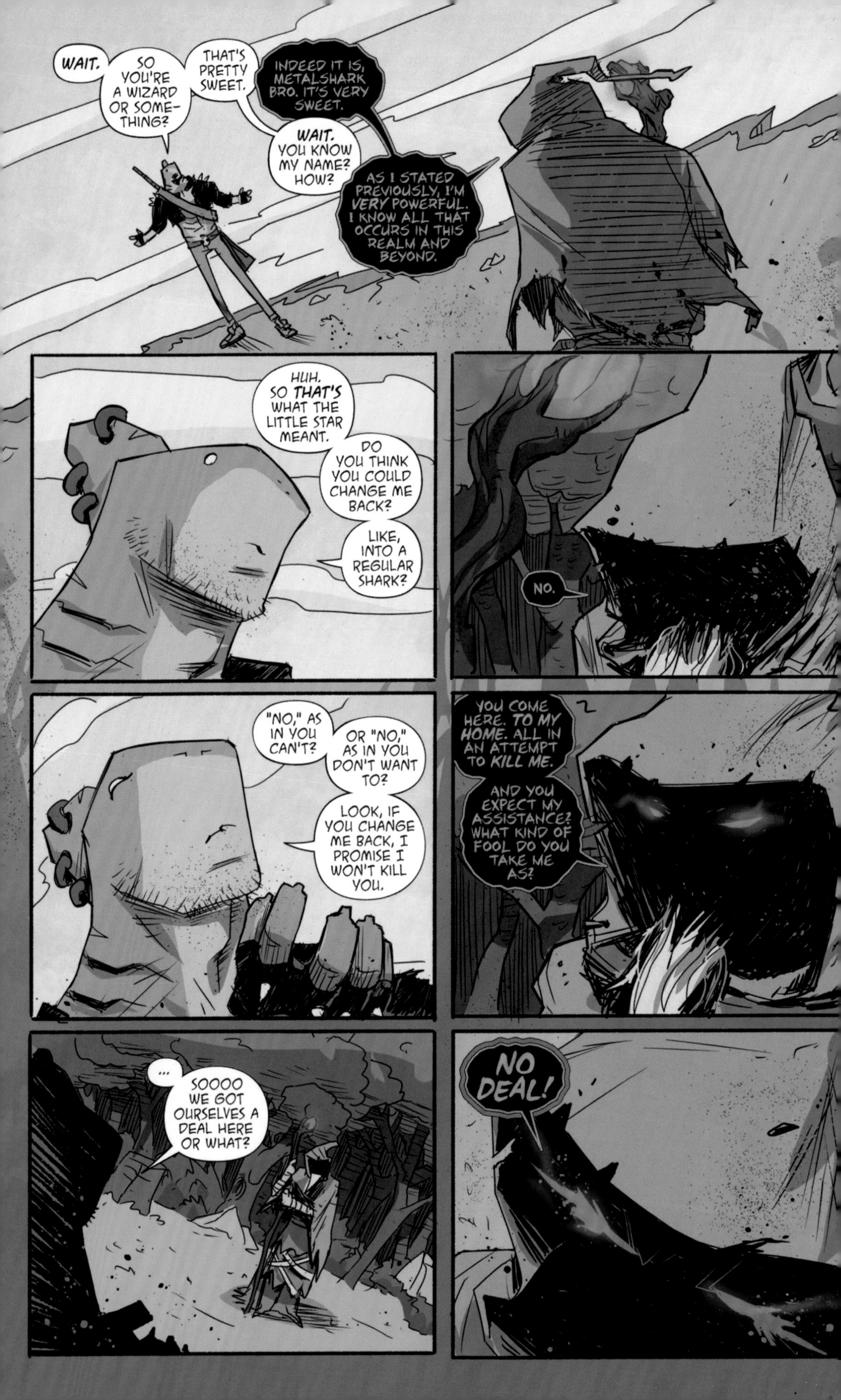
WAIT.
SO YOU'RE A WIZARD OR SOME-THING?
THAT'S PRETTY SWEET.
INDEED IT IS, METALSHARK BRO. IT'S VERY SWEET.
WAIT. YOU KNOW MY NAME? HOW?
AS I STATED PREVIOUSLY, I'M VERY POWERFUL. I KNOW ALL THAT OCCURS IN THIS REALM AND BEYOND.
HUH. SO THAT'S WHAT THE LITTLE STAR MEANT.
DO YOU THINK YOU COULD CHANGE ME BACK?
LIKE, INTO A REGULAR SHARK?
NO.
"NO," AS IN YOU CAN'T?
OR "NO," AS IN YOU DON'T WANT TO?
LOOK, IF YOU CHANGE ME BACK, I PROMISE I WON'T KILL YOU.
YOU COME HERE. TO MY HOME. ALL IN AN ATTEMPT TO KILL ME.
AND YOU EXPECT MY ASSISTANCE? WHAT KIND OF FOOL DO YOU TAKE ME AS?
...
SOOOO WE GOT OURSELVES A DEAL HERE OR WHAT?
NO DEAL!

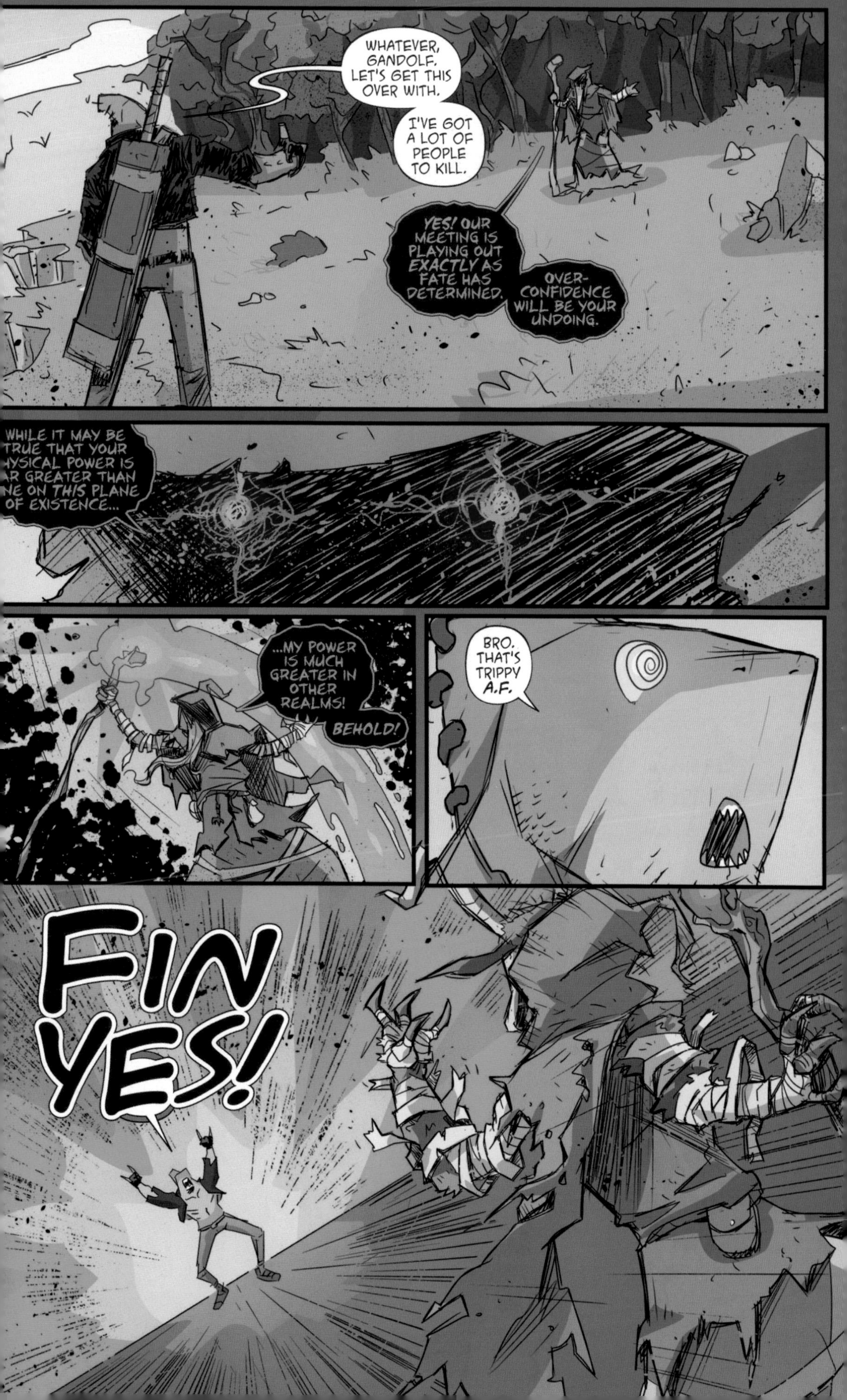
WHATEVER, GANDOLF. LET'S GET THIS OVER WITH.
I'VE GOT A LOT OF PEOPLE TO KILL.
YES! OUR MEETING IS PLAYING OUT EXACTLY AS FATE HAS DETERMINED.
OVER-CONFIDENCE WILL BE YOUR UNDOING.
WHILE IT MAY BE TRUE THAT YOUR PHYSICAL POWER IS FAR GREATER THAN ONE ON THIS PLANE OF EXISTENCE...
...MY POWER IS MUCH GREATER IN OTHER REALMS!
BEHOLD!
BRO. THAT'S TRIPPY A.F.
FIN YES!

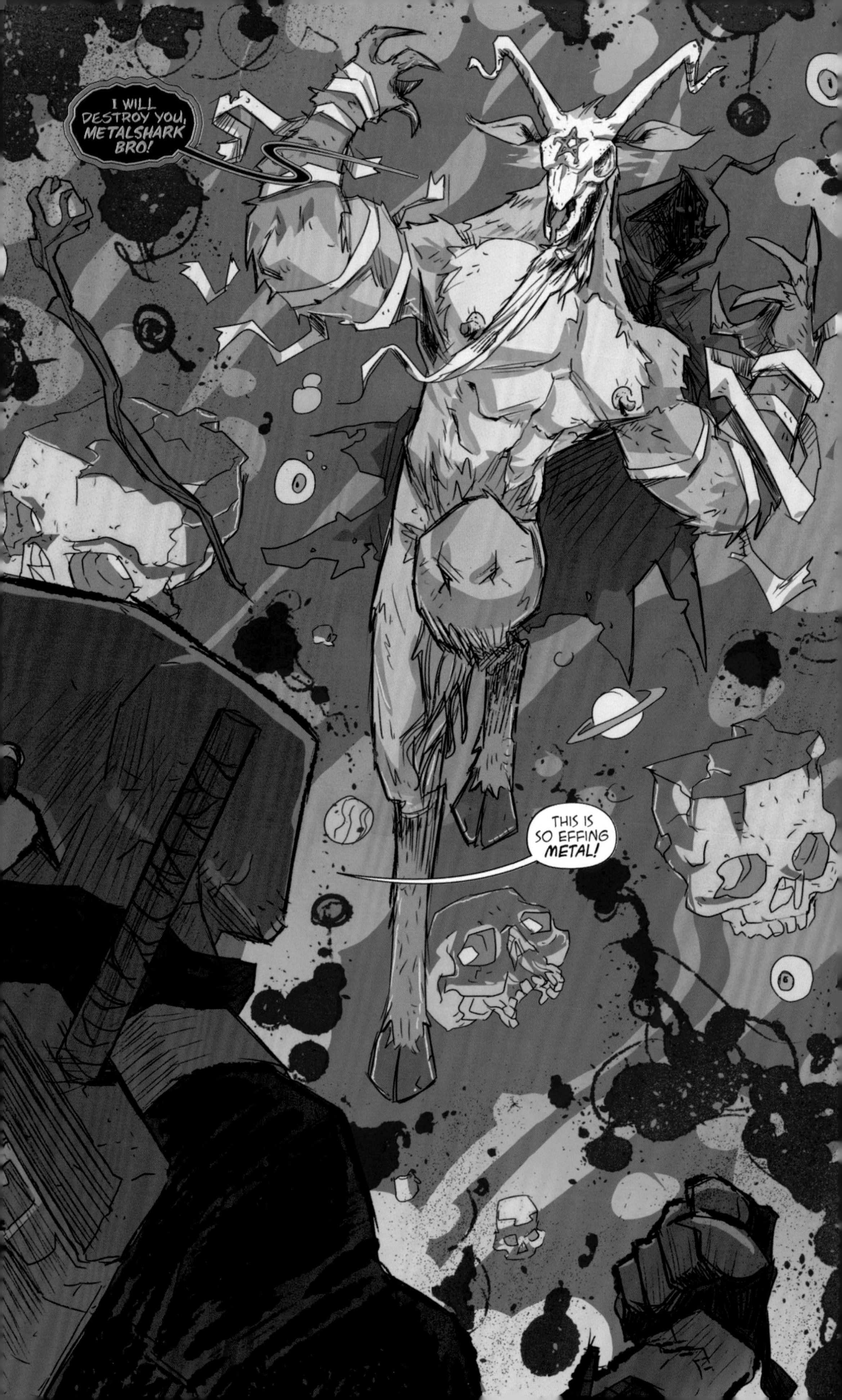
I WILL DESTROY YOU, METALSHARK BRO!
THIS IS SO EFFING METAL!

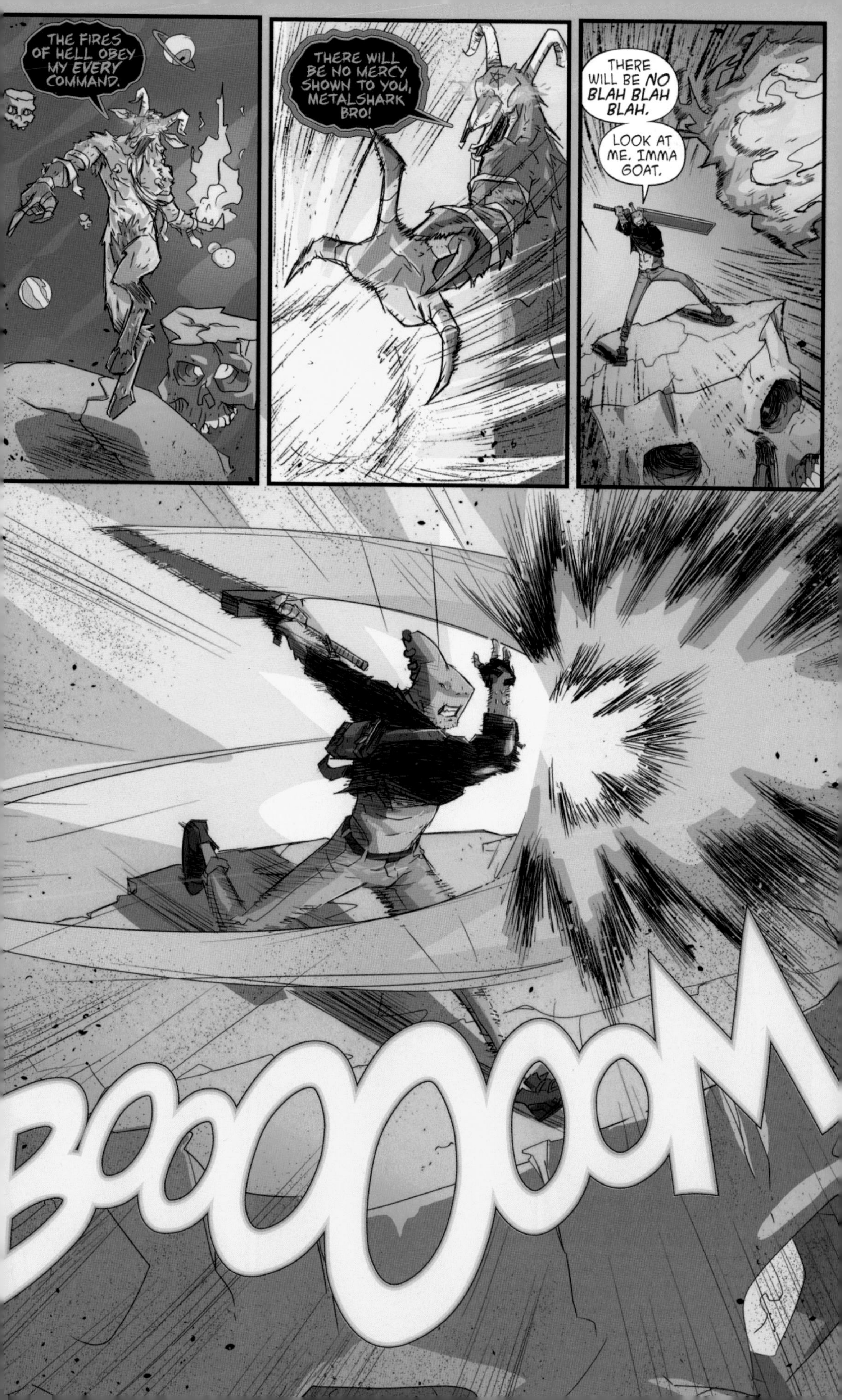
THE FIRES OF HELL OBEY MY EVERY COMMAND.
THERE WILL BE NO MERCY SHOWN TO YOU, METALSHARK BRO!
THERE WILL BE NO BLAH BLAH BLAH.
LOOK AT ME. IMMA GOAT.
BOOOOOM

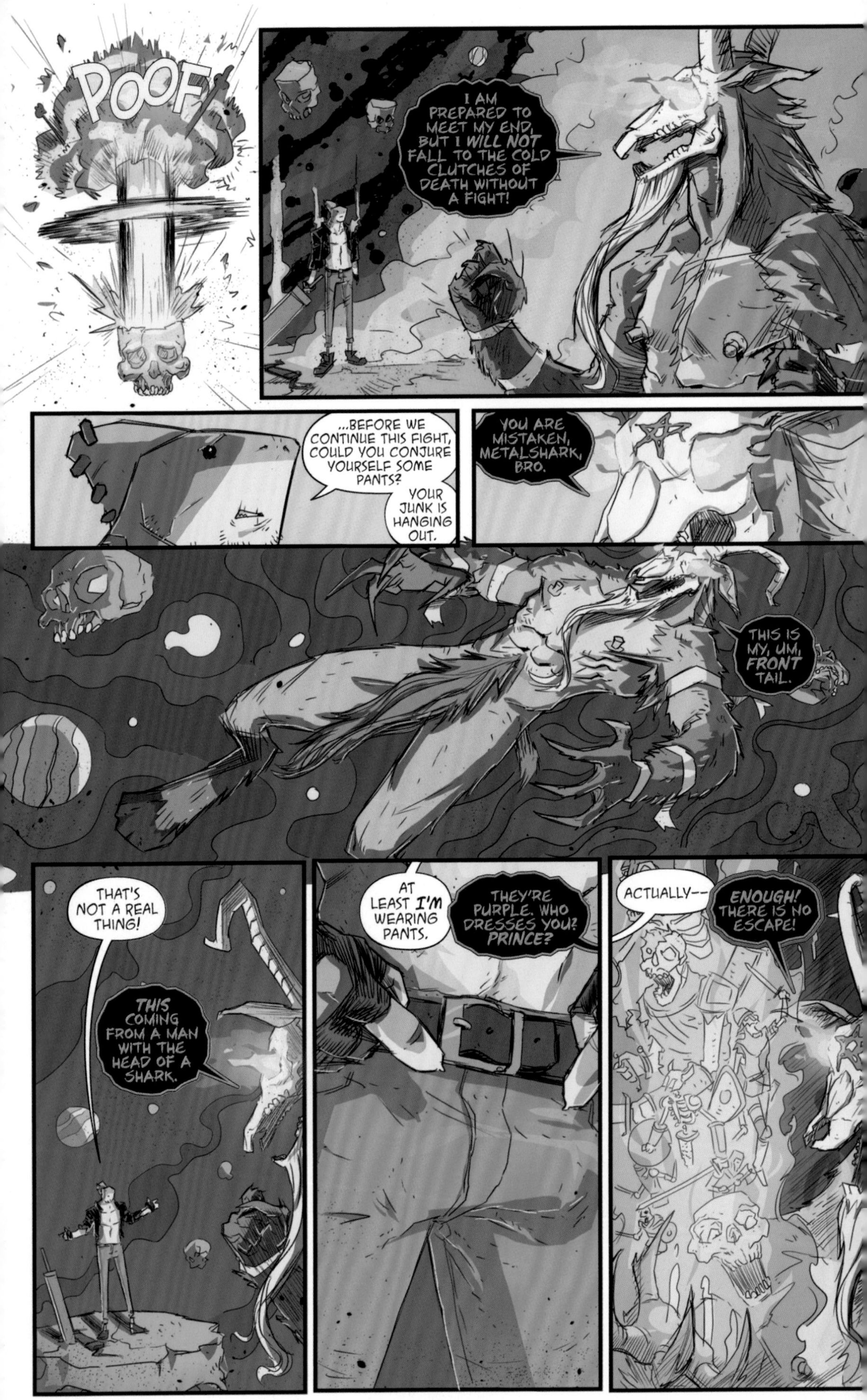
POOF
I AM PREPARED TO MEET MY END, BUT I WILL NOT FALL TO THE COLD CLUTCHES OF DEATH WITHOUT A FIGHT!
...BEFORE WE CONTINUE THIS FIGHT, COULD YOU CONJURE YOURSELF SOME PANTS?
YOUR JUNK IS HANGING OUT.
YOU ARE MISTAKEN, METALSHARK, BRO.
THIS IS MY, UM, FRONT TAIL.
THAT'S NOT A REAL THING!
THIS COMING FROM A MAN WITH THE HEAD OF A SHARK.
AT LEAST I'M WEARING PANTS.
THEY'RE PURPLE. WHO DRESSES YOU? PRINCE?
ACTUALLY--
ENOUGH! THERE IS NO ESCAPE!

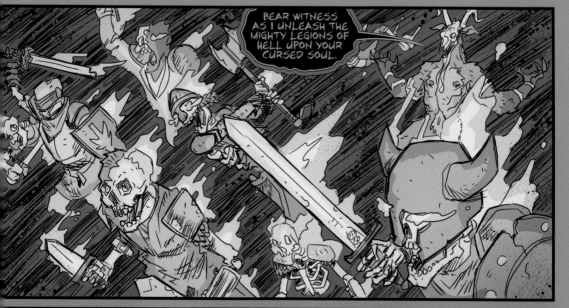

BEAR WITNESS AS I UNLEASH THE MIGHTY LEGIONS OF HELL UPON YOUR CURSED SOUL.

DID YOU STEAL THAT ONE OUT OF THE GRIM-*BORE?*

EAT SWORD, VAPE-SMOKE BRO!

DUDE! YOU'RE MESSING UP MY LEATHER!

IT'S VINTAGE!

SHOW SOME **RESPECT!**

WHOA. MY BLADE HAS NO EFFECT ON THESE SKELETON SPIRIT DUDES.

WHAT THE HELL?

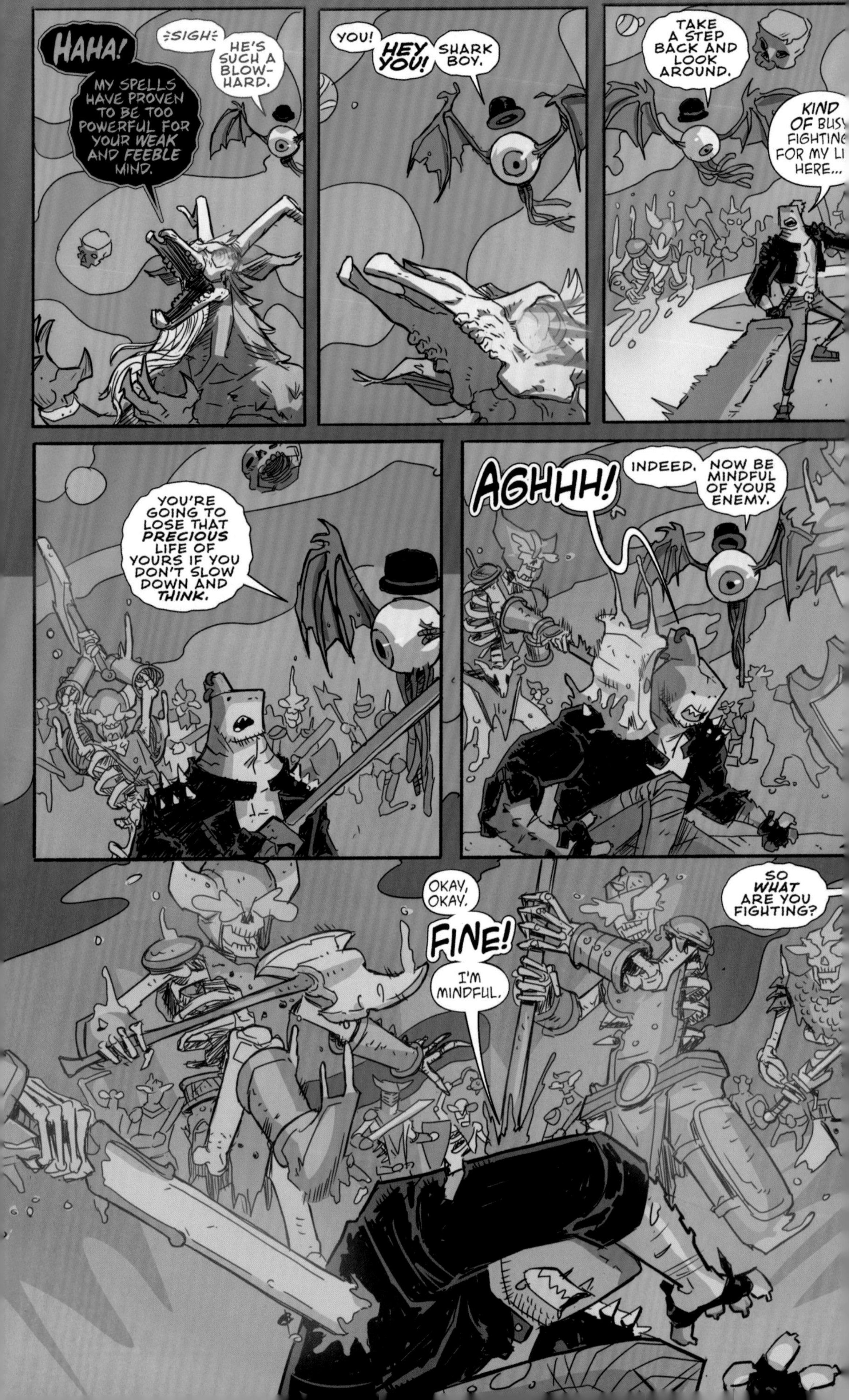
HAHA!
MY SPELLS HAVE PROVEN TO BE TOO POWERFUL FOR YOUR WEAK AND FEEBLE MIND.
SIGH
HE'S SUCH A BLOW-HARD.
YOU!
HEY YOU!
SHARK BOY.
TAKE A STEP BACK AND LOOK AROUND.
KIND OF BUSY FIGHTING FOR MY LI... HERE...
YOU'RE GOING TO LOSE THAT PRECIOUS LIFE OF YOURS IF YOU DON'T SLOW DOWN AND THINK.
AGHHH!
INDEED.
NOW BE MINDFUL OF YOUR ENEMY.
OKAY, OKAY.
FINE!
I'M MINDFUL.
SO WHAT ARE YOU FIGHTING?

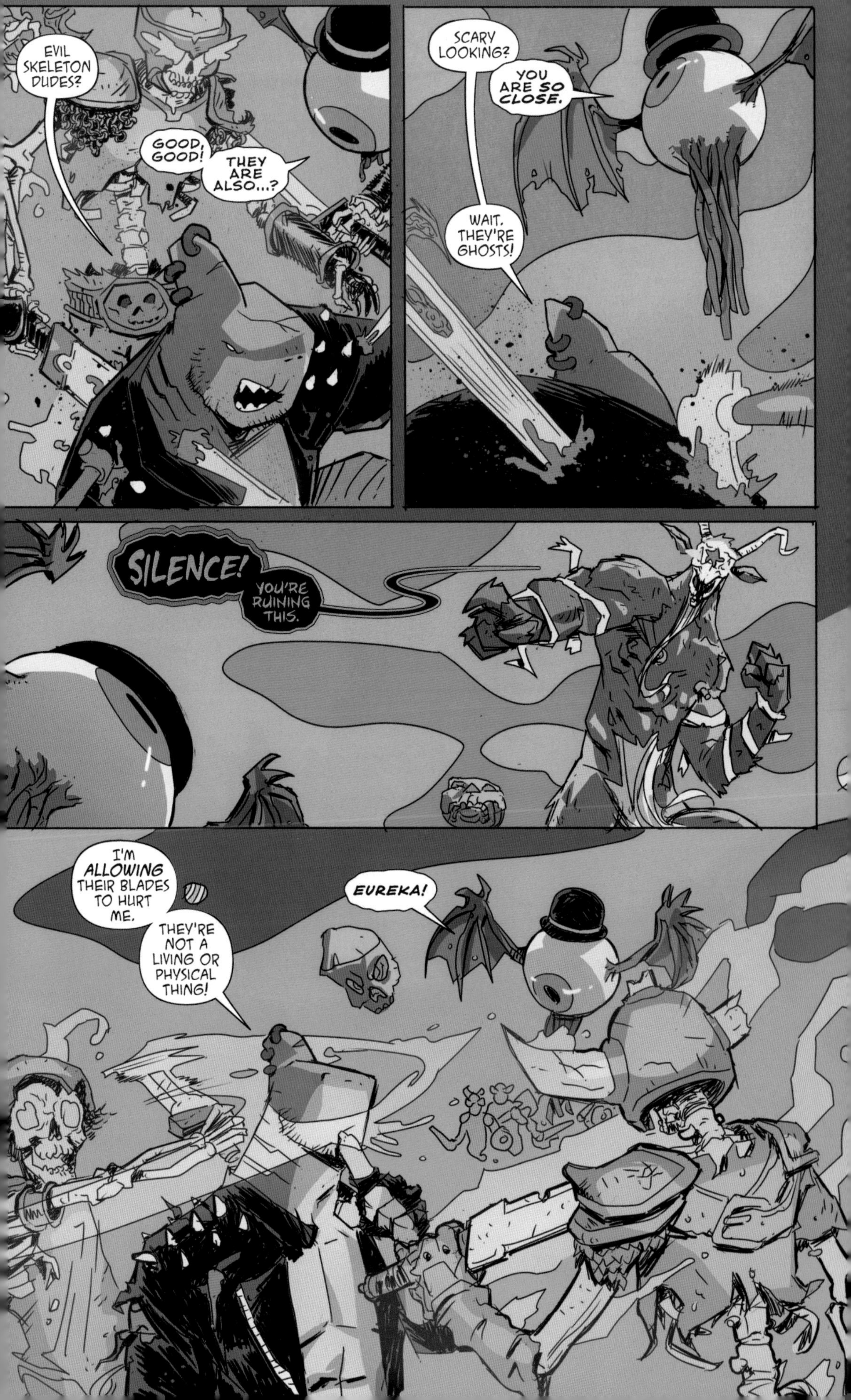
EVIL SKELETON DUDES?
GOOD, GOOD!
THEY ARE ALSO...?
SCARY LOOKING?
YOU ARE SO CLOSE.
WAIT. THEY'RE GHOSTS!
SILENCE!
YOU'RE RUINING THIS.
I'M ALLOWING THEIR BLADES TO HURT ME.
THEY'RE NOT A LIVING OR PHYSICAL THING!
EUREKA!

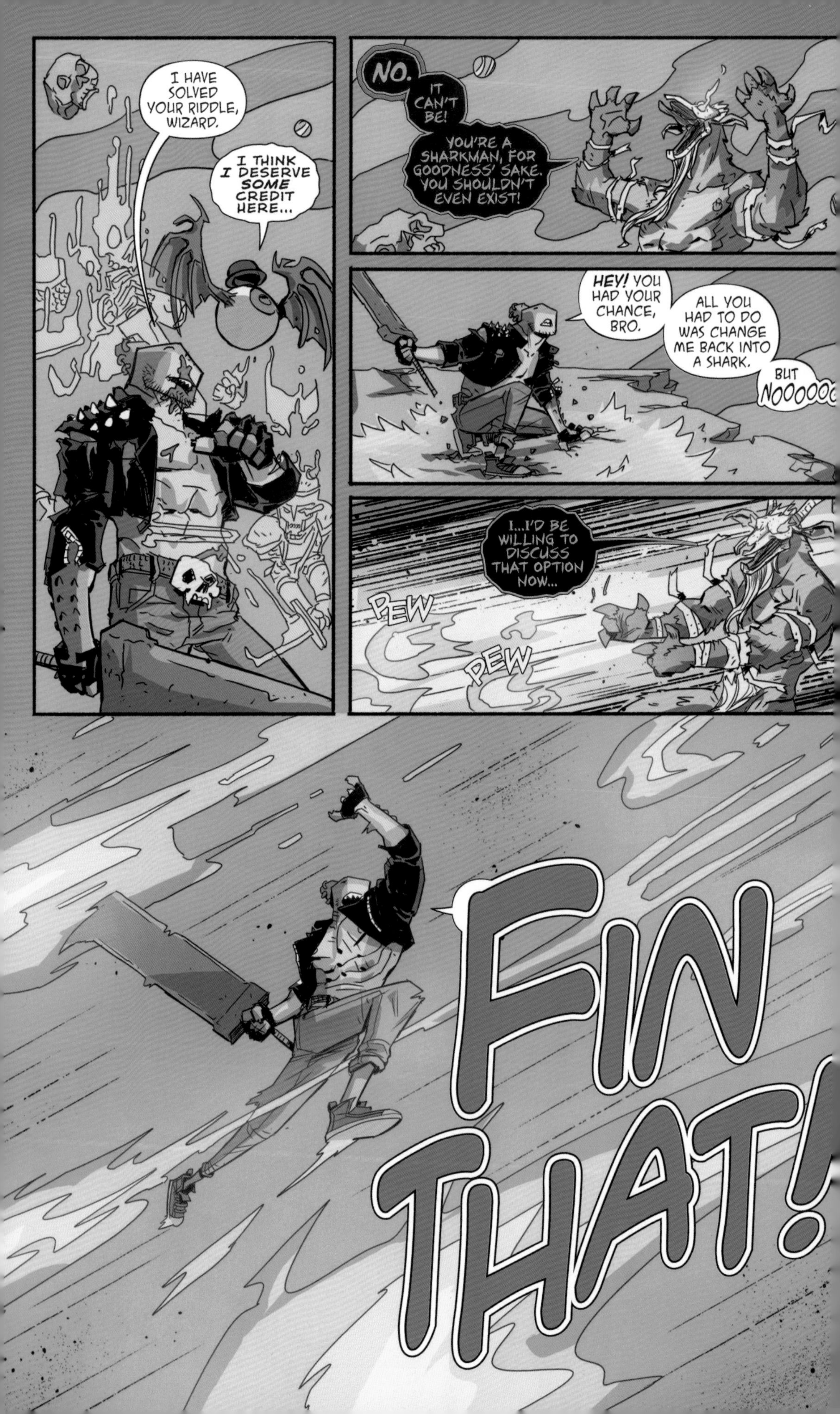
I HAVE SOLVED YOUR RIDDLE, WIZARD.
I THINK *I* DESERVE ***SOME*** CREDIT HERE...
NO.
IT CAN'T BE!
YOU'RE A SHARKMAN, FOR GOODNESS' SAKE. YOU SHOULDN'T EVEN EXIST!
HEY! YOU HAD YOUR CHANCE, BRO.
ALL YOU HAD TO DO WAS CHANGE ME BACK INTO A SHARK.
BUT NOOOOO
I...I'D BE WILLING TO DISCUSS THAT OPTION NOW...
PEW
PEW
FIN THAT!

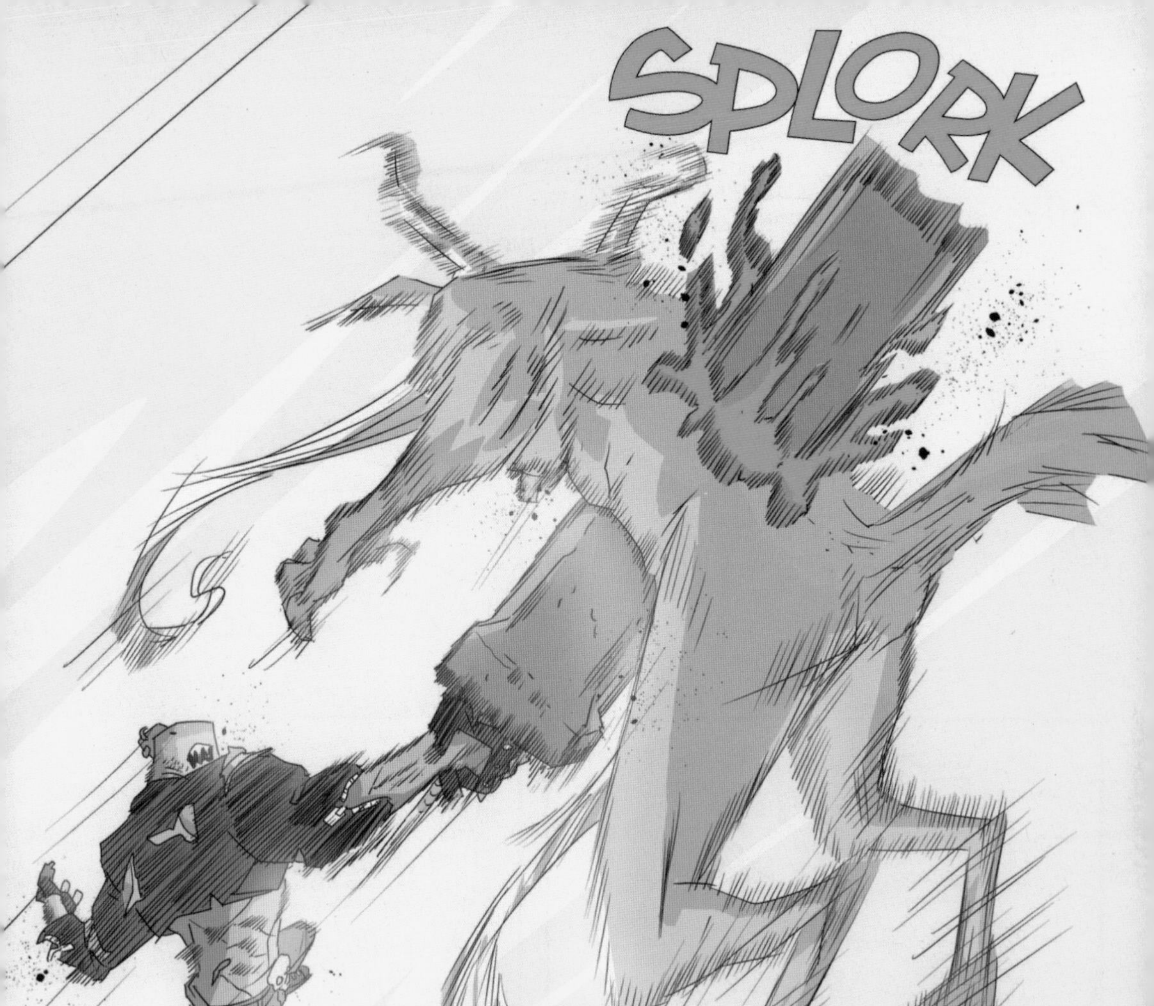
SPLORK

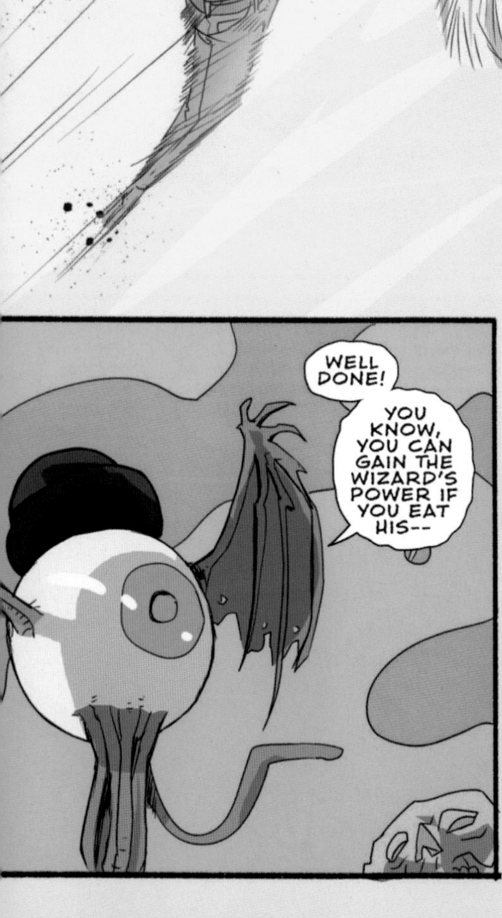
WELL DONE!
YOU KNOW, YOU CAN GAIN THE WIZARD'S POWER IF YOU EAT HIS--

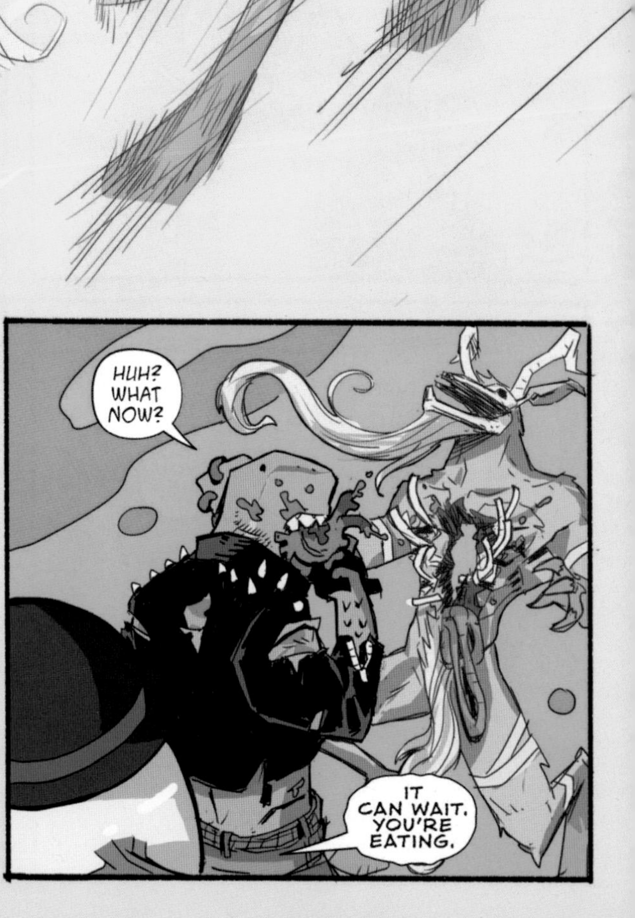
HUH? WHAT NOW?
IT CAN WAIT. YOU'RE EATING.

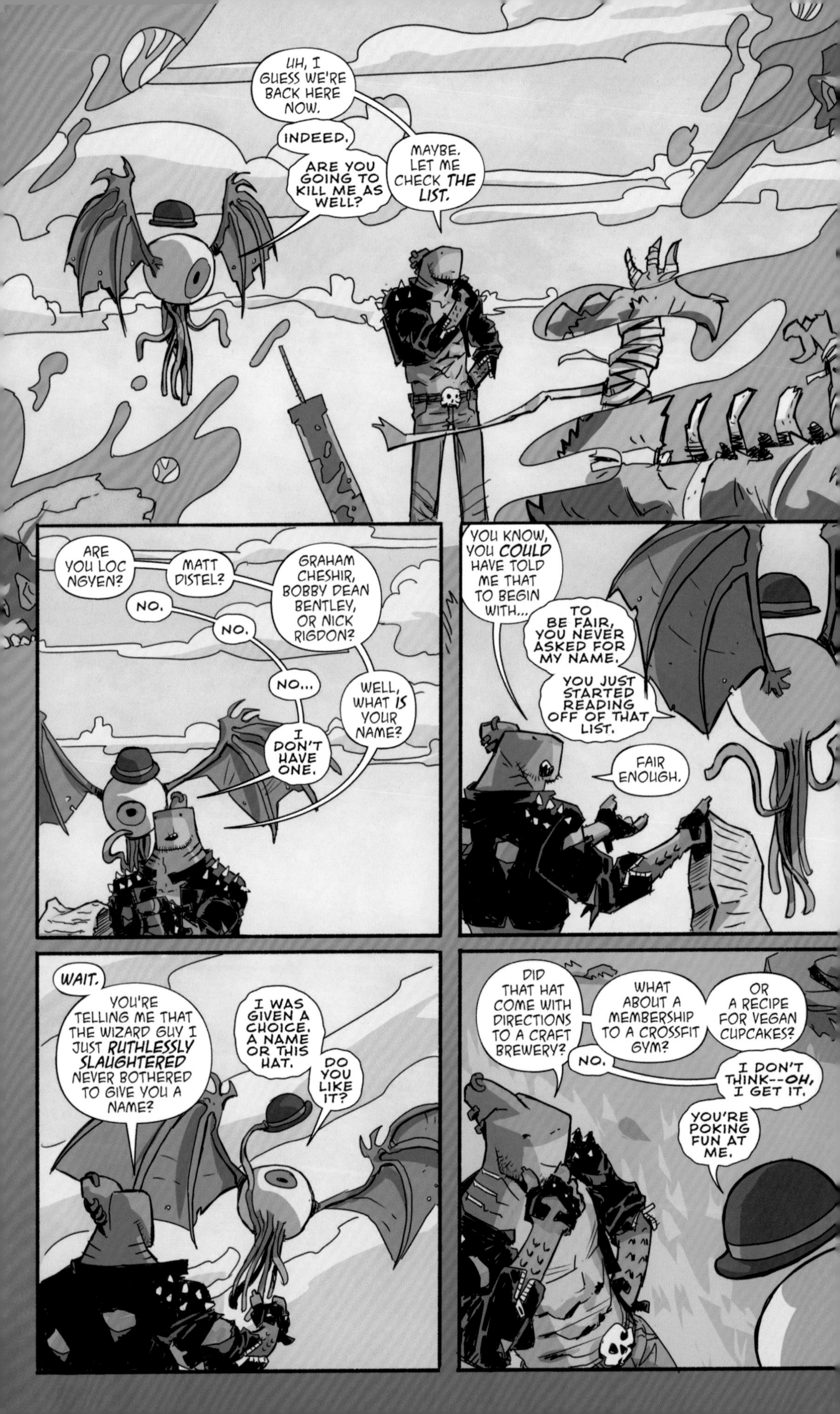
UH, I GUESS WE'RE BACK HERE NOW.
INDEED.
ARE YOU GOING TO KILL ME AS WELL?
MAYBE. LET ME CHECK THE LIST.
ARE YOU LOC NGYEN?
NO.
MATT DISTEL?
NO.
GRAHAM CHESHIR, BOBBY DEAN BENTLEY, OR NICK RIGDON?
NO...
WELL, WHAT IS YOUR NAME?
I DON'T HAVE ONE.
YOU KNOW, YOU COULD HAVE TOLD ME THAT TO BEGIN WITH...
TO BE FAIR, YOU NEVER ASKED FOR MY NAME.
YOU JUST STARTED READING OFF OF THAT LIST.
FAIR ENOUGH.
WAIT.
YOU'RE TELLING ME THAT THE WIZARD GUY I JUST RUTHLESSLY SLAUGHTERED NEVER BOTHERED TO GIVE YOU A NAME?
I WAS GIVEN A CHOICE. A NAME OR THIS HAT.
DO YOU LIKE IT?
DID THAT HAT COME WITH DIRECTIONS TO A CRAFT BREWERY?
NO.
WHAT ABOUT A MEMBERSHIP TO A CROSSFIT GYM?
OR A RECIPE FOR VEGAN CUPCAKES?
I DON'T THINK--OH, I GET IT.
YOU'RE POKING FUN AT ME.

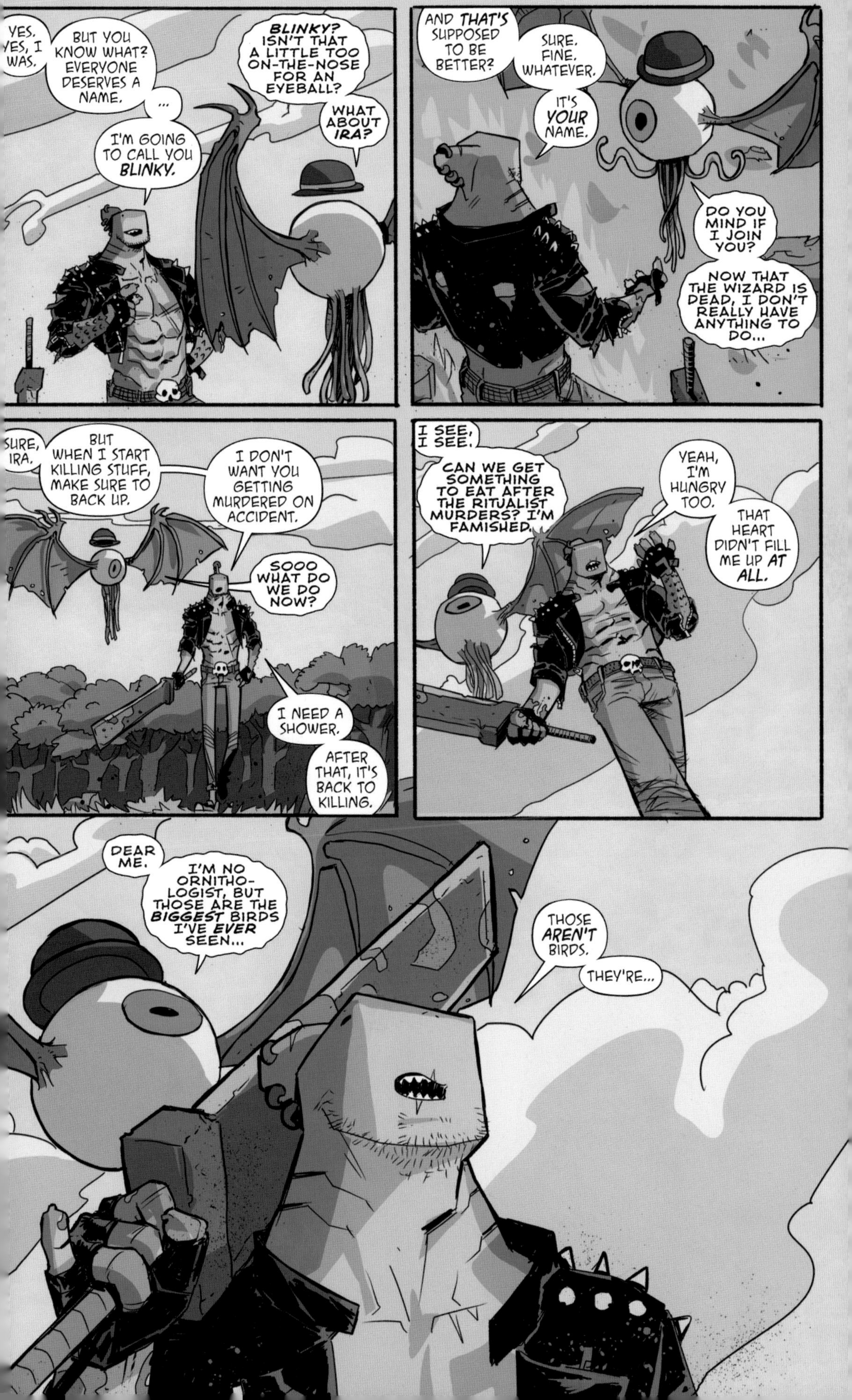
YES. YES, I WAS.
BUT YOU KNOW WHAT? EVERYONE DESERVES A NAME.
...
I'M GOING TO CALL YOU **BLINKY.**
BLINKY? ISN'T THAT A LITTLE TOO ON-THE-NOSE FOR AN EYEBALL?
WHAT ABOUT ***IRA?***
AND ***THAT'S*** SUPPOSED TO BE BETTER?
SURE. FINE. WHATEVER.
IT'S ***YOUR*** NAME.
DO YOU MIND IF I JOIN YOU?
NOW THAT THE WIZARD IS DEAD, I DON'T REALLY HAVE ANYTHING TO DO...
SURE, IRA.
BUT WHEN I START KILLING STUFF, MAKE SURE TO BACK UP.
I DON'T WANT YOU GETTING MURDERED ON ACCIDENT.
SOOO WHAT DO WE DO NOW?
I NEED A SHOWER.
AFTER THAT, IT'S BACK TO KILLING.
I SEE, I SEE.
CAN WE GET SOMETHING TO EAT AFTER THE RITUALIST MURDERS? I'M FAMISHED.
YEAH, I'M HUNGRY TOO.
THAT HEART DIDN'T FILL ME UP ***AT ALL.***
DEAR ME.
I'M NO ORNITHOLOGIST, BUT THOSE ARE THE ***BIGGEST*** BIRDS I'VE ***EVER*** SEEN...
THOSE ***AREN'T*** BIRDS.
THEY'RE...

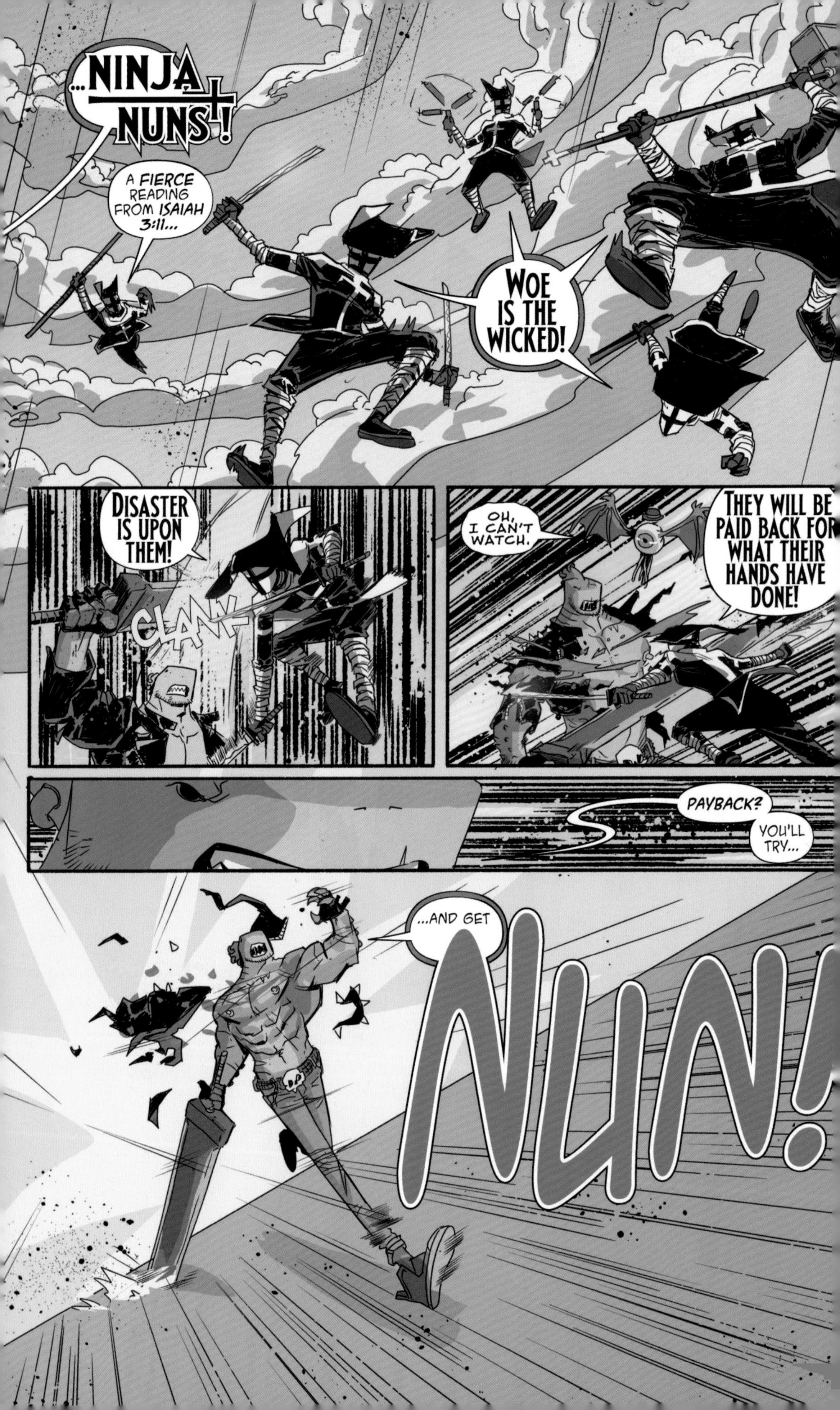
...NINJA NUNS!
A FIERCE READING FROM ISAIAH 3:11...
WOE IS THE WICKED!
DISASTER IS UPON THEM!
CLANK
OH, I CAN'T WATCH.
THEY WILL BE PAID BACK FOR WHAT THEIR HANDS HAVE DONE!
PAYBACK?
YOU'LL TRY...
...AND GET
NUN!

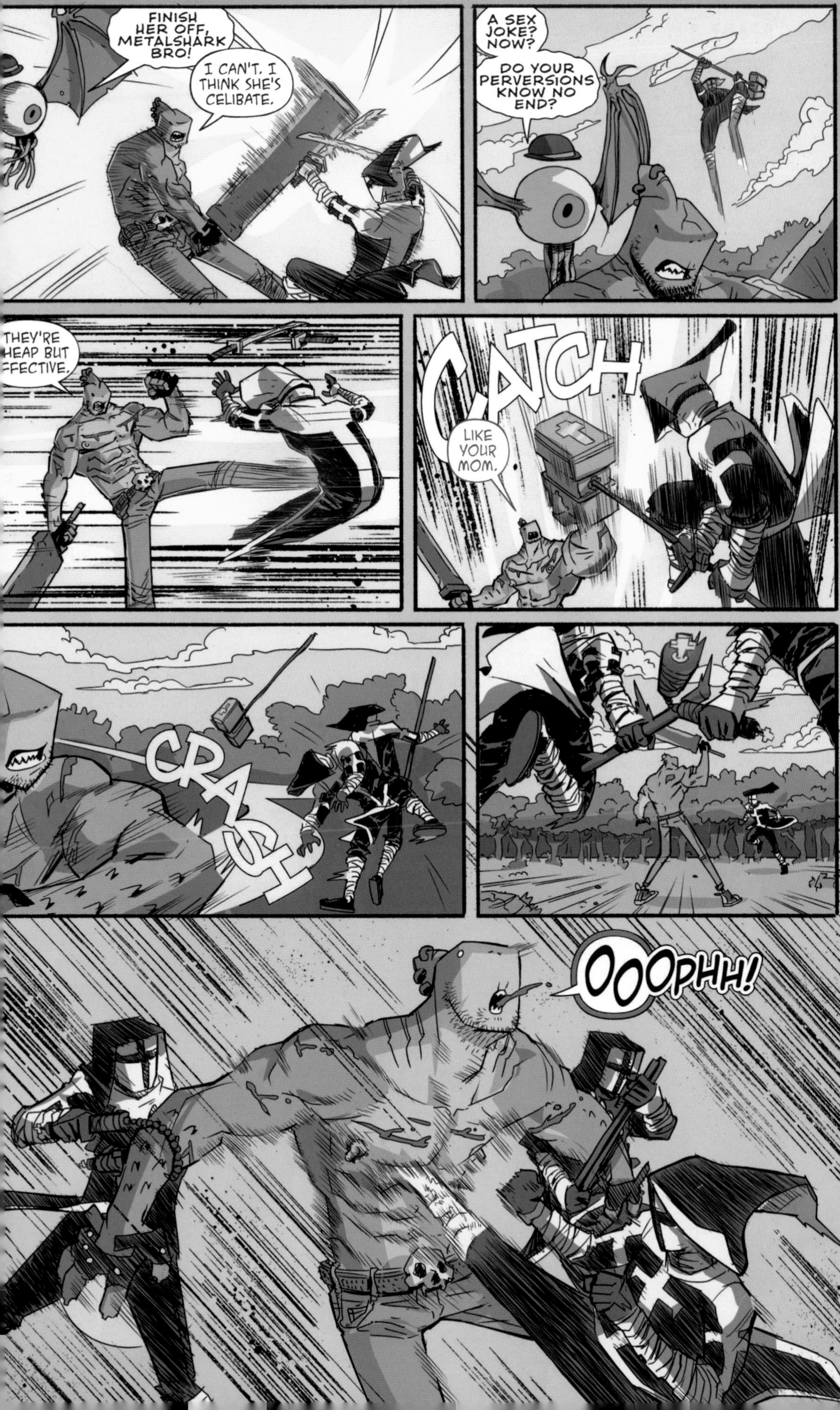
FINISH HER OFF, METALSHARK BRO!
I CAN'T. I THINK SHE'S CELIBATE.
A SEX JOKE? NOW?
DO YOUR PERVERSIONS KNOW NO END?
THEY'RE HEAP BUT FFECTIVE.
CATCH
LIKE YOUR MOM.
CRASH
OOOPHH!

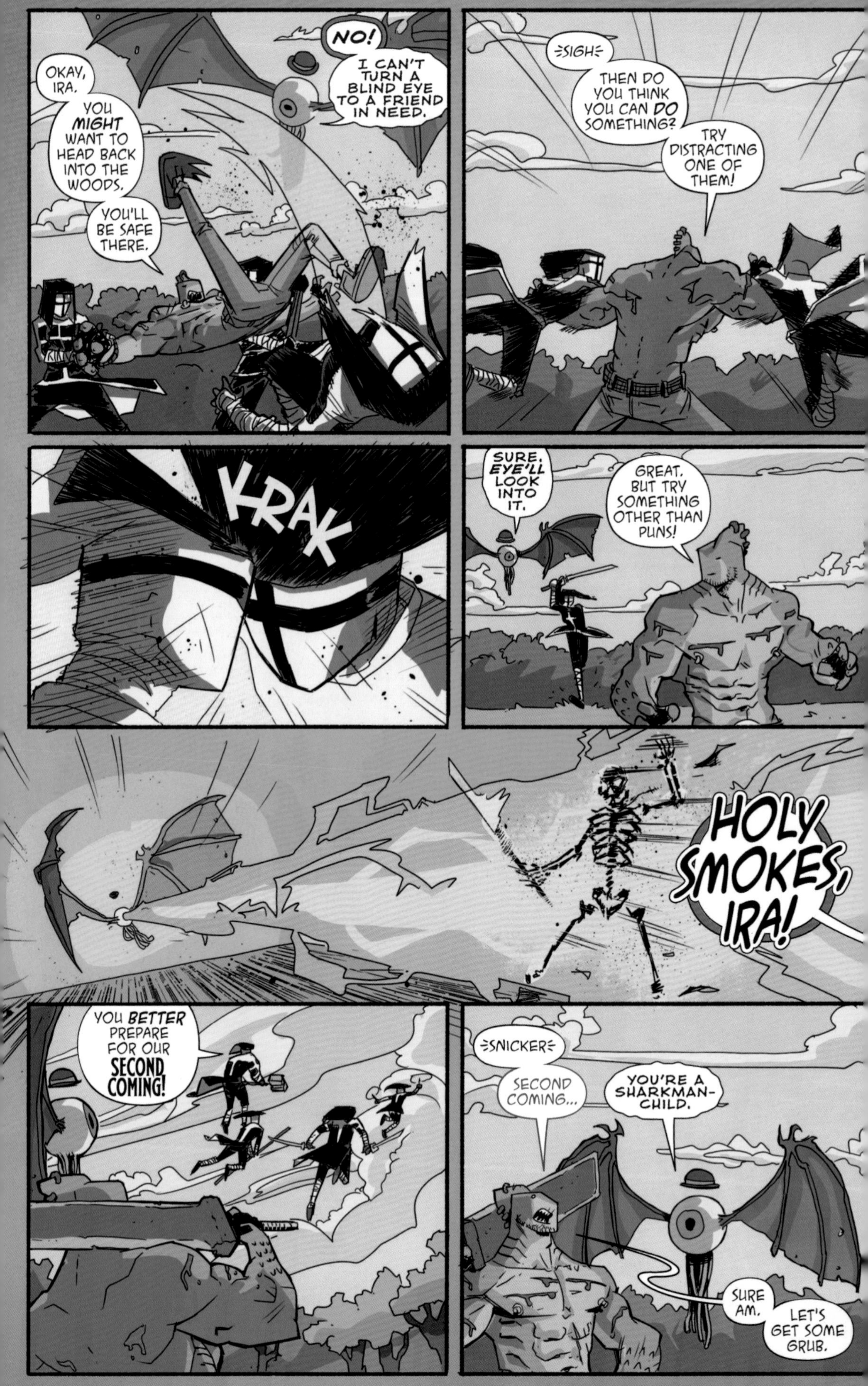
OKAY, IRA.
YOU MIGHT WANT TO HEAD BACK INTO THE WOODS.
YOU'LL BE SAFE THERE.
NO!
I CAN'T TURN A BLIND EYE TO A FRIEND IN NEED.
≡SIGH≡
THEN DO YOU THINK YOU CAN DO SOMETHING?
TRY DISTRACTING ONE OF THEM!
KRAK
SURE. EYE'LL LOOK INTO IT.
GREAT, BUT TRY SOMETHING OTHER THAN PUNS!
HOLY SMOKES, IRA!
YOU BETTER PREPARE FOR OUR SECOND COMING!
≡SNICKER≡
SECOND COMING...
YOU'RE A SHARKMAN-CHILD.
SURE AM.
LET'S GET SOME GRUB.

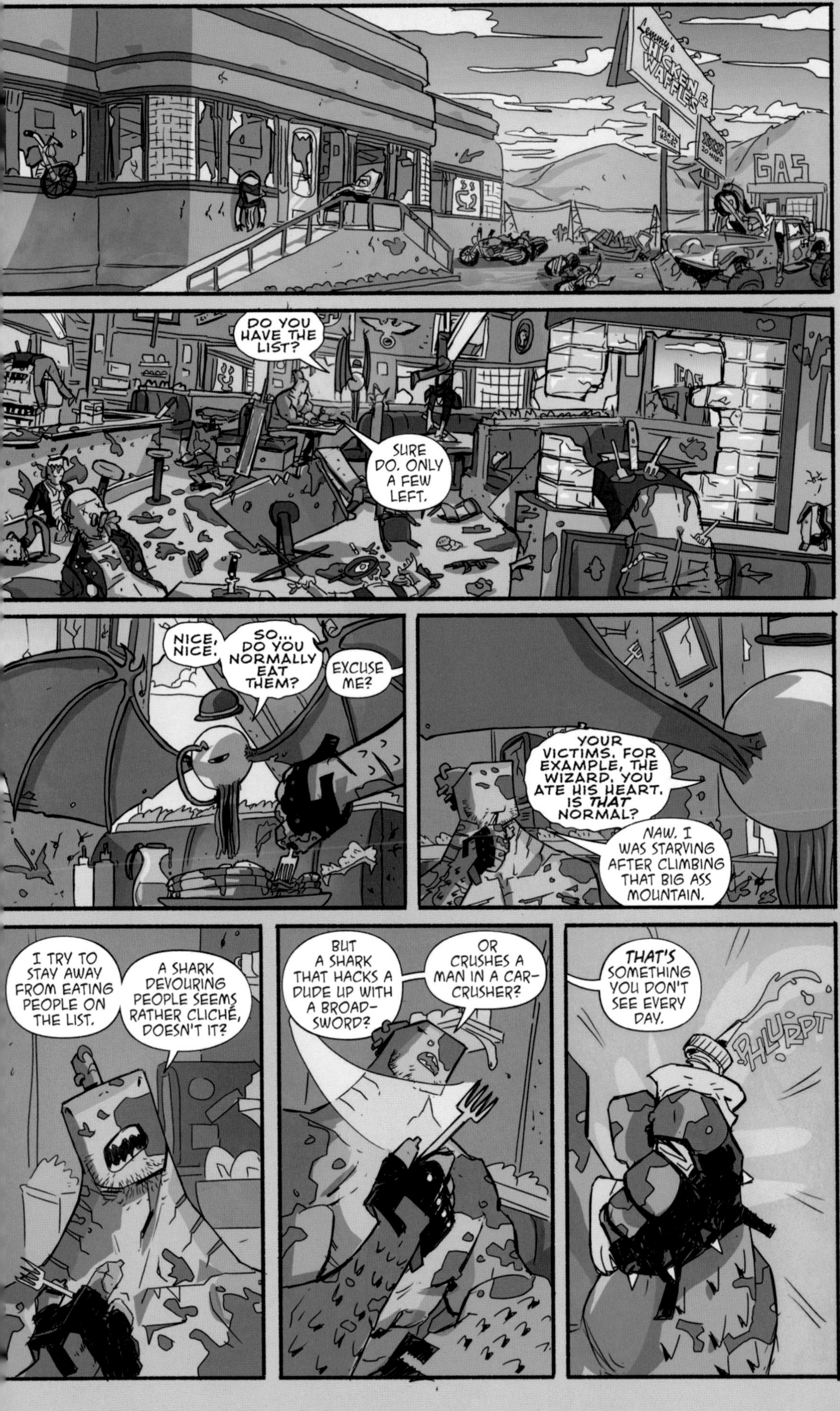
Lemmy's CHICKEN & WAFFLES
OPEN 24 HOURS
XXX
GAS
DO YOU HAVE THE LIST?
SURE DO. ONLY A FEW LEFT.
NICE, NICE.
SO... DO YOU NORMALLY EAT THEM?
EXCUSE ME?
YOUR VICTIMS. FOR EXAMPLE, THE WIZARD. YOU ATE HIS HEART. IS *THAT* NORMAL?
NAW. I WAS STARVING AFTER CLIMBING THAT BIG ASS MOUNTAIN.
I TRY TO STAY AWAY FROM EATING PEOPLE ON THE LIST.
A SHARK DEVOURING PEOPLE SEEMS RATHER CLICHÉ, DOESN'T IT?
BUT A SHARK THAT HACKS A DUDE UP WITH A BROAD-SWORD?
OR CRUSHES A MAN IN A CAR-CRUSHER?
THAT'S SOMETHING YOU DON'T SEE EVERY DAY.
PHLURPT

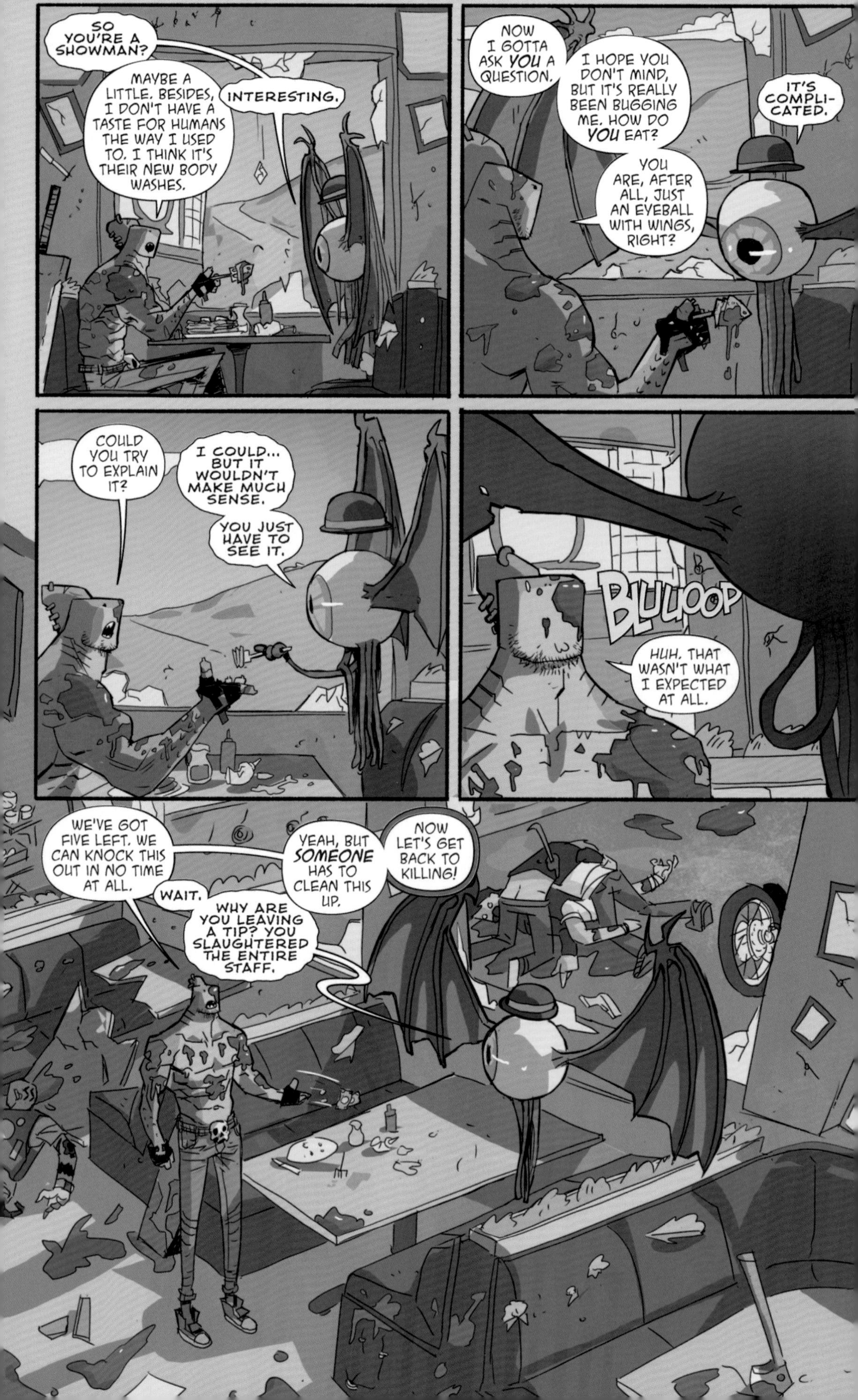
SO YOU'RE A SHOWMAN?
MAYBE A LITTLE. BESIDES, I DON'T HAVE A TASTE FOR HUMANS THE WAY I USED TO. I THINK IT'S THEIR NEW BODY WASHES.
INTERESTING.
NOW I GOTTA ASK YOU A QUESTION.
I HOPE YOU DON'T MIND, BUT IT'S REALLY BEEN BUGGING ME. HOW DO YOU EAT?
YOU ARE, AFTER ALL, JUST AN EYEBALL WITH WINGS, RIGHT?
IT'S COMPLICATED.
COULD YOU TRY TO EXPLAIN IT?
I COULD... BUT IT WOULDN'T MAKE MUCH SENSE.
YOU JUST HAVE TO SEE IT.
BLULOOP
HUH. THAT WASN'T WHAT I EXPECTED AT ALL.
WE'VE GOT FIVE LEFT. WE CAN KNOCK THIS OUT IN NO TIME AT ALL.
WAIT.
WHY ARE YOU LEAVING A TIP? YOU SLAUGHTERED THE ENTIRE STAFF.
YEAH, BUT SOMEONE HAS TO CLEAN THIS UP.
NOW LET'S GET BACK TO KILLING!

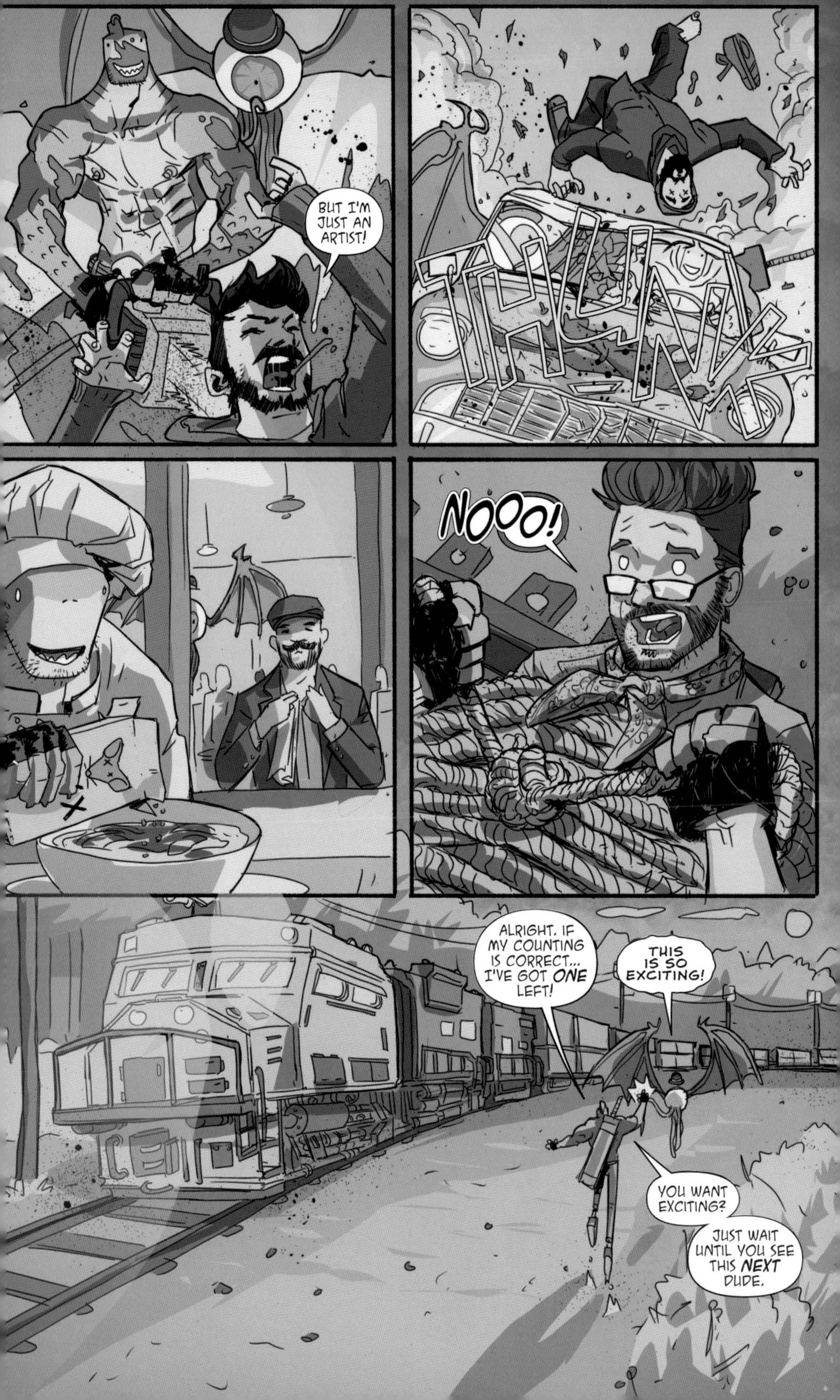
BUT I'M JUST AN ARTIST!
THUNK
NOOO!
ALRIGHT. IF MY COUNTING IS CORRECT... I'VE GOT *ONE* LEFT!
THIS IS SO EXCITING!
YOU WANT EXCITING?
JUST WAIT UNTIL YOU SEE THIS *NEXT* DUDE.

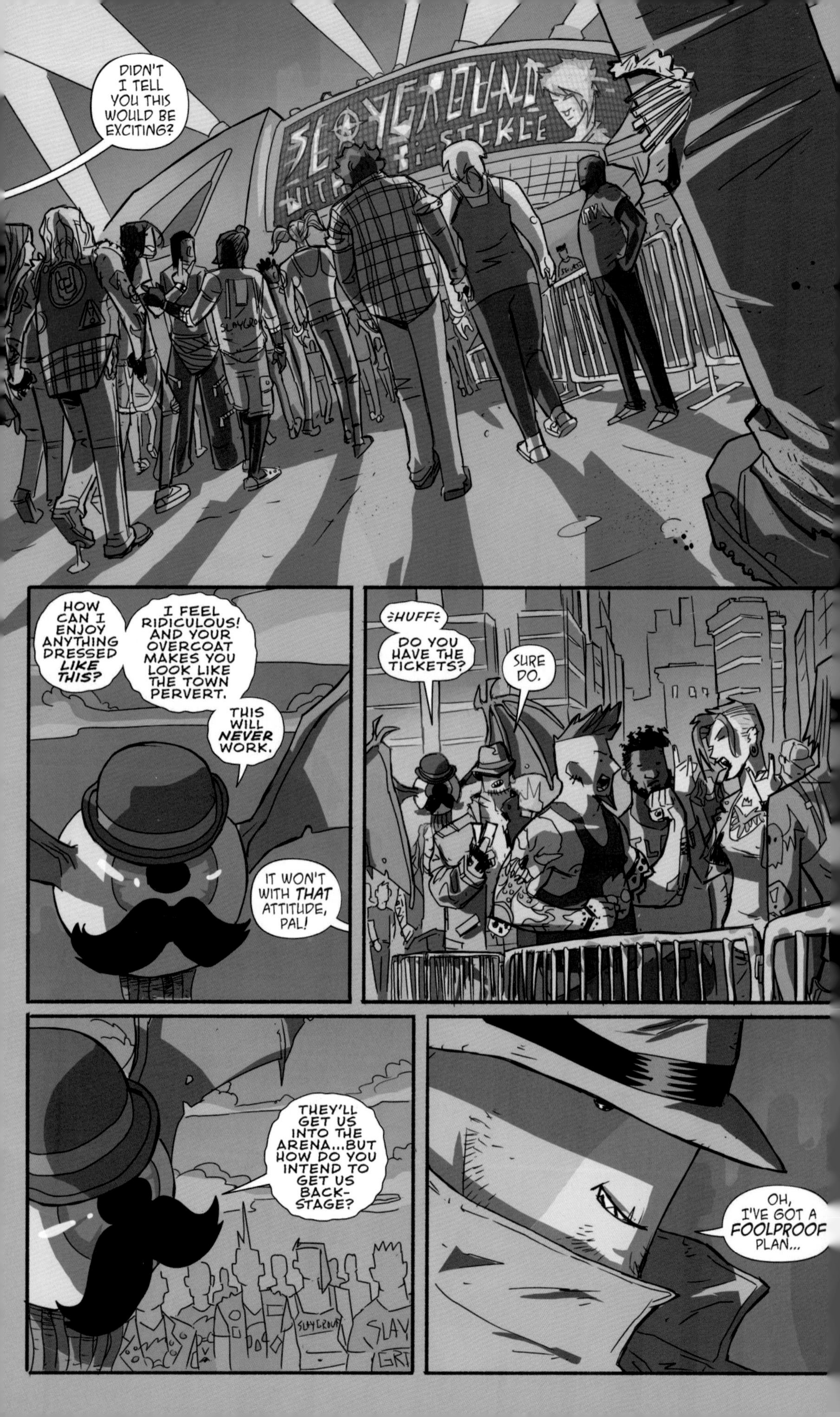

DIDN'T I TELL YOU THIS WOULD BE EXCITING?
HOW CAN I ENJOY ANYTHING DRESSED *LIKE THIS?*
I FEEL RIDICULOUS! AND YOUR OVERCOAT MAKES YOU LOOK LIKE THE TOWN PERVERT.
THIS WILL *NEVER* WORK.
IT WON'T WITH *THAT* ATTITUDE, PAL!
HUFF
DO YOU HAVE THE TICKETS?
SURE DO.
THEY'LL GET US INTO THE ARENA...BUT HOW DO YOU INTEND TO GET US BACK-STAGE?
OH, I'VE GOT A **FOOLPROOF** PLAN...

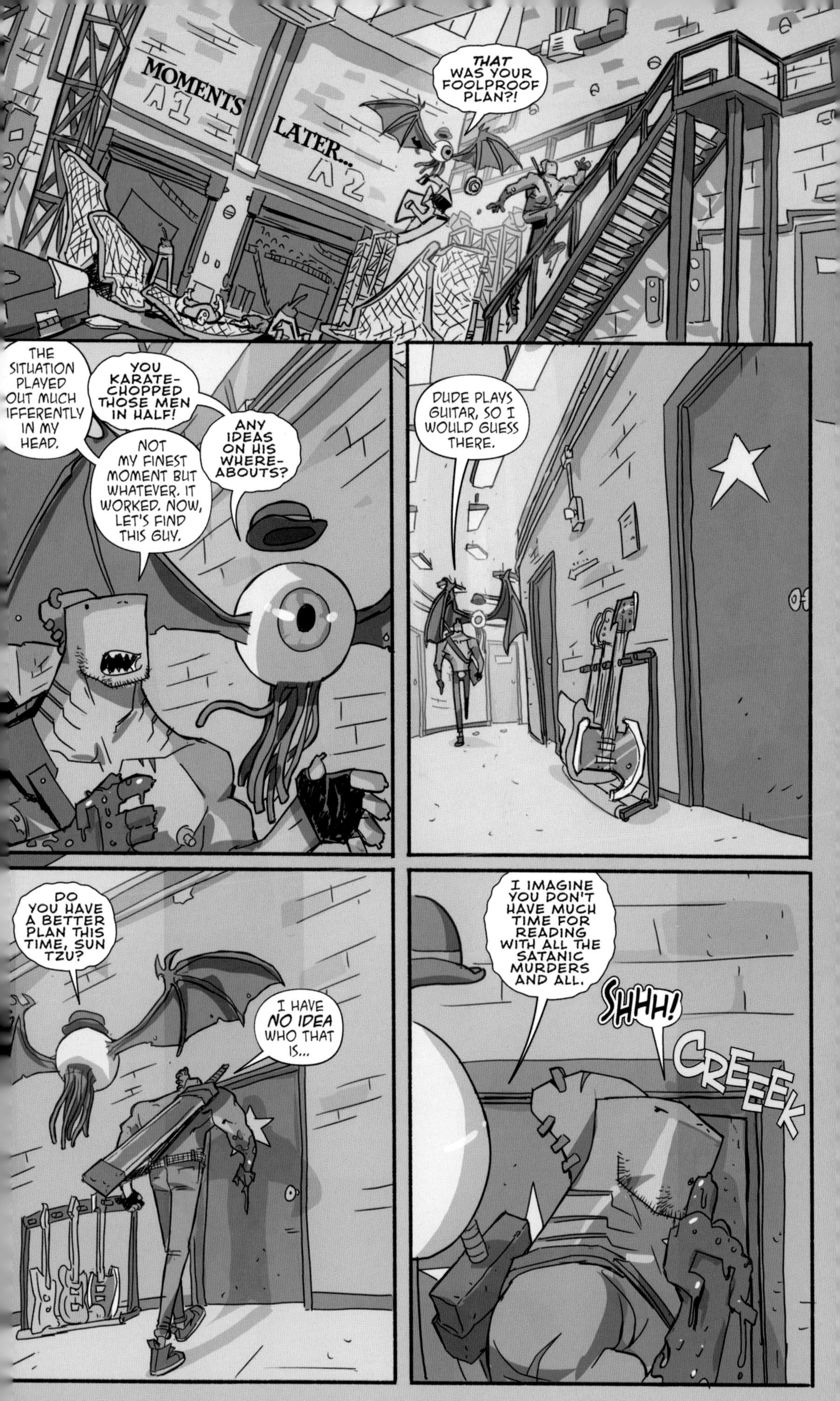
MOMENTS LATER...
A1
A2
THAT WAS YOUR FOOLPROOF PLAN?!
THE SITUATION PLAYED OUT MUCH IFFERENTLY IN MY HEAD.
YOU KARATE-CHOPPED THOSE MEN IN HALF!
NOT MY FINEST MOMENT BUT WHATEVER. IT WORKED. NOW, LET'S FIND THIS GUY.
ANY IDEAS ON HIS WHERE-ABOUTS?
DUDE PLAYS GUITAR, SO I WOULD GUESS THERE.
DO YOU HAVE A BETTER PLAN THIS TIME, SUN TZU?
I HAVE NO IDEA WHO THAT IS...
I IMAGINE YOU DON'T HAVE MUCH TIME FOR READING WITH ALL THE SATANIC MURDERS AND ALL.
SHHH!
CREEEK

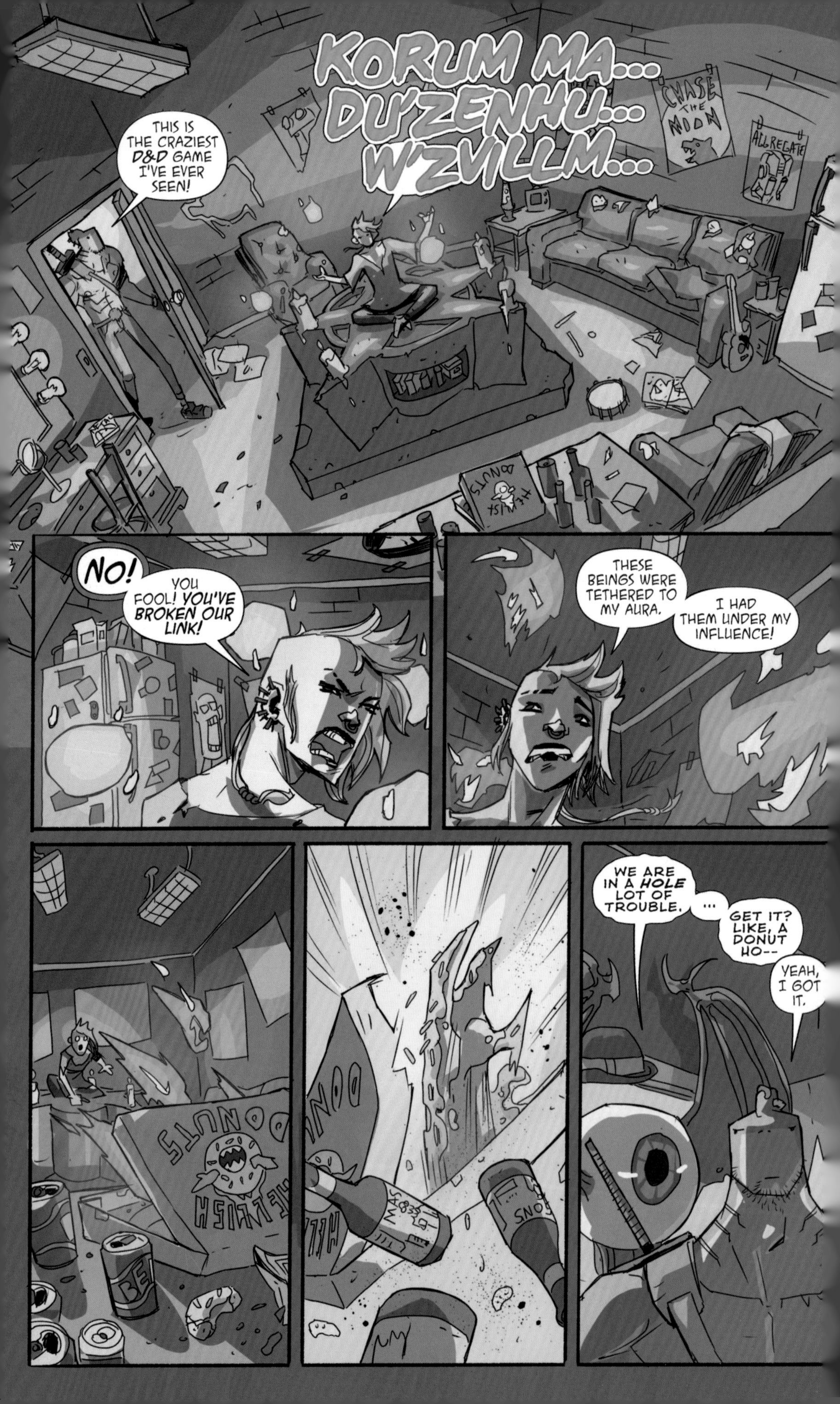
KORUM MA... DU'ZENHU... W'ZVILLM...
THIS IS THE CRAZIEST D&D GAME I'VE EVER SEEN!
CHASE THE MOON
AGGREGATE
DONUTS
NO!
YOU FOOL! YOU'VE BROKEN OUR LINK!
THESE BEINGS WERE TETHERED TO MY AURA.
I HAD THEM UNDER MY INFLUENCE!
DONUTS
WE ARE IN A HOLE LOT OF TROUBLE.
...
GET IT? LIKE, A DONUT HO--
YEAH, I GOT IT.

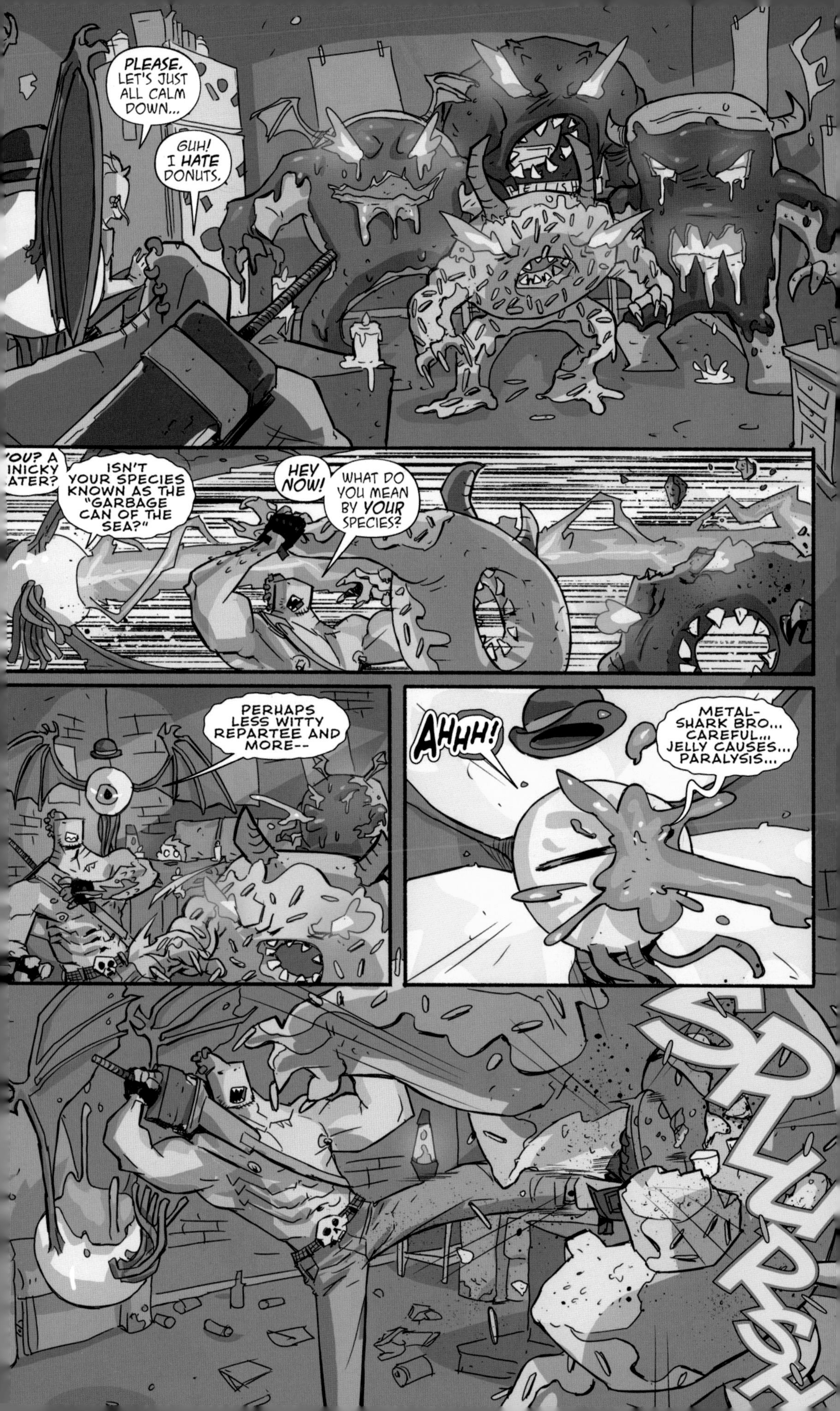
PLEASE. LET'S JUST ALL CALM DOWN...
GUH! I HATE DONUTS.
OU? A INICKY ATER?
ISN'T YOUR SPECIES KNOWN AS THE "GARBAGE CAN OF THE SEA?"
HEY NOW!
WHAT DO YOU MEAN BY YOUR SPECIES?
PERHAPS LESS WITTY REPARTEE AND MORE--
AHHH!
METAL-SHARK BRO... CAREFUL... JELLY CAUSES... PARALYSIS...

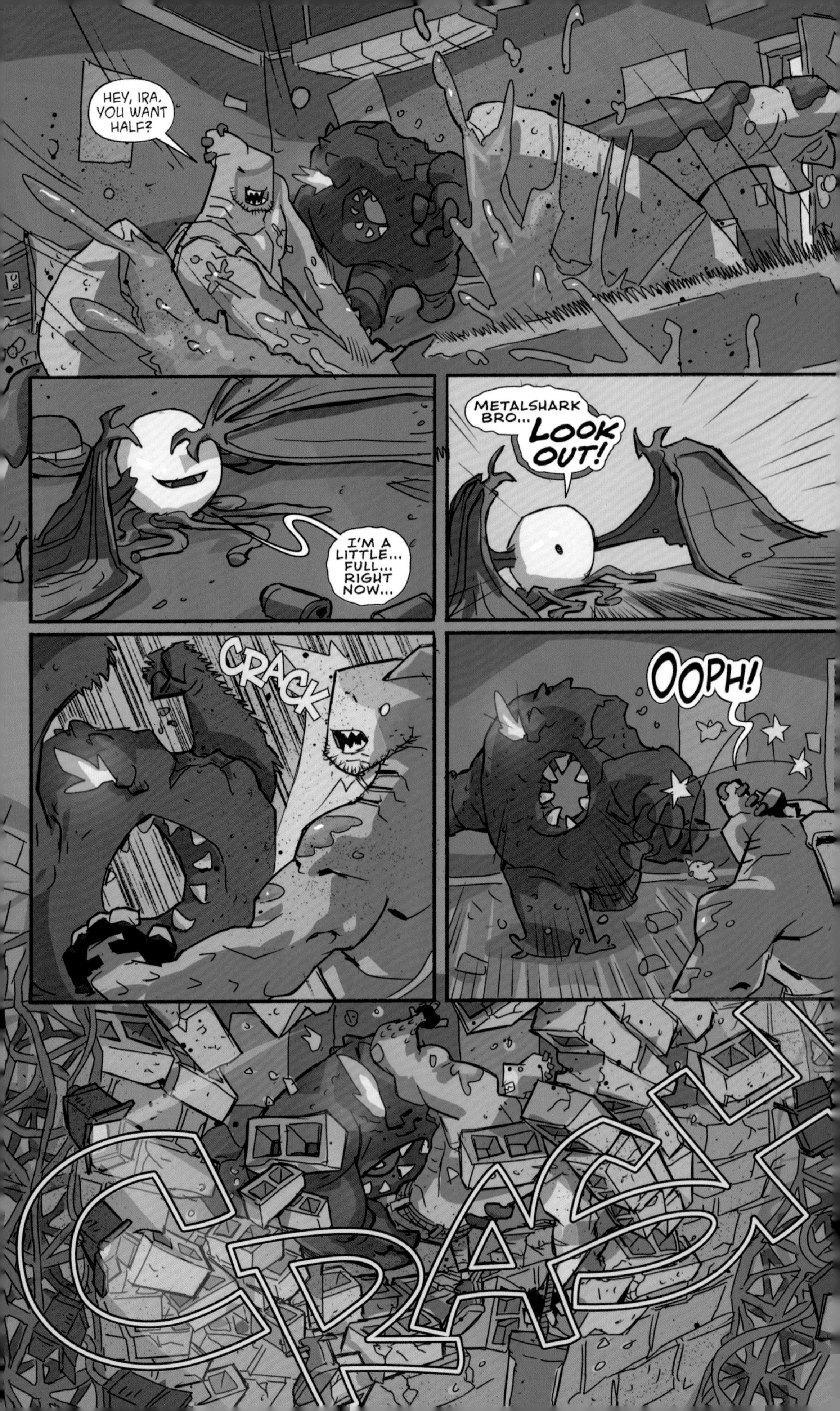
HEY, IRA, YOU WANT HALF?
I'M A LITTLE... FULL... RIGHT NOW...
METALSHARK BRO... LOOK OUT!
CRACK
OOPH!
CRASH

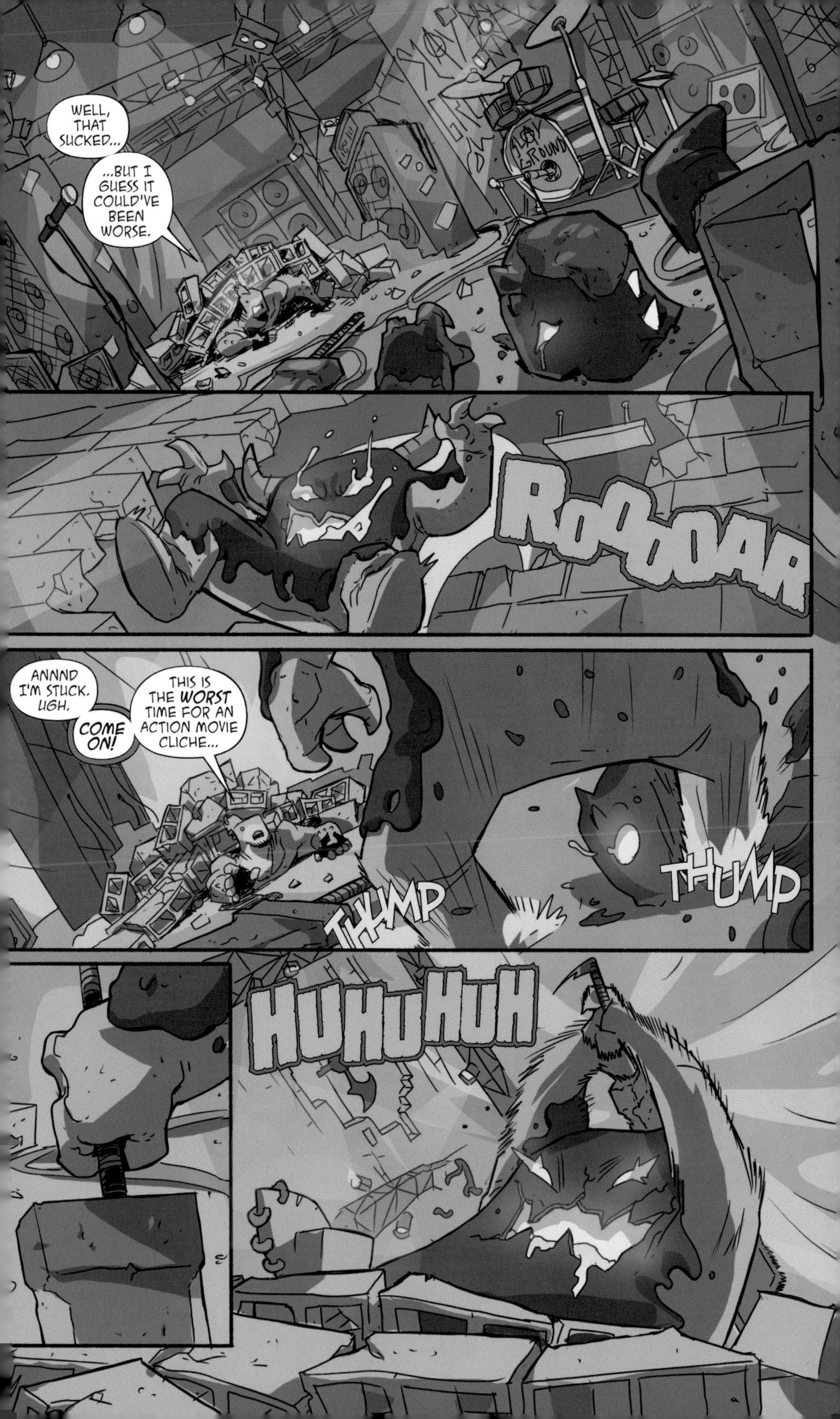
WELL, THAT SUCKED...
...BUT I GUESS IT COULD'VE BEEN WORSE.
ROOOOAR
ANNND I'M STUCK. UGH.
COME ON!
THIS IS THE WORST TIME FOR AN ACTION MOVIE CLICHE...
THUMP
THUMP
HUHUHUH

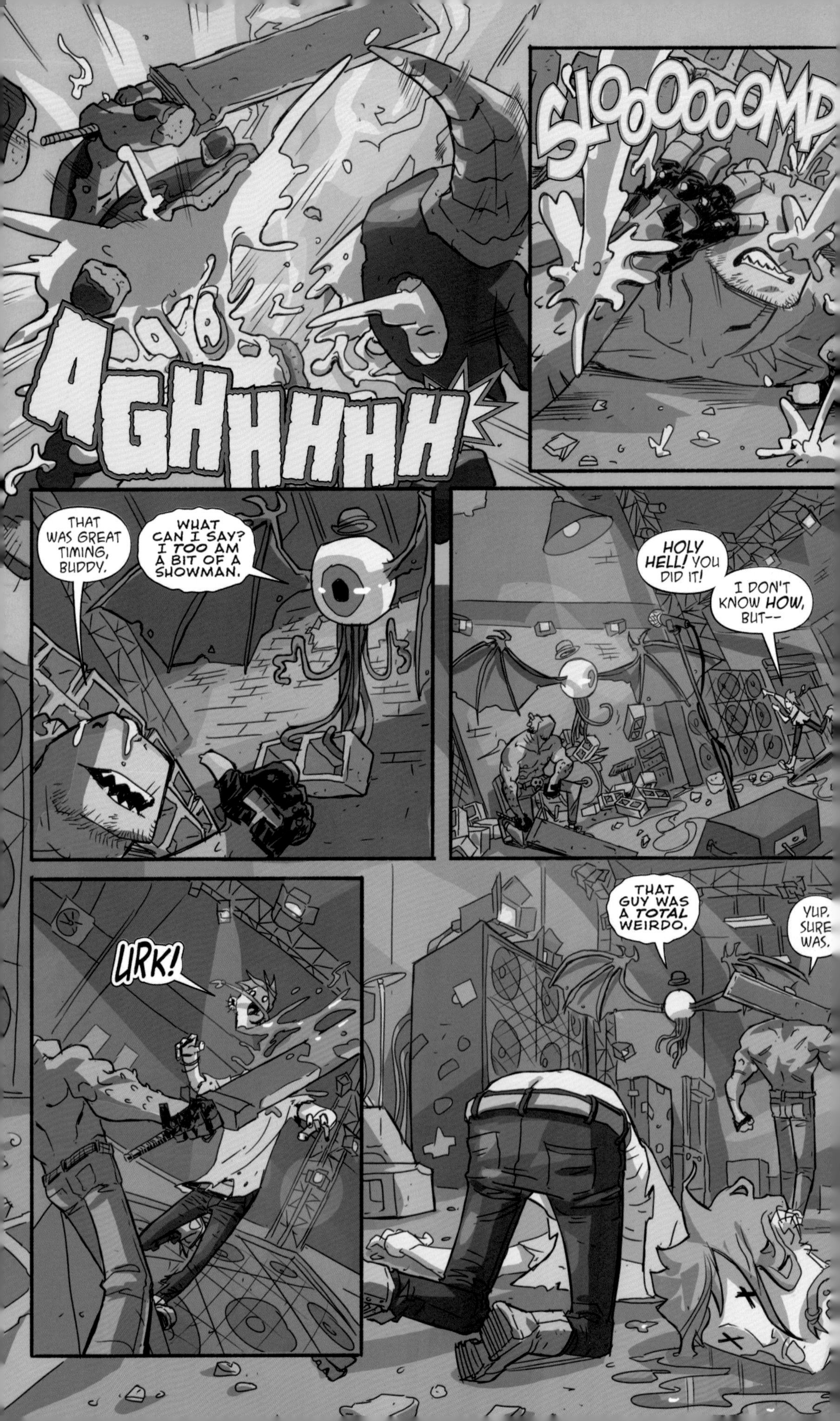
AGHHHHH
SLOOOOOOMP
THAT WAS GREAT TIMING, BUDDY.
WHAT CAN I SAY? I TOO AM A BIT OF A SHOWMAN.
HOLY HELL! YOU DID IT!
I DON'T KNOW HOW, BUT--
URK!
THAT GUY WAS A TOTAL WEIRDO.
YUP. SURE WAS.

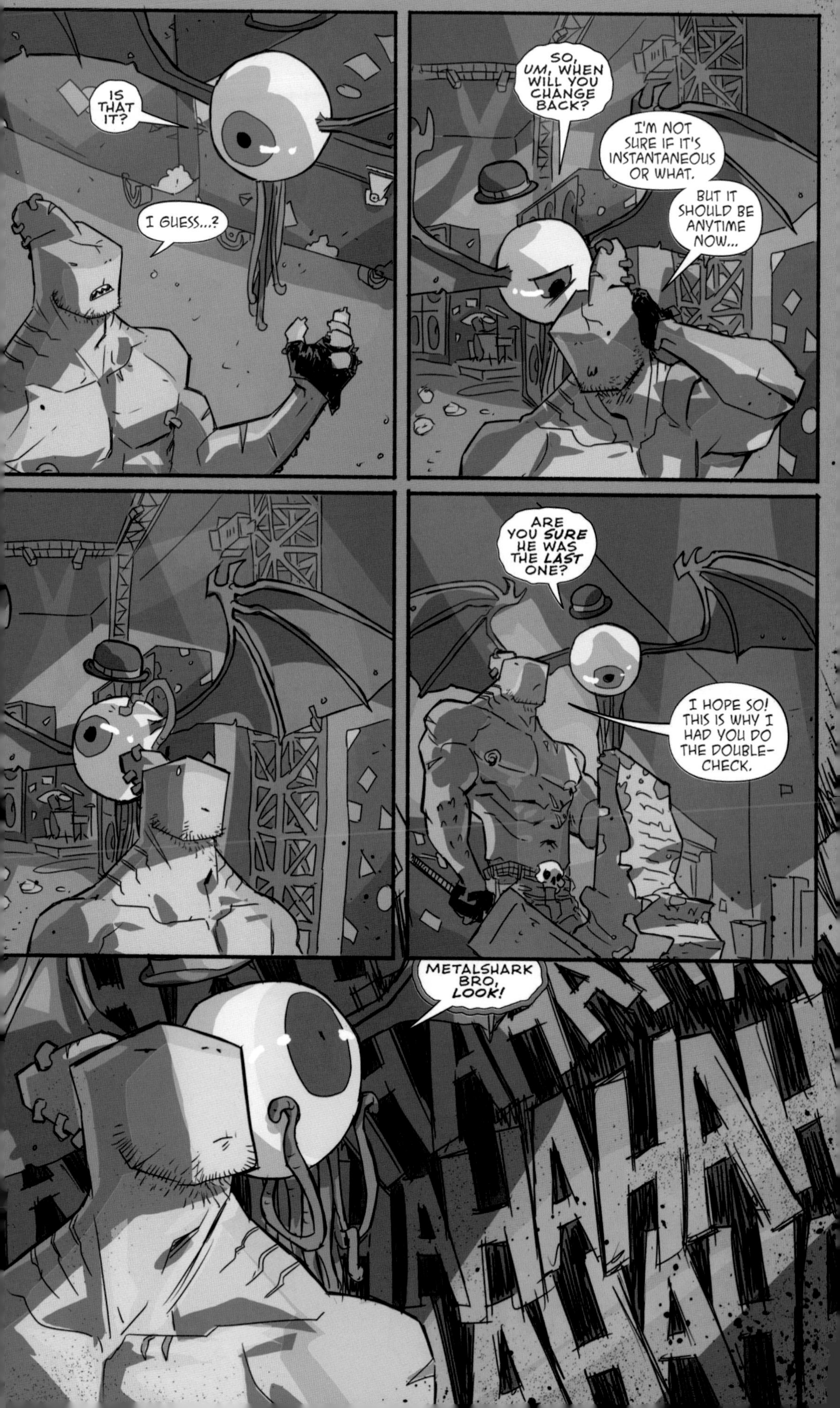
IS THAT IT?
I GUESS...?
SO, UM, WHEN WILL YOU CHANGE BACK?
I'M NOT SURE IF IT'S INSTANTANEOUS OR WHAT.
BUT IT SHOULD BE ANYTIME NOW...
ARE YOU SURE HE WAS THE LAST ONE?
I HOPE SO! THIS IS WHY I HAD YOU DO THE DOUBLE-CHECK.
METALSHARK BRO, LOOK!

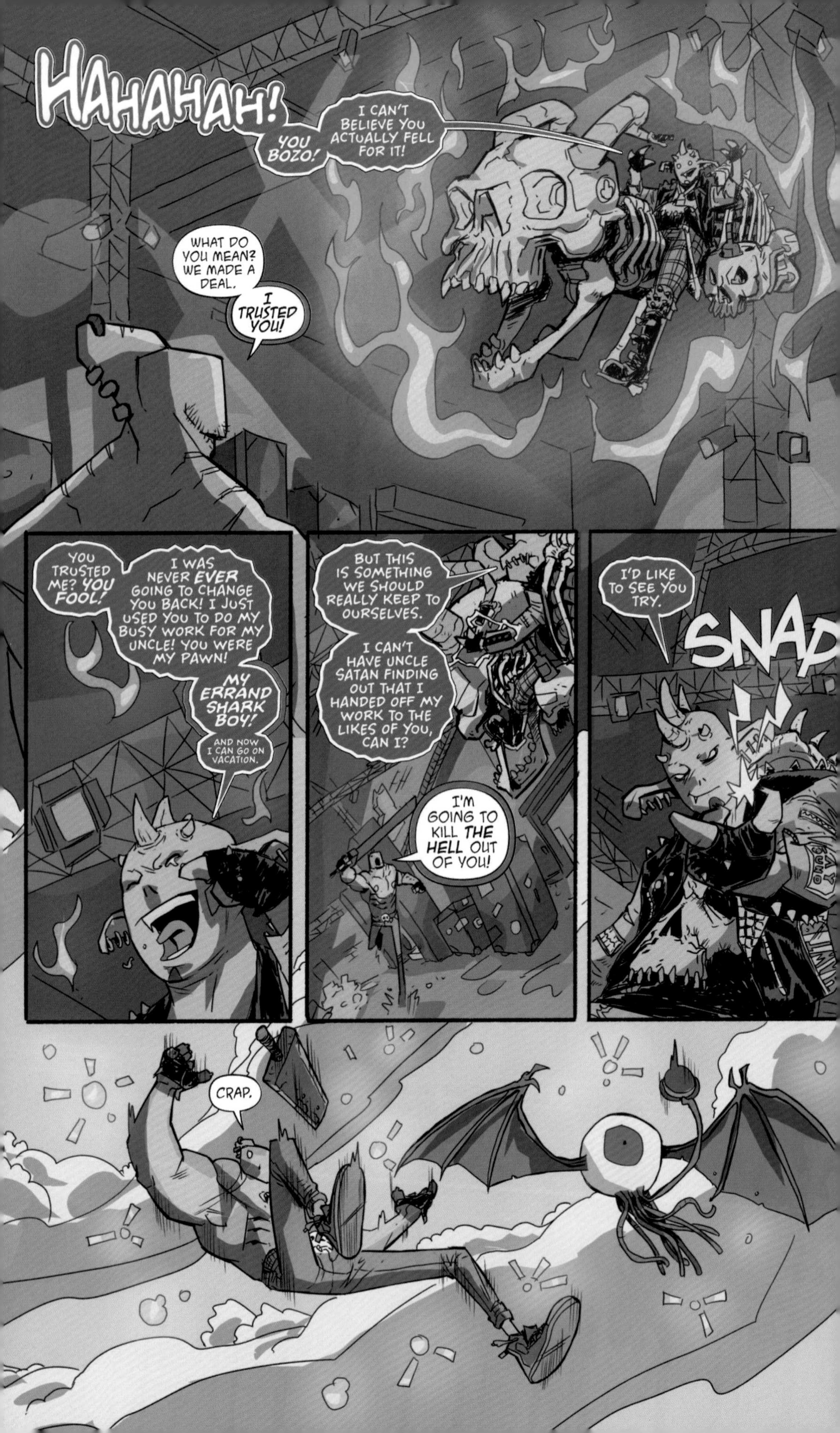
HAHAHAH!
YOU BOZO!
I CAN'T BELIEVE YOU ACTUALLY FELL FOR IT!
WHAT DO YOU MEAN? WE MADE A DEAL.
I TRUSTED YOU!
YOU TRUSTED ME? YOU FOOL!
I WAS NEVER EVER GOING TO CHANGE YOU BACK! I JUST USED YOU TO DO MY BUSY WORK FOR MY UNCLE! YOU WERE MY PAWN!
MY ERRAND SHARK BOY!
AND NOW I CAN GO ON VACATION.
BUT THIS IS SOMETHING WE SHOULD REALLY KEEP TO OURSELVES.
I CAN'T HAVE UNCLE SATAN FINDING OUT THAT I HANDED OFF MY WORK TO THE LIKES OF YOU, CAN I?
I'M GOING TO KILL THE HELL OUT OF YOU!
I'D LIKE TO SEE YOU TRY.
SNAP
CRAP.

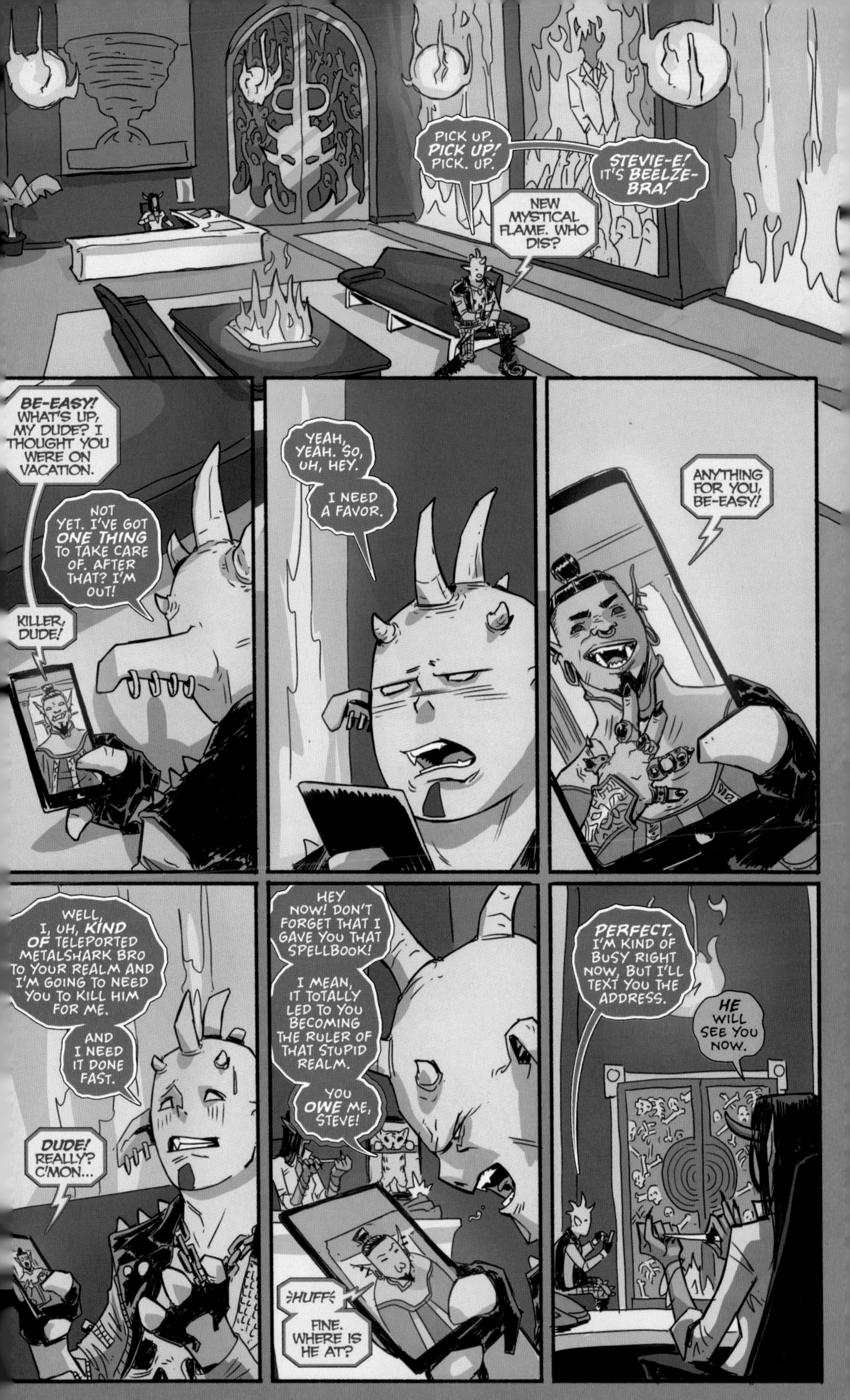
PICK UP. PICK UP! PICK. UP.
STEVIE-E! IT'S BEELZE-BRA!
NEW MYSTICAL FLAME. WHO DIS?
BE-EASY! WHAT'S UP, MY DUDE? I THOUGHT YOU WERE ON VACATION.
NOT YET. I'VE GOT ONE THING TO TAKE CARE OF. AFTER THAT? I'M OUT!
KILLER, DUDE!
YEAH, YEAH. SO, UH, HEY.
I NEED A FAVOR.
ANYTHING FOR YOU, BE-EASY!
WELL, I, UH, KIND OF TELEPORTED METALSHARK BRO TO YOUR REALM AND I'M GOING TO NEED YOU TO KILL HIM FOR ME.
AND I NEED IT DONE FAST.
DUDE! REALLY? C'MON...
HEY NOW! DON'T FORGET THAT I GAVE YOU THAT SPELLBOOK!
I MEAN, IT TOTALLY LED TO YOU BECOMING THE RULER OF THAT STUPID REALM.
YOU OWE ME, STEVE!
HUFF
FINE. WHERE IS HE AT?
PERFECT. I'M KIND OF BUSY RIGHT NOW, BUT I'LL TEXT YOU THE ADDRESS.
HE WILL SEE YOU NOW.

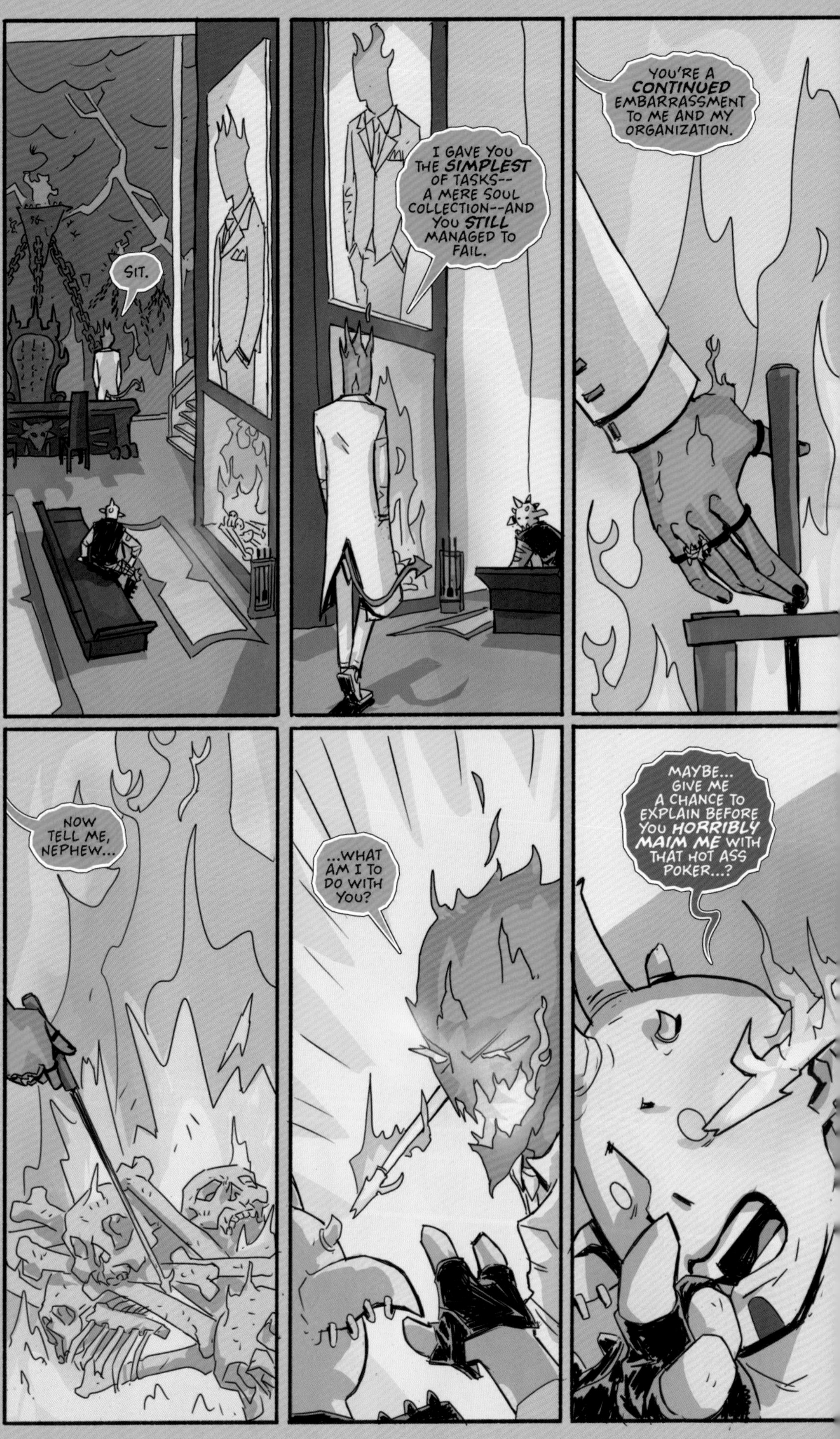
SIT.
I GAVE YOU THE **SIMPLEST** OF TASKS-- A MERE SOUL COLLECTION--AND YOU **STILL** MANAGED TO FAIL.
YOU'RE A **CONTINUED** EMBARRASSMENT TO ME AND MY ORGANIZATION.
NOW TELL ME, NEPHEW...
...WHAT AM I TO DO WITH YOU?
MAYBE... GIVE ME A CHANCE TO EXPLAIN BEFORE YOU **HORRIBLY MAIM ME** WITH THAT HOT ASS POKER...?

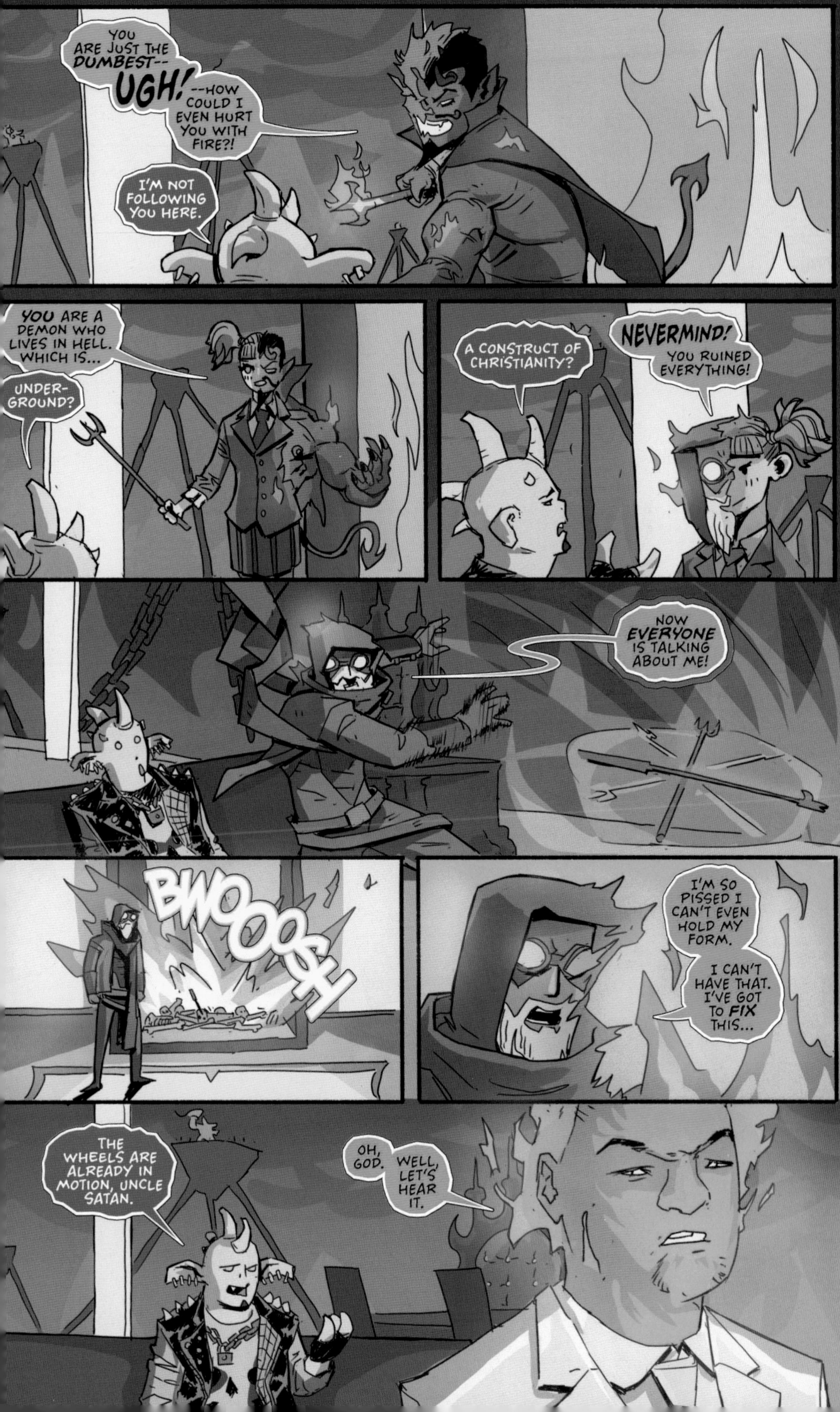
YOU ARE JUST THE DUMBEST--
UGH!
--HOW COULD I EVEN HURT YOU WITH FIRE?!
I'M NOT FOLLOWING YOU HERE.
YOU ARE A DEMON WHO LIVES IN HELL. WHICH IS...
UNDER-GROUND?
A CONSTRUCT OF CHRISTIANITY?
NEVERMIND!
YOU RUINED EVERYTHING!
NOW EVERYONE IS TALKING ABOUT ME!
BWOOOSH
I'M SO PISSED I CAN'T EVEN HOLD MY FORM.
I CAN'T HAVE THAT. I'VE GOT TO FIX THIS...
THE WHEELS ARE ALREADY IN MOTION, UNCLE SATAN.
OH, GOD.
WELL, LET'S HEAR IT.

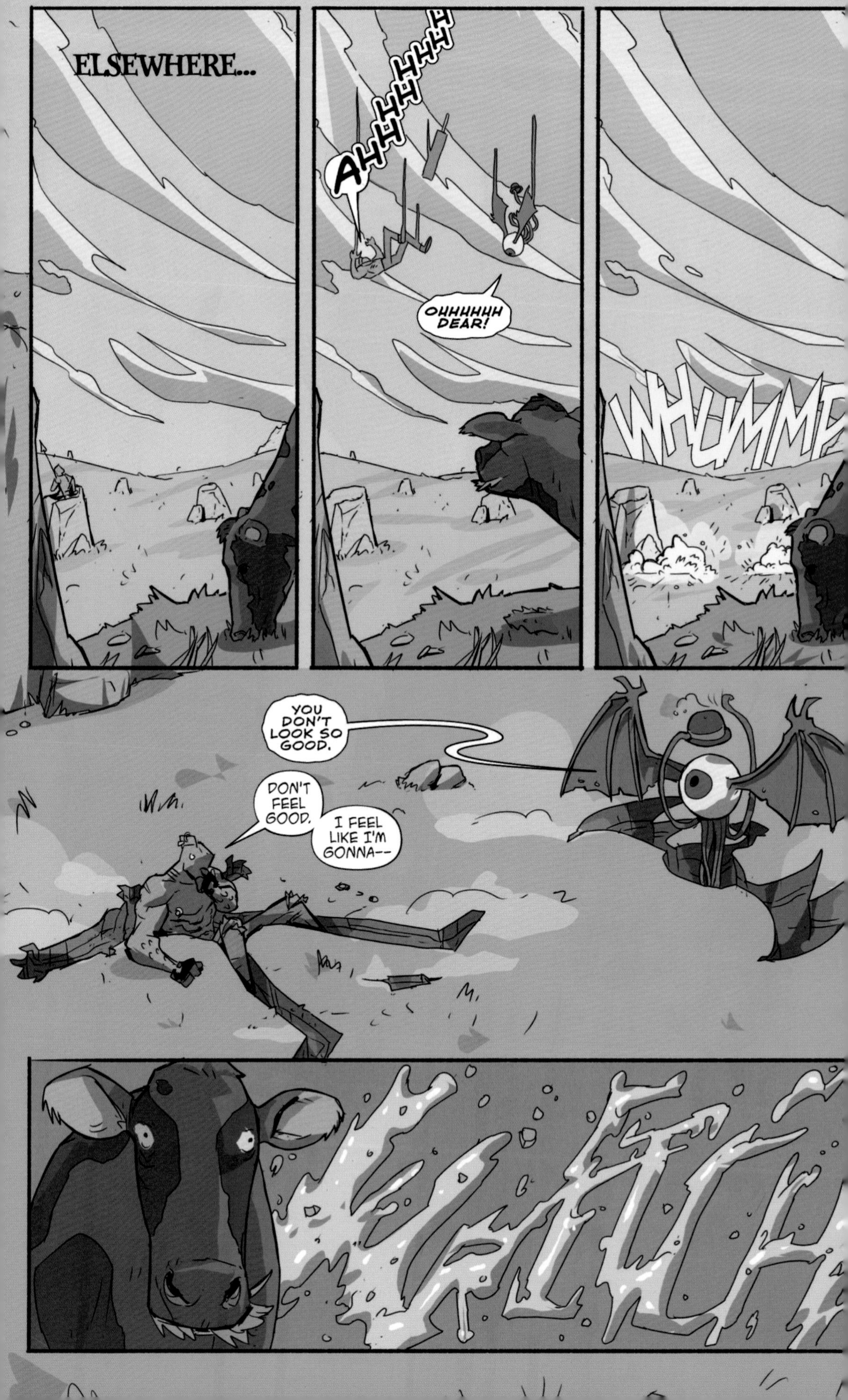

ELSEWHERE...
AHHHHHHH
OHHHHHH DEAR!
WHUMMP
YOU DON'T LOOK SO GOOD.
DON'T FEEL GOOD.
I FEEL LIKE I'M GONNA--

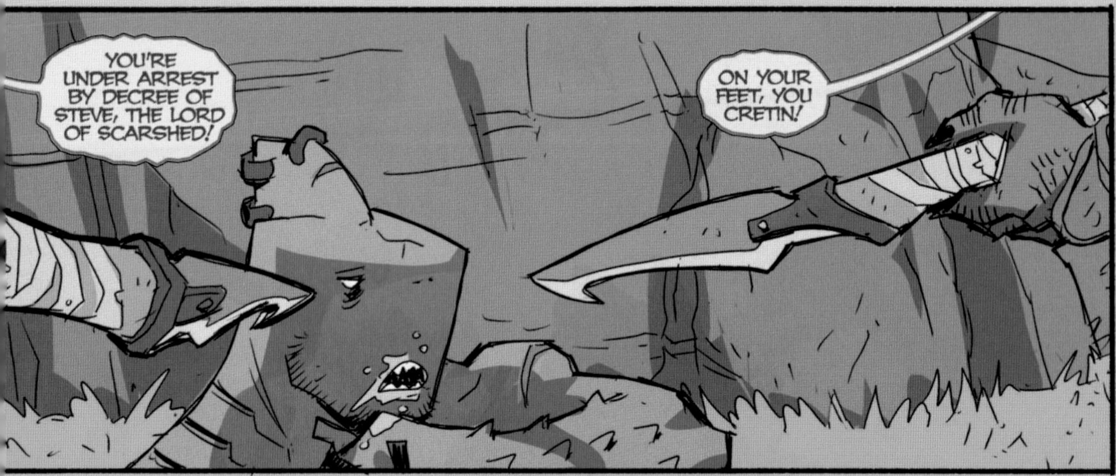
YOU'RE UNDER ARREST BY DECREE OF STEVE, THE LORD OF SCARSHED!
ON YOUR FEET, YOU CRETIN!
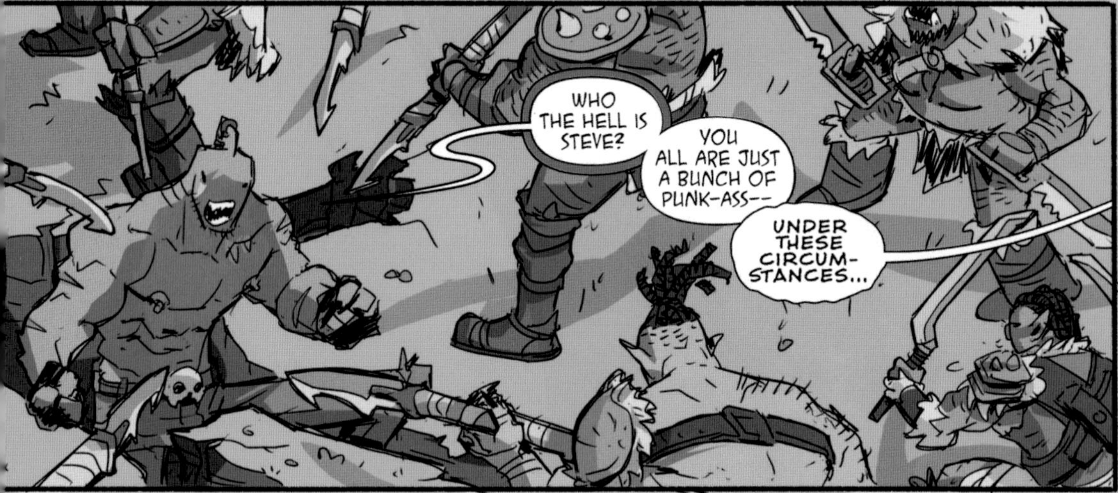
WHO THE HELL IS STEVE?
YOU ALL ARE JUST A BUNCH OF PUNK-ASS--
UNDER THESE CIRCUM-STANCES...
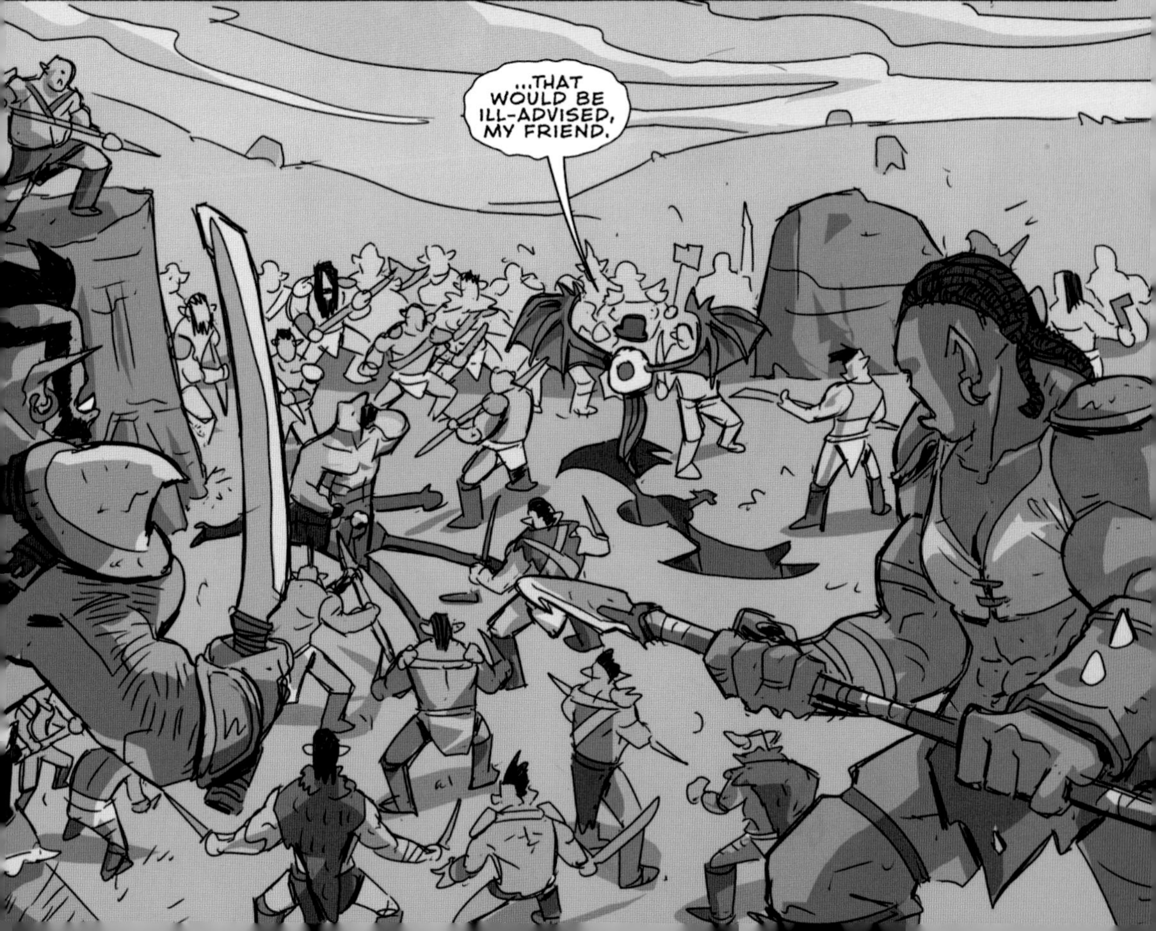
...THAT WOULD BE ILL-ADVISED, MY FRIEND.

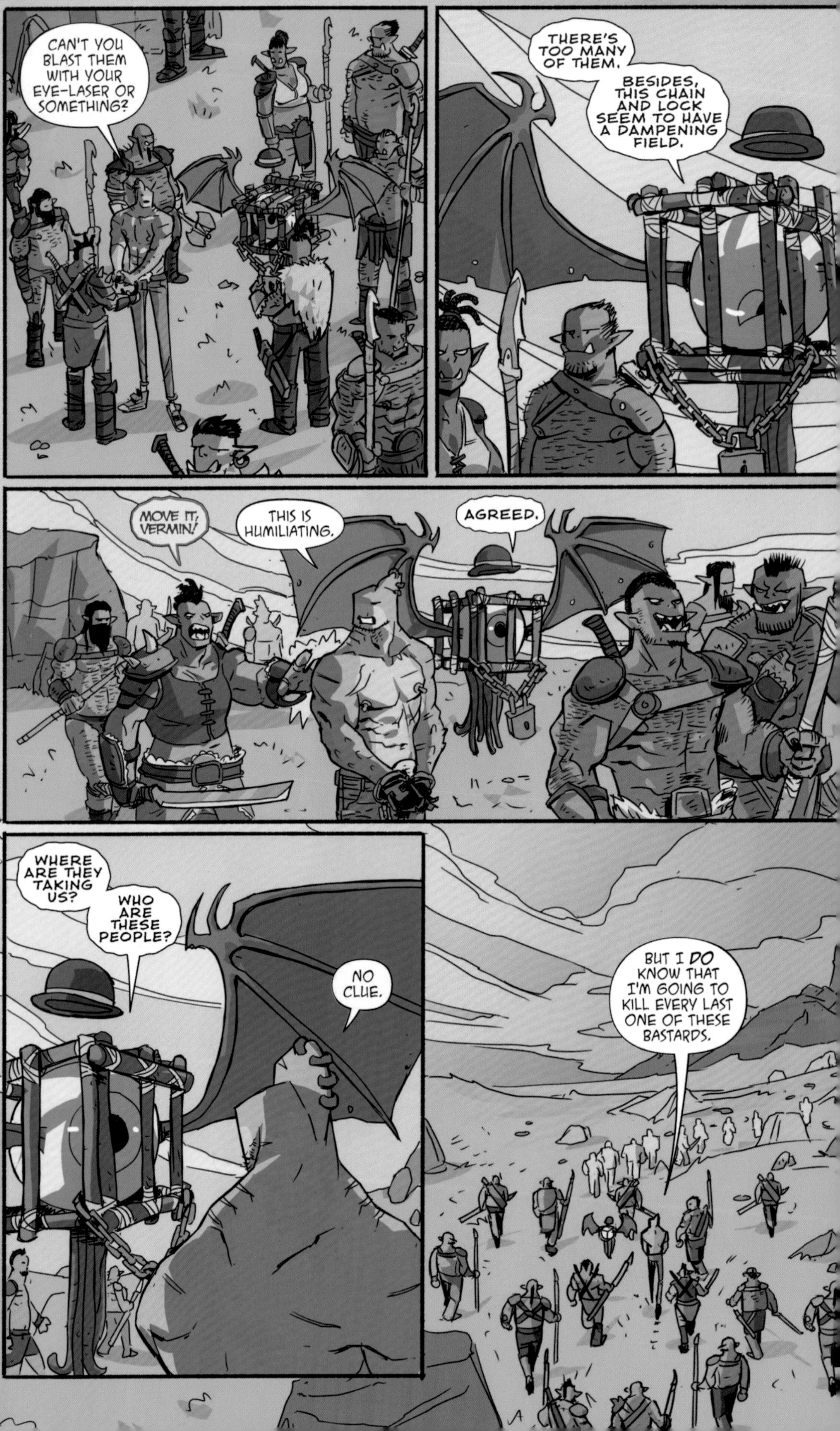
CAN'T YOU BLAST THEM WITH YOUR EYE-LASER OR SOMETHING?
THERE'S TOO MANY OF THEM.
BESIDES, THIS CHAIN AND LOCK SEEM TO HAVE A DAMPENING FIELD.
MOVE IT, VERMIN!
THIS IS HUMILIATING.
AGREED.
WHERE ARE THEY TAKING US?
WHO ARE THESE PEOPLE?
NO CLUE.
BUT I DO KNOW THAT I'M GOING TO KILL EVERY LAST ONE OF THESE BASTARDS.

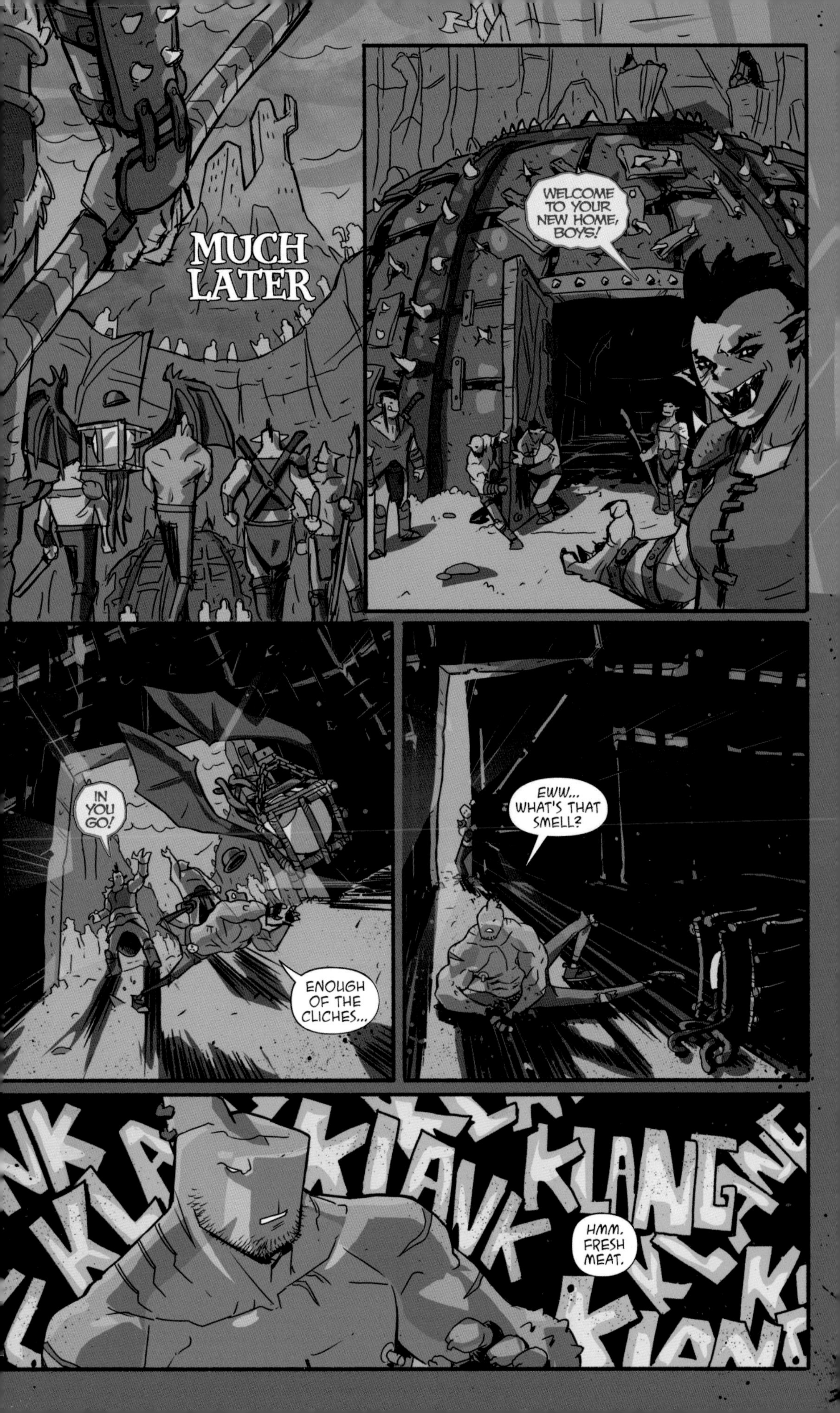
MUCH LATER
WELCOME TO YOUR NEW HOME, BOYS!
IN YOU GO!
ENOUGH OF THE CLICHES...
EWW... WHAT'S THAT SMELL?
KLANK
KLANG
HMM. FRESH MEAT.

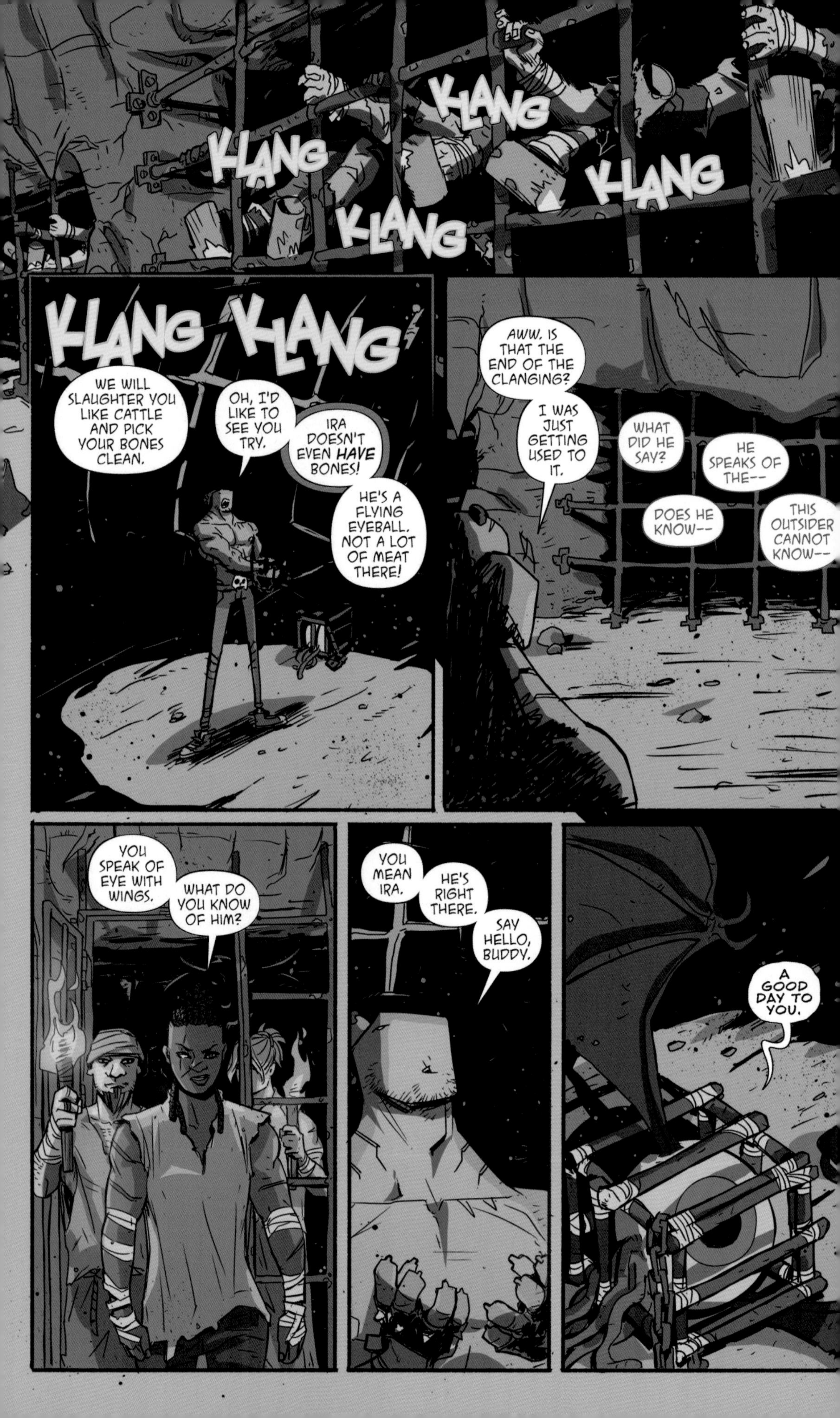
KLANG
KLANG
KLANG
KLANG
KLANG KLANG
WE WILL SLAUGHTER YOU LIKE CATTLE AND PICK YOUR BONES CLEAN.
OH, I'D LIKE TO SEE YOU TRY.
IRA DOESN'T EVEN HAVE BONES!
HE'S A FLYING EYEBALL. NOT A LOT OF MEAT THERE!
AWW. IS THAT THE END OF THE CLANGING?
I WAS JUST GETTING USED TO IT.
WHAT DID HE SAY?
HE SPEAKS OF THE--
DOES HE KNOW--
THIS OUTSIDER CANNOT KNOW--
YOU SPEAK OF EYE WITH WINGS.
WHAT DO YOU KNOW OF HIM?
YOU MEAN IRA.
HE'S RIGHT THERE.
SAY HELLO, BUDDY.
A GOOD DAY TO YOU.

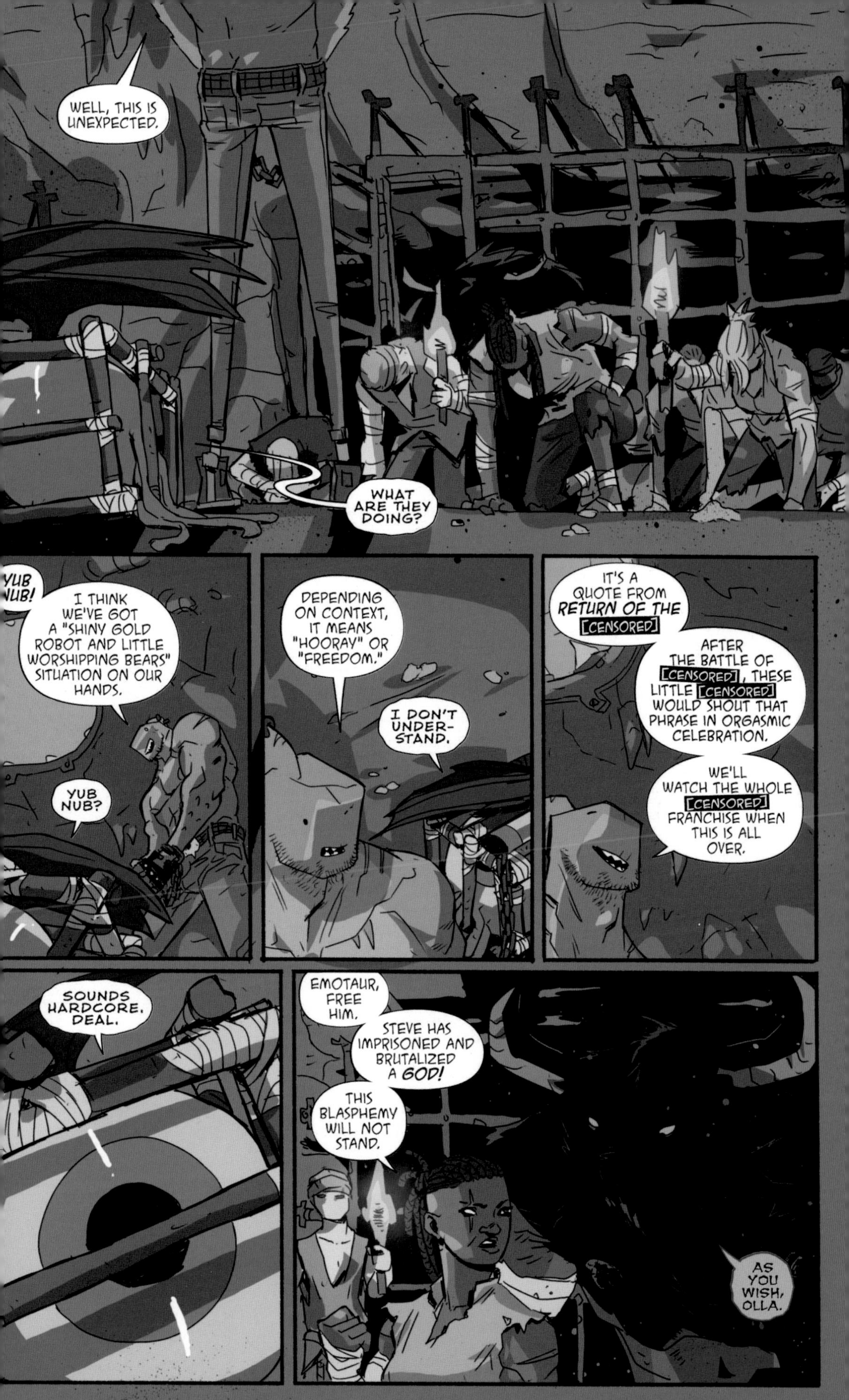

WELL, THIS IS UNEXPECTED.
WHAT ARE THEY DOING?
YUB NUB!
I THINK WE'VE GOT A "SHINY GOLD ROBOT AND LITTLE WORSHIPPING BEARS" SITUATION ON OUR HANDS.
YUB NUB?
DEPENDING ON CONTEXT, IT MEANS "HOORAY" OR "FREEDOM."
I DON'T UNDERSTAND.
IT'S A QUOTE FROM ***RETURN OF THE*** [CENSORED]
AFTER THE BATTLE OF [CENSORED], THESE LITTLE [CENSORED] WOULD SHOUT THAT PHRASE IN ORGASMIC CELEBRATION.
WE'LL WATCH THE WHOLE [CENSORED] FRANCHISE WHEN THIS IS ALL OVER.
SOUNDS HARDCORE. DEAL.
EMOTAUR, FREE HIM.
STEVE HAS IMPRISONED AND BRUTALIZED A ***GOD!***
THIS BLASPHEMY WILL NOT STAND.
AS YOU WISH, OLLA.

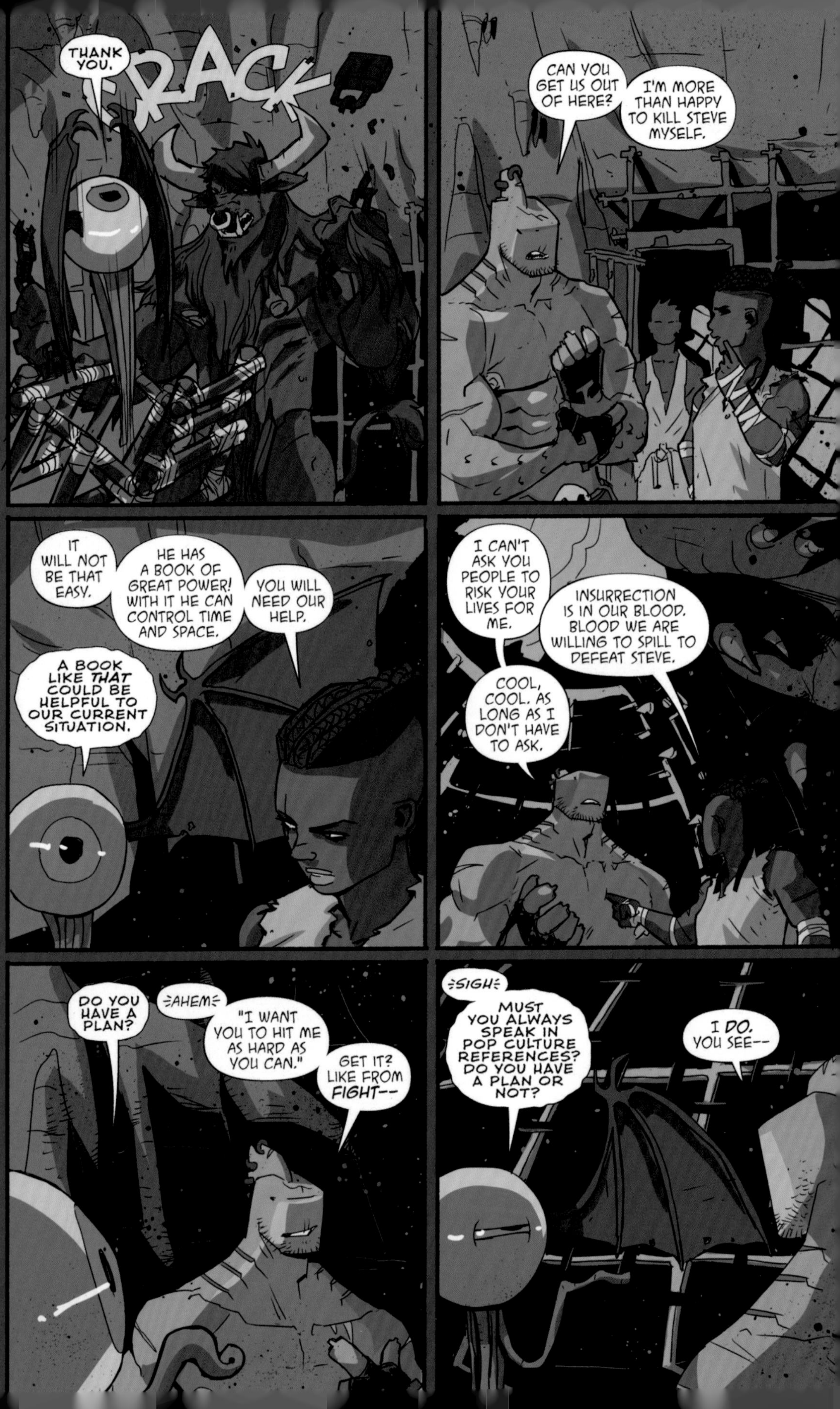
THANK YOU.
CRACK
CAN YOU GET US OUT OF HERE?
I'M MORE THAN HAPPY TO KILL STEVE MYSELF.
IT WILL NOT BE THAT EASY.
HE HAS A BOOK OF GREAT POWER! WITH IT HE CAN CONTROL TIME AND SPACE.
YOU WILL NEED OUR HELP.
A BOOK LIKE *THAT* COULD BE HELPFUL TO OUR CURRENT SITUATION.
I CAN'T ASK YOU PEOPLE TO RISK YOUR LIVES FOR ME.
INSURRECTION IS IN OUR BLOOD. BLOOD WE ARE WILLING TO SPILL TO DEFEAT STEVE.
COOL, COOL. AS LONG AS I DON'T HAVE TO ASK.
DO YOU HAVE A PLAN?
AHEM
"I WANT YOU TO HIT ME AS HARD AS YOU CAN."
GET IT? LIKE FROM *FIGHT*--
SIGH
MUST YOU ALWAYS SPEAK IN POP CULTURE REFERENCES? DO YOU HAVE A PLAN OR NOT?
I *DO*. YOU SEE--

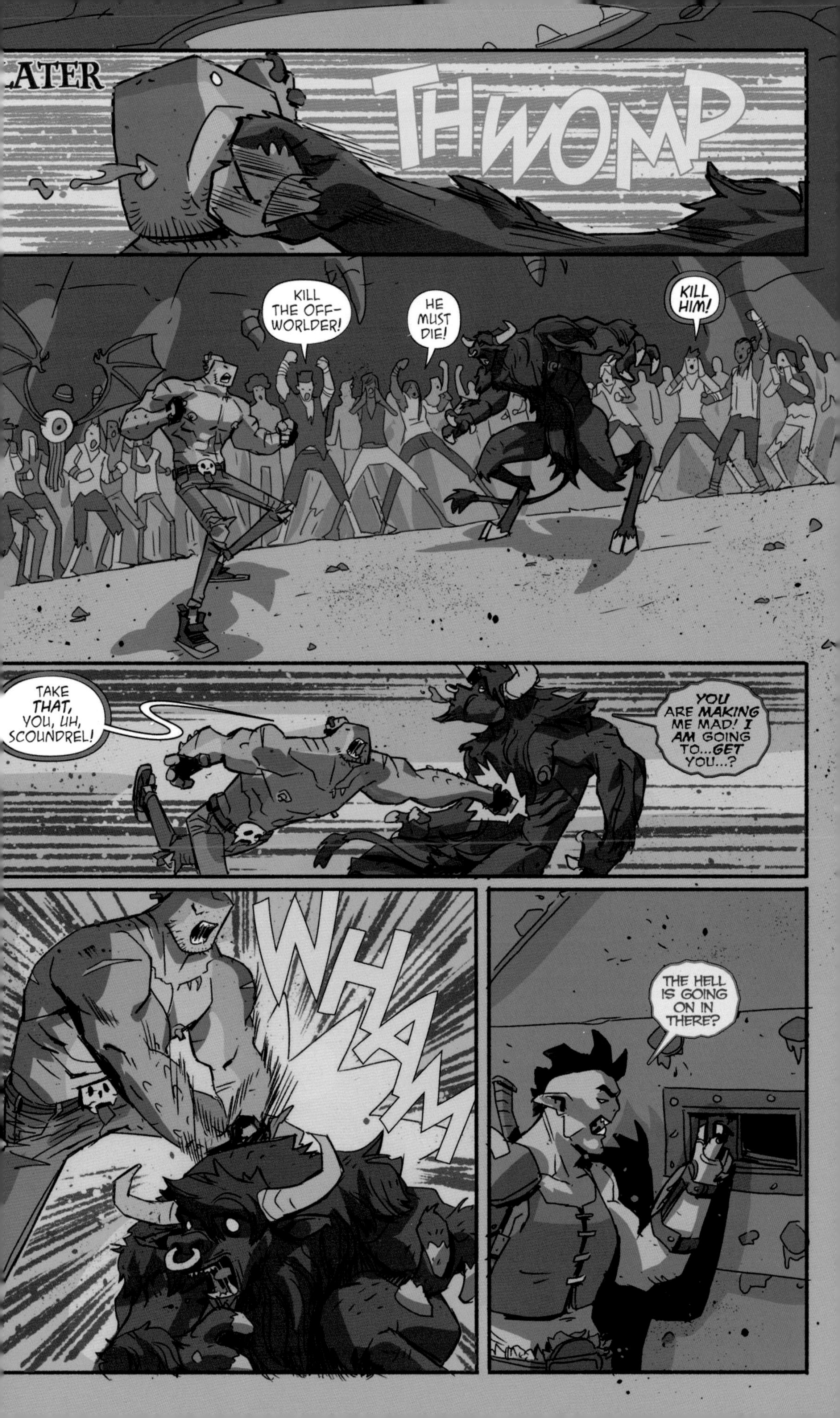

LATER
THWOMP
KILL THE OFF-WORLDER!
HE MUST DIE!
KILL HIM!
TAKE THAT, YOU, UH, SCOUNDREL!
YOU ARE MAKING ME MAD! I AM GOING TO...GET YOU...?
WHAM
THE HELL IS GOING ON IN THERE?

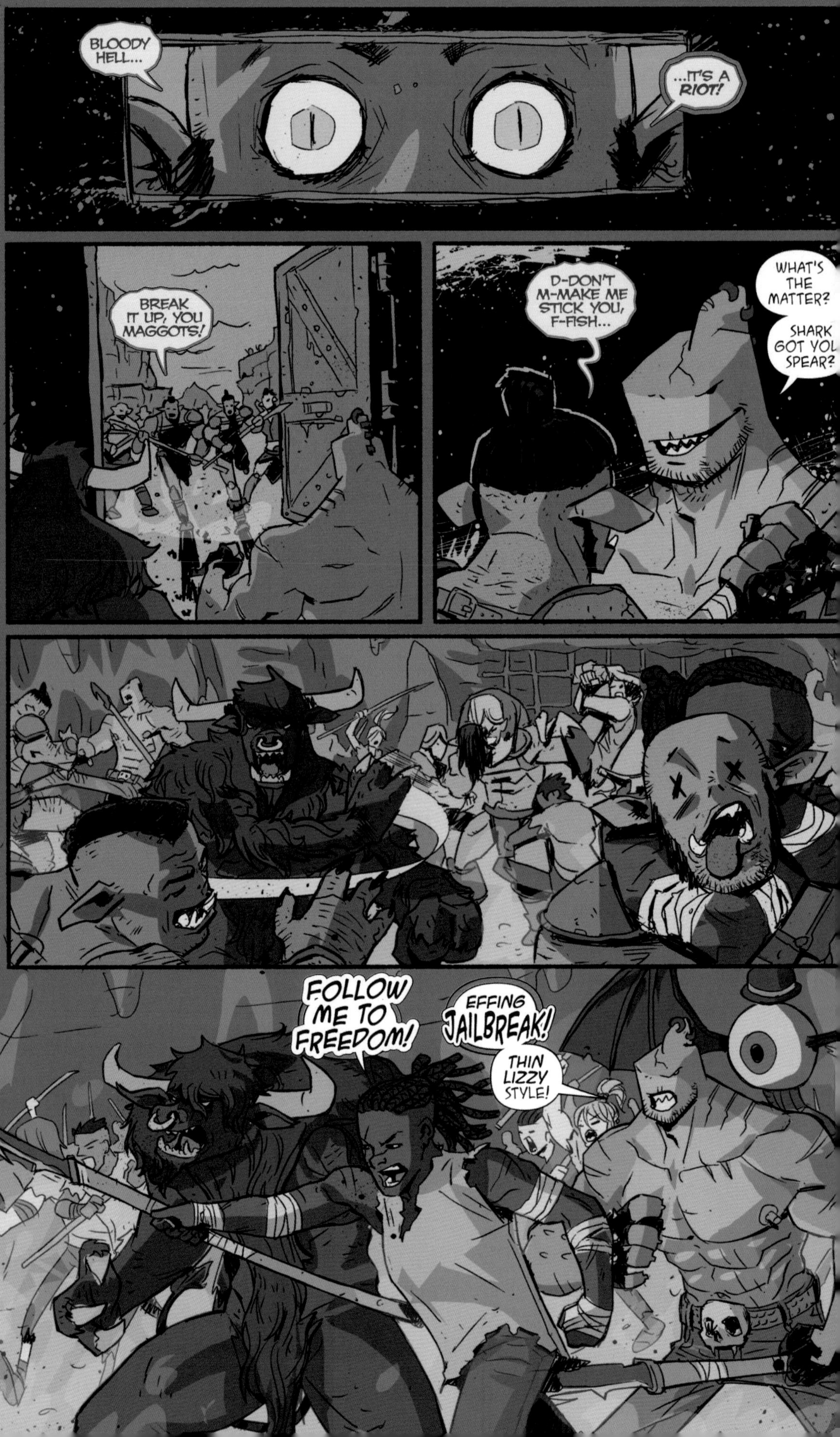
BLOODY HELL...
...IT'S A RIOT!
BREAK IT UP, YOU MAGGOTS!
D-DON'T M-MAKE ME STICK YOU, F-FISH...
WHAT'S THE MATTER?
SHARK GOT YOU SPEAR?
FOLLOW ME TO FREEDOM!
EFFING JAILBREAK!
THIN LIZZY STYLE!

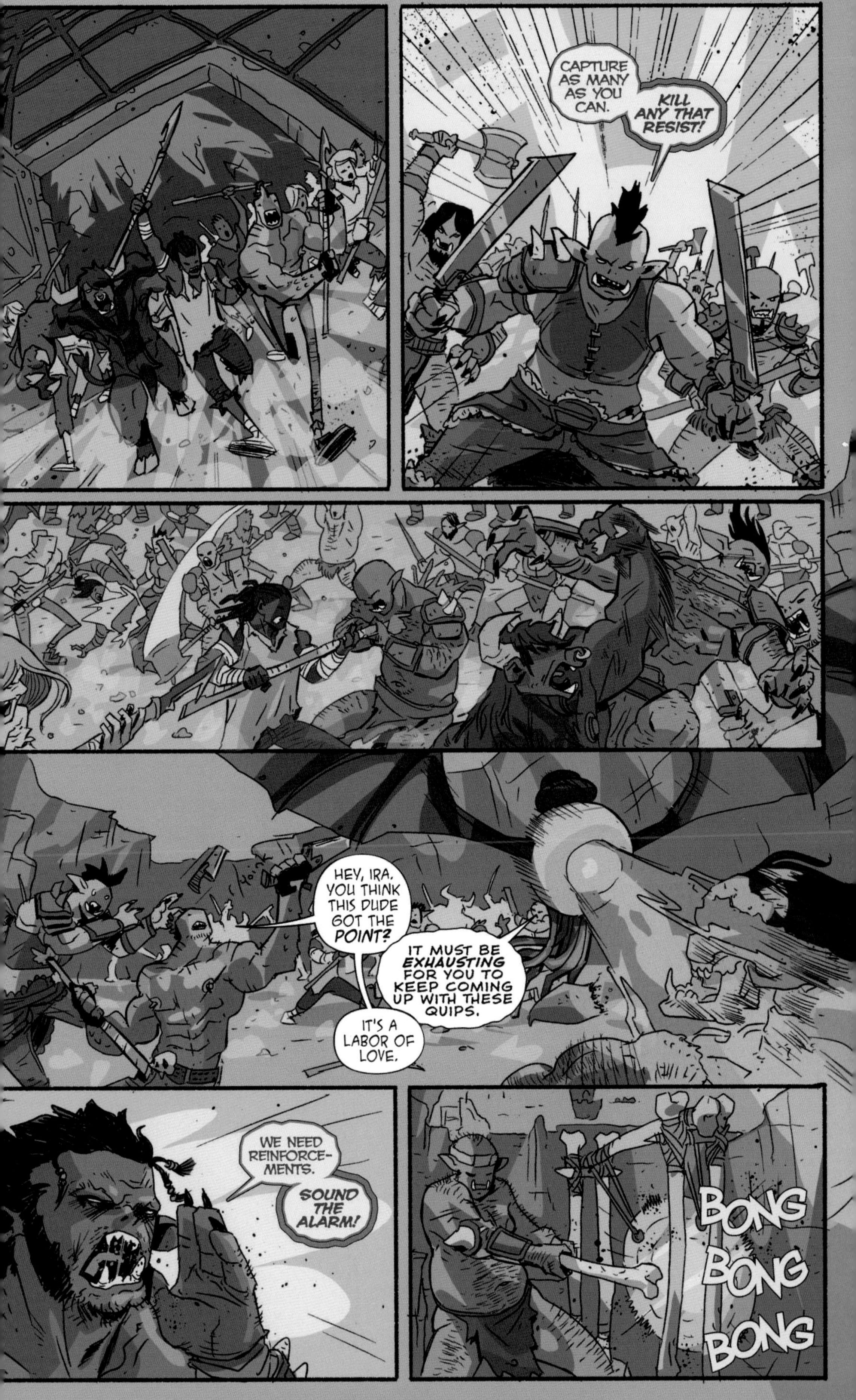
CAPTURE AS MANY AS YOU CAN.
KILL ANY THAT RESIST!
HEY, IRA, YOU THINK THIS DUDE GOT THE POINT?
IT MUST BE EXHAUSTING FOR YOU TO KEEP COMING UP WITH THESE QUIPS.
IT'S A LABOR OF LOVE.
WE NEED REINFORCE-MENTS.
SOUND THE ALARM!
BONG
BONG
BONG

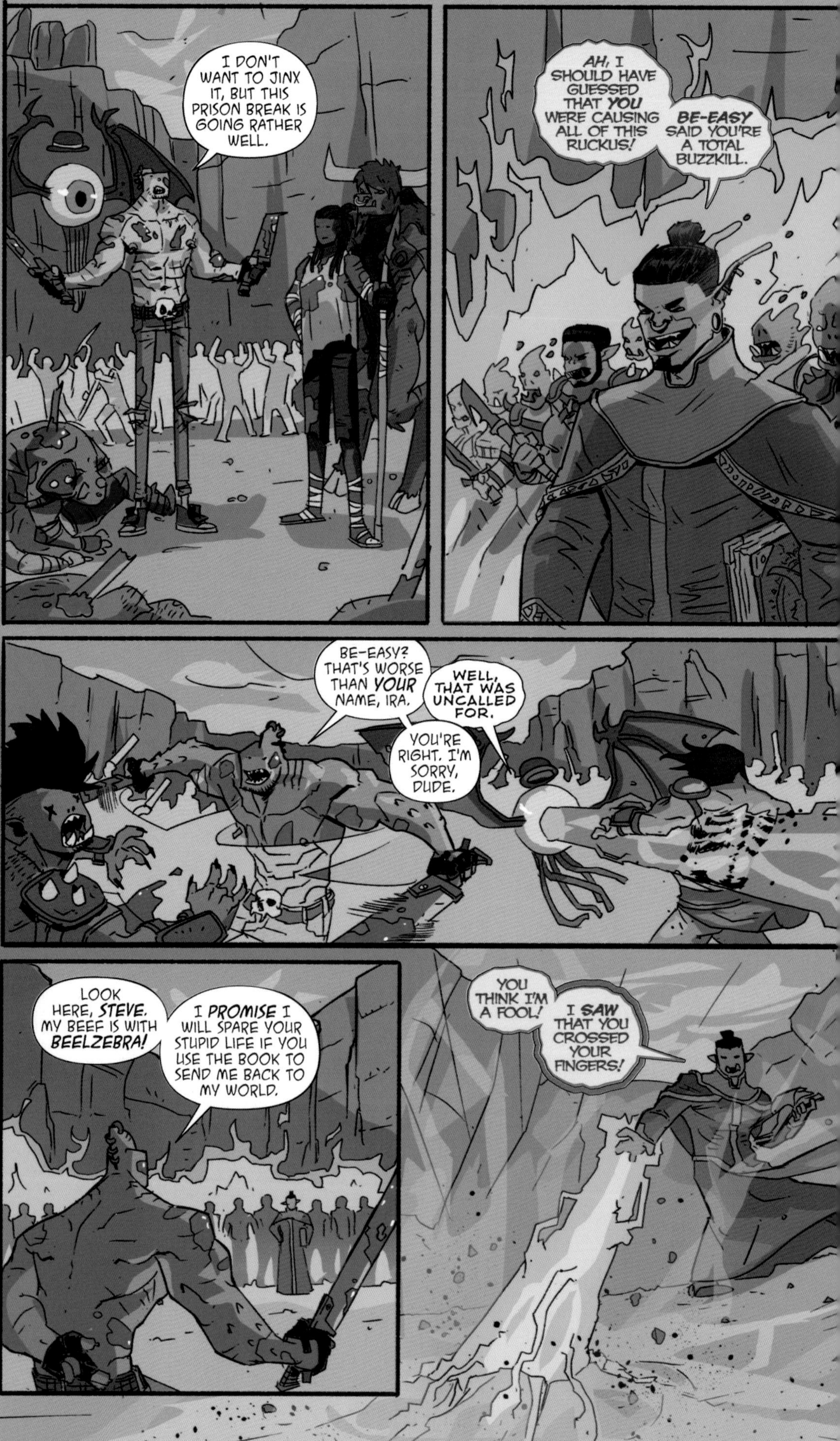
I DON'T WANT TO JINX IT, BUT THIS PRISON BREAK IS GOING RATHER WELL.
AH, I SHOULD HAVE GUESSED THAT YOU WERE CAUSING ALL OF THIS RUCKUS!
BE-EASY SAID YOU'RE A TOTAL BUZZKILL.
BE-EASY? THAT'S WORSE THAN YOUR NAME, IRA.
WELL, THAT WAS UNCALLED FOR.
YOU'RE RIGHT. I'M SORRY, DUDE.
LOOK HERE, STEVE. MY BEEF IS WITH BEELZEBRA!
I PROMISE I WILL SPARE YOUR STUPID LIFE IF YOU USE THE BOOK TO SEND ME BACK TO MY WORLD.
YOU THINK I'M A FOOL!
I SAW THAT YOU CROSSED YOUR FINGERS!

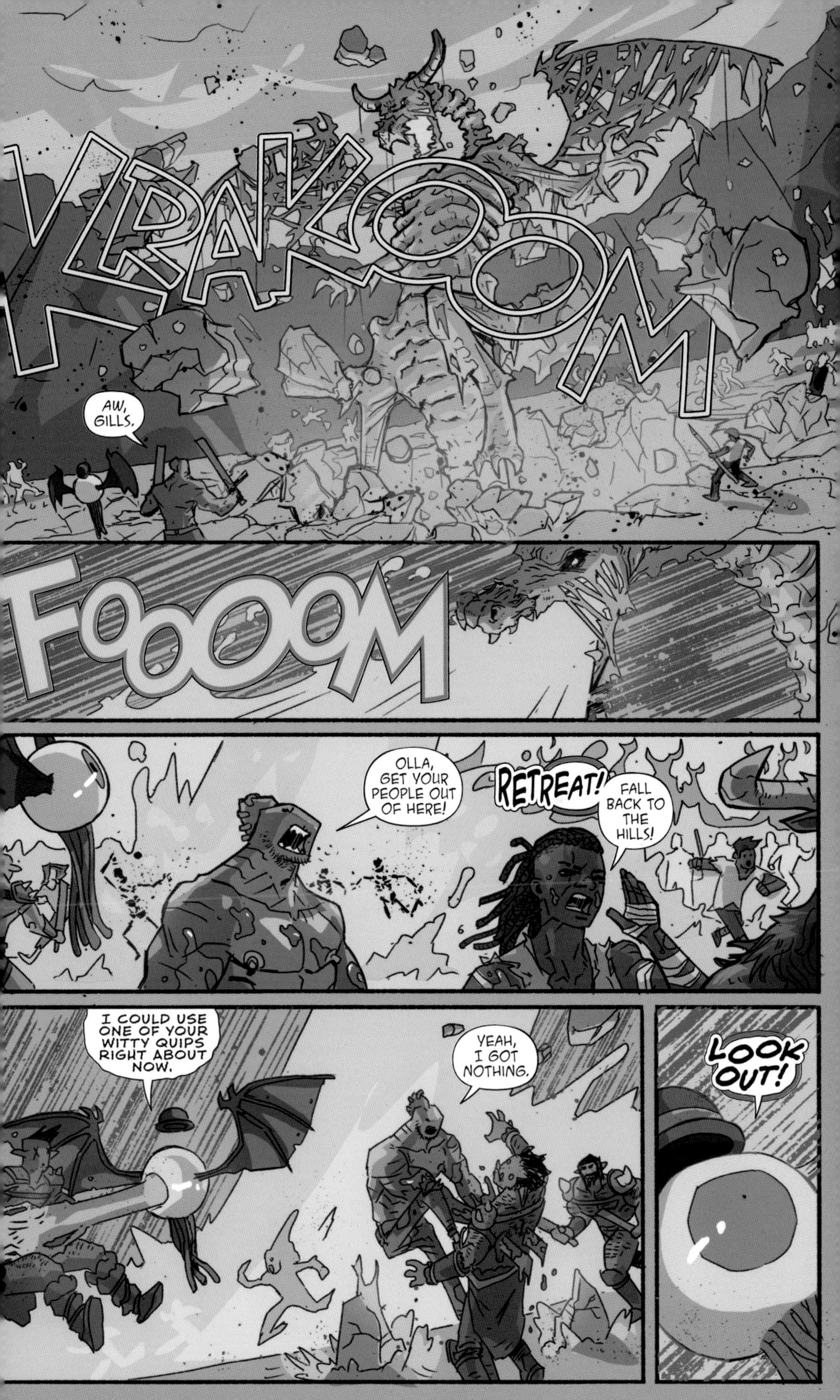
VLRAKOOOM
AW, GILLS.
FOOOOM
OLLA, GET YOUR PEOPLE OUT OF HERE!
RETREAT!
FALL BACK TO THE HILLS!
I COULD USE ONE OF YOUR WITTY QUIPS RIGHT ABOUT NOW.
YEAH, I GOT NOTHING.
LOOK OUT!

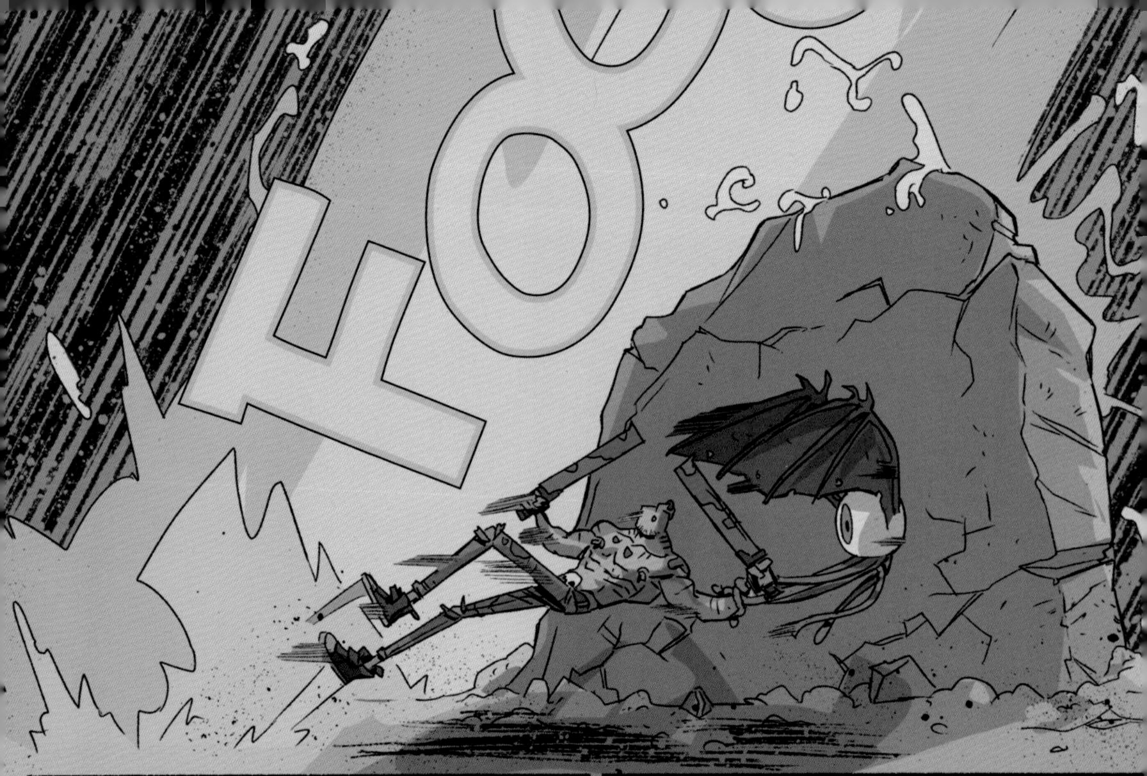
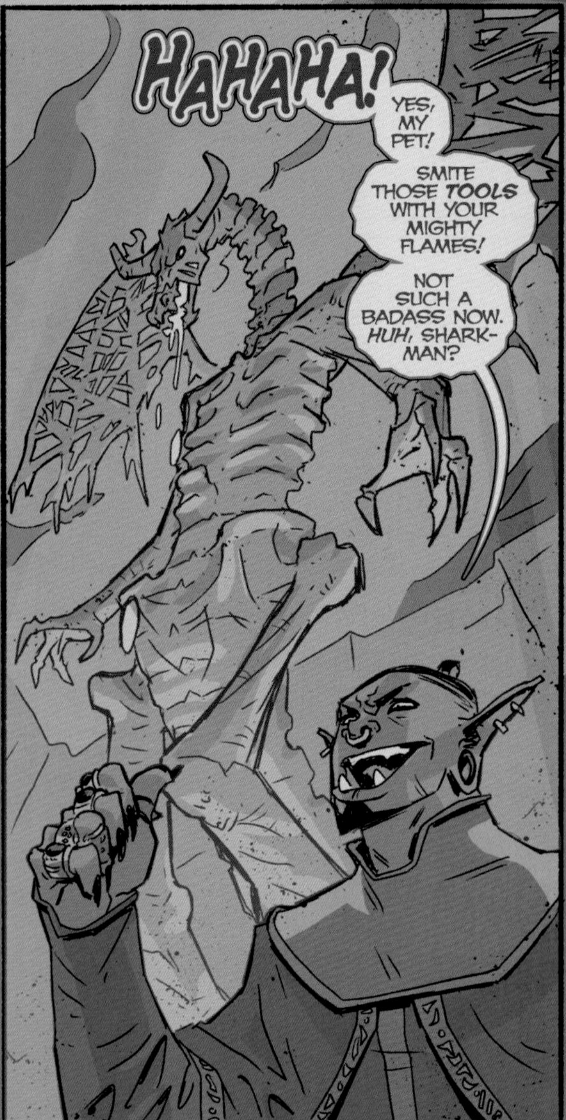
HAHAHA!
YES, MY PET!
SMITE THOSE *TOOLS* WITH YOUR MIGHTY FLAMES!
NOT SUCH A BADASS NOW. *HUH,* SHARK-MAN?
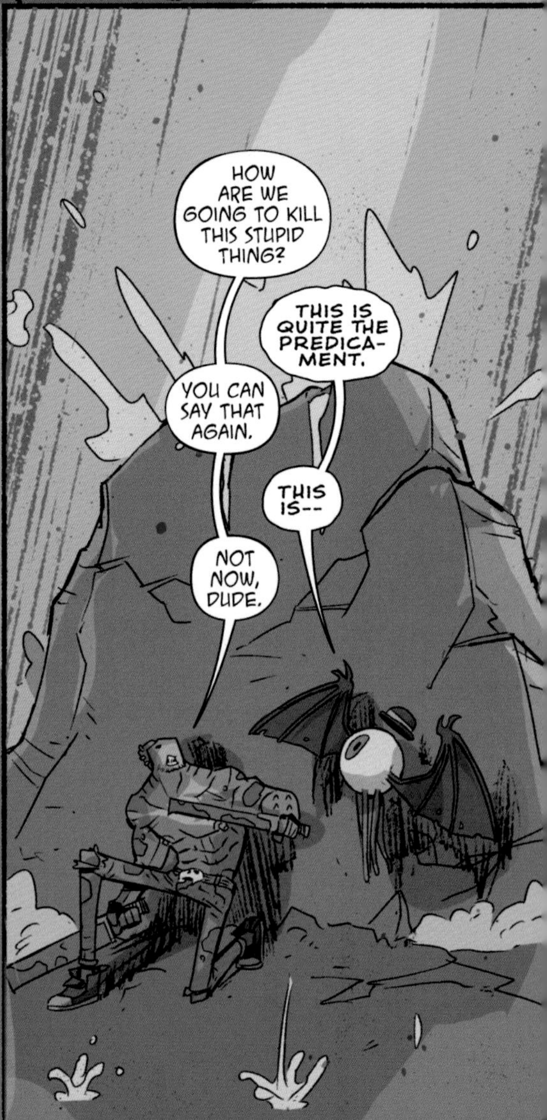
HOW ARE WE GOING TO KILL THIS STUPID THING?
THIS IS QUITE THE PREDICAMENT.
YOU CAN SAY THAT AGAIN.
THIS IS--
NOT NOW, DUDE.

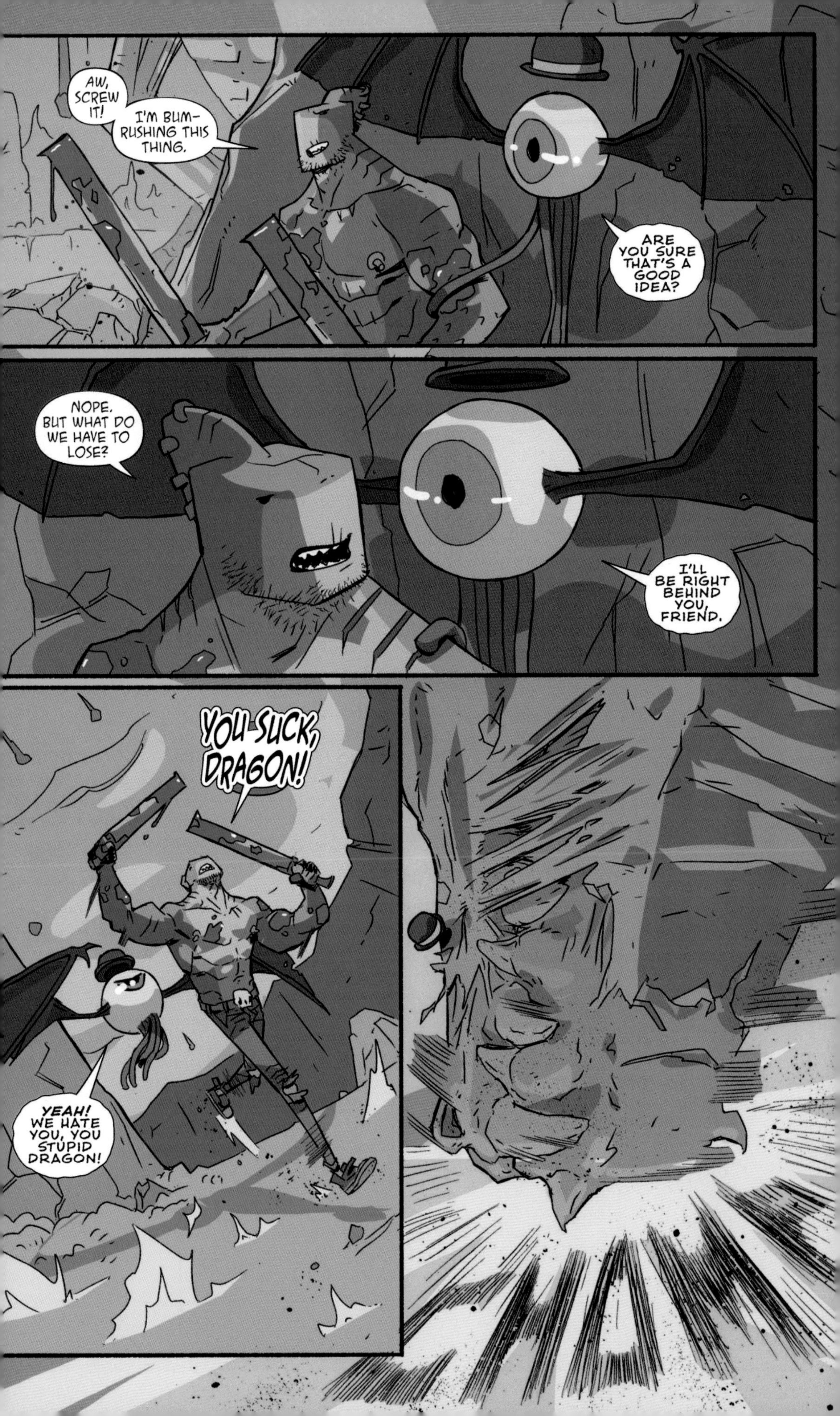
AW, SCREW IT!
I'M BUM-RUSHING THIS THING.
ARE YOU SURE THAT'S A GOOD IDEA?
NOPE. BUT WHAT DO WE HAVE TO LOSE?
I'LL BE RIGHT BEHIND YOU, FRIEND.
YOU SUCK, DRAGON!
YEAH! WE HATE YOU, YOU STUPID DRAGON!

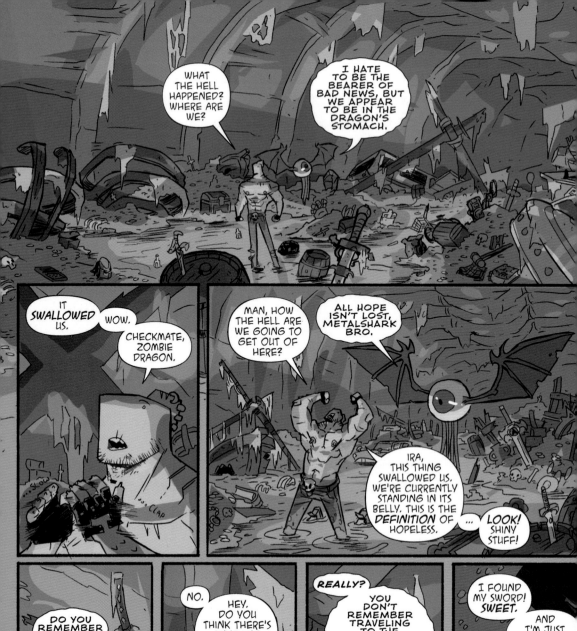

WHAT THE HELL HAPPENED? WHERE ARE WE?

I HATE TO BE THE BEARER OF BAD NEWS, BUT WE APPEAR TO BE IN THE DRAGON'S STOMACH.

IT *SWALLOWED* US.

WOW. CHECKMATE, ZOMBIE DRAGON.

MAN, HOW THE HELL ARE WE GOING TO GET OUT OF HERE?

ALL HOPE ISN'T LOST, METALSHARK BRO.

IRA, THIS THING SWALLOWED US, WE'RE CURRENTLY STANDING IN ITS BELLY. THIS IS THE *DEFINITION* OF HOPELESS.

... *LOOK!* SHINY STUFF!

DO YOU REMEMBER KILLING THE WIZARD?

NO.

HEY. DO YOU THINK THERE'S ANYTHING GOOD STASHED IN HERE?

REALLY?

YOU DON'T REMEMBER TRAVELING TO THE NETHERWORLD, BATTLING SKELETON SOLDIERS, DEFEATING THE POWERFUL GOAT WIZARD, AND MEETING *ME* IN THE PROCESS?

I FOUND MY SWORD! *SWEET.*

AND I'M JUST MESSING WITH YOU.

NOW *WHAT* ABOUT A GOAT?

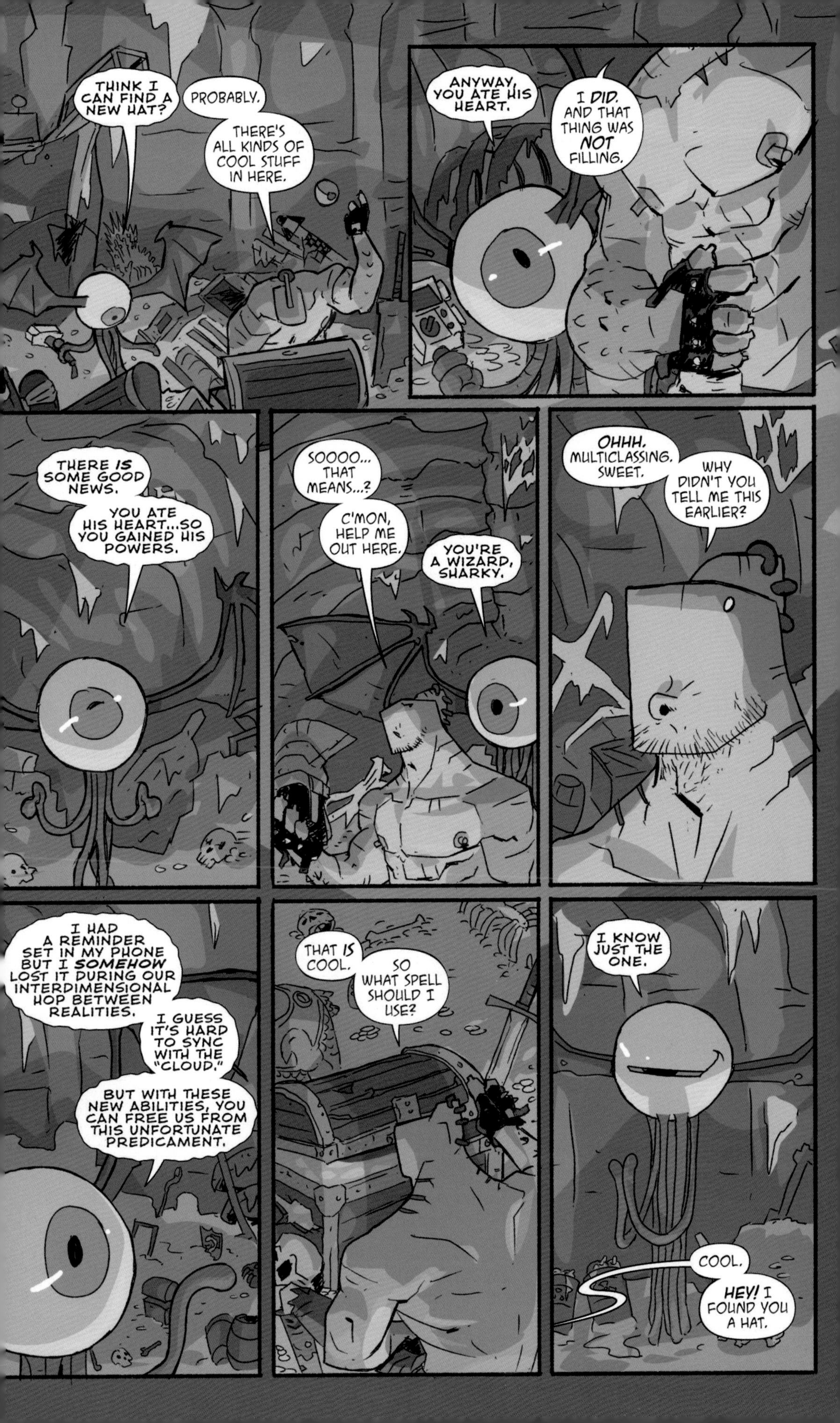
THINK I CAN FIND A NEW HAT?
PROBABLY.
THERE'S ALL KINDS OF COOL STUFF IN HERE.
ANYWAY, YOU ATE HIS HEART.
I DID. AND THAT THING WAS NOT FILLING.
THERE IS SOME GOOD NEWS.
YOU ATE HIS HEART...SO YOU GAINED HIS POWERS.
SOOOO... THAT MEANS...?
C'MON, HELP ME OUT HERE.
YOU'RE A WIZARD, SHARKY.
OHHH. MULTICLASSING. SWEET.
WHY DIDN'T YOU TELL ME THIS EARLIER?
I HAD A REMINDER SET IN MY PHONE BUT I SOMEHOW LOST IT DURING OUR INTERDIMENSIONAL HOP BETWEEN REALITIES.
I GUESS IT'S HARD TO SYNC WITH THE "CLOUD."
BUT WITH THESE NEW ABILITIES, YOU CAN FREE US FROM THIS UNFORTUNATE PREDICAMENT.
THAT IS COOL.
SO WHAT SPELL SHOULD I USE?
I KNOW JUST THE ONE.
COOL.
HEY! I FOUND YOU A HAT.

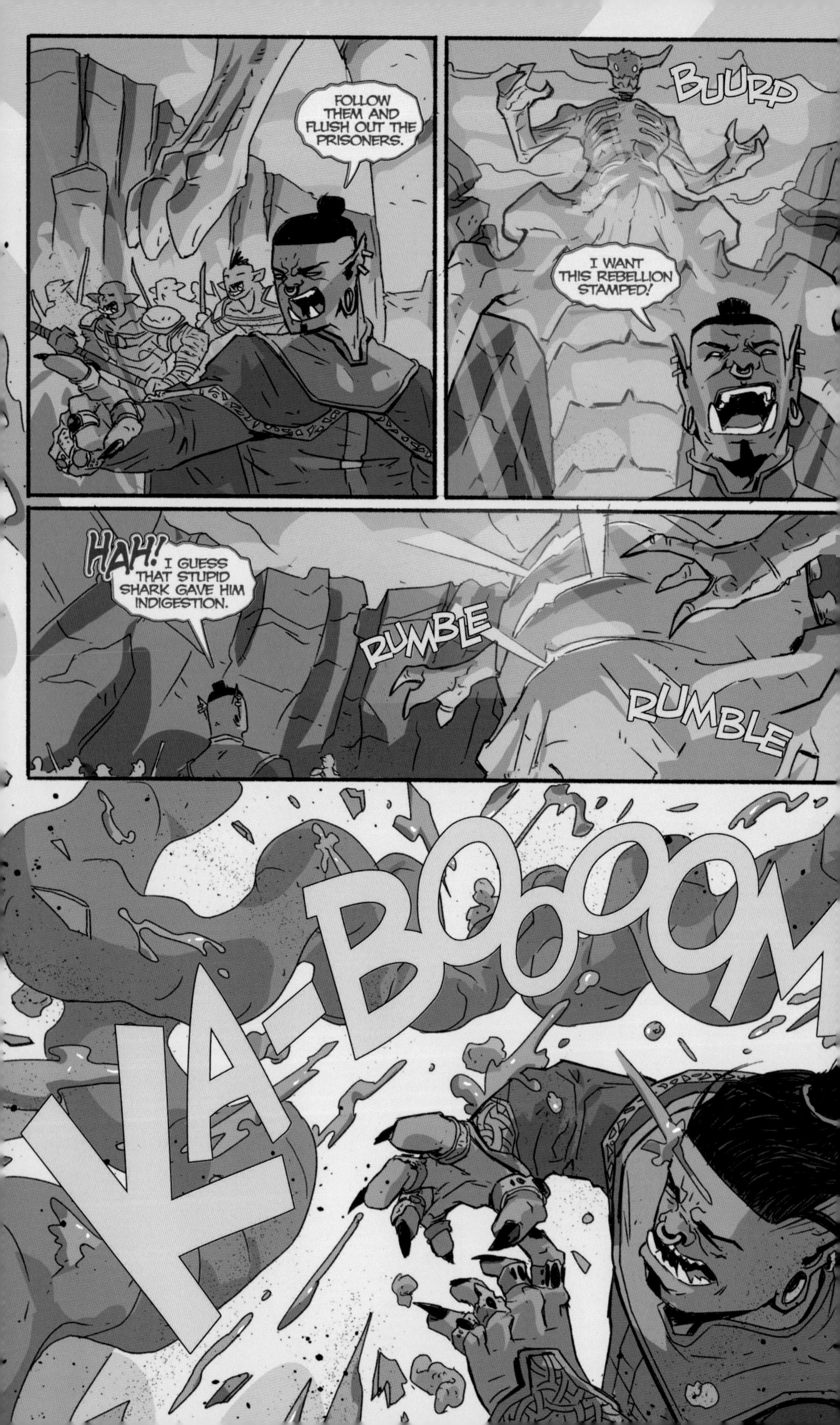
FOLLOW THEM AND FLUSH OUT THE PRISONERS.
BUURP
I WANT THIS REBELLION STAMPED!
HAH! I GUESS THAT STUPID SHARK GAVE HIM INDIGESTION.
RUMBLE
RUMBLE
KA-BOOOOM

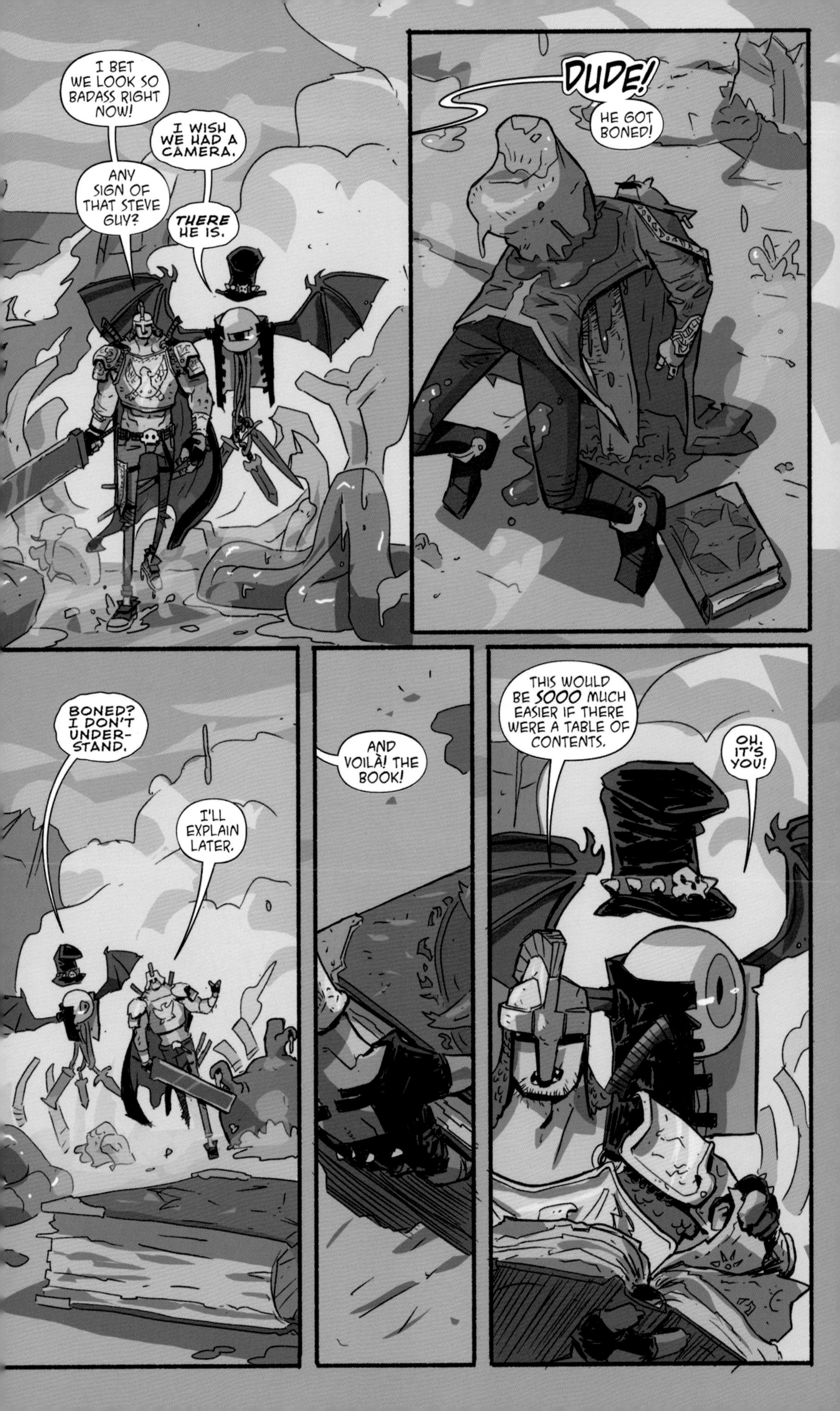

I BET WE LOOK SO BADASS RIGHT NOW!
I WISH WE HAD A CAMERA.
ANY SIGN OF THAT STEVE GUY?
THERE HE IS.
DUDE!
HE GOT BONED!
BONED? I DON'T UNDER-STAND.
I'LL EXPLAIN LATER.
AND VOILÀ! THE BOOK!
THIS WOULD BE SOOO MUCH EASIER IF THERE WERE A TABLE OF CONTENTS.
OH. IT'S YOU!

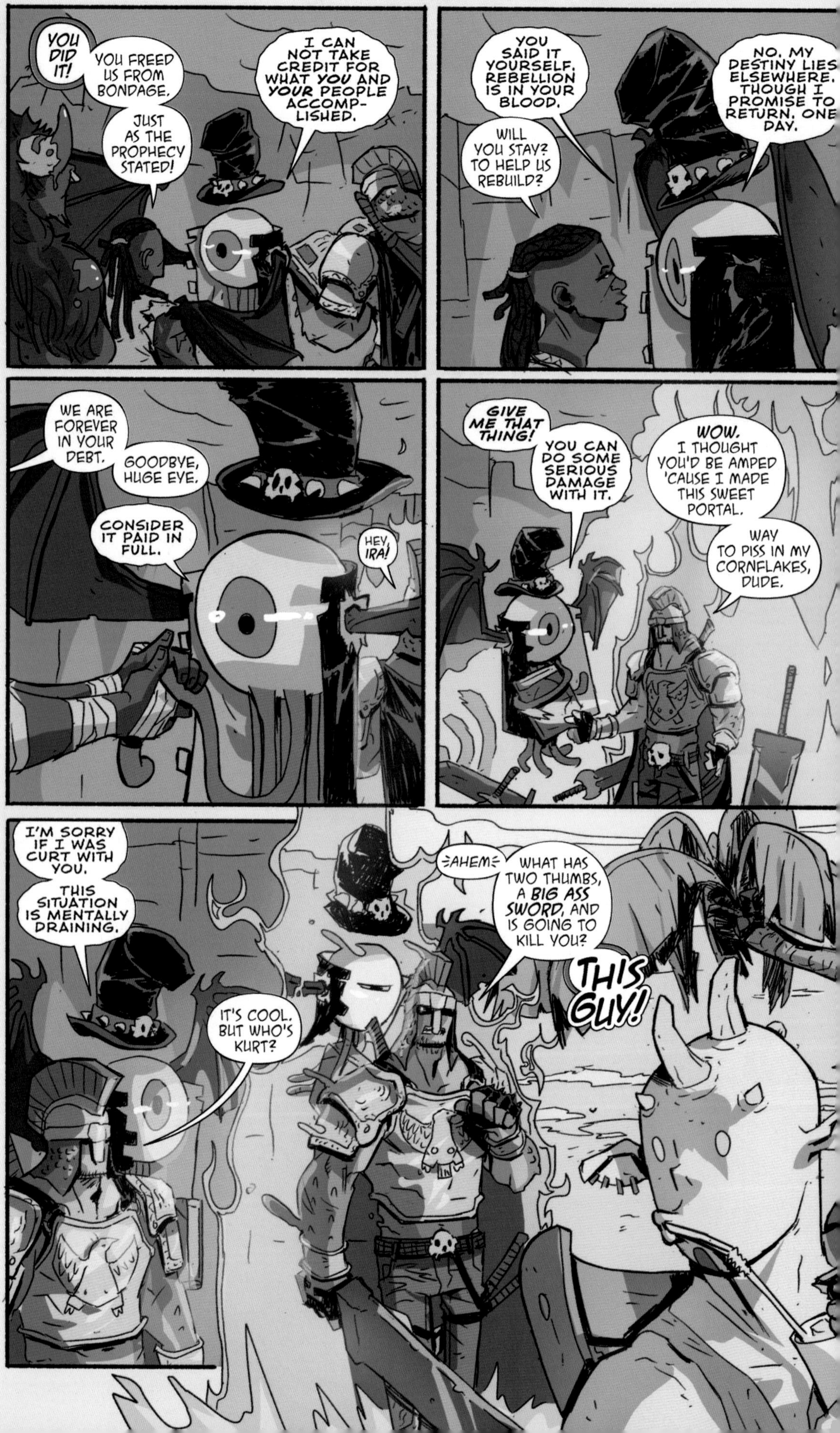
YOU DID IT!
YOU FREED US FROM BONDAGE.
JUST AS THE PROPHECY STATED!
I CAN NOT TAKE CREDIT FOR WHAT YOU AND YOUR PEOPLE ACCOMPLISHED.
YOU SAID IT YOURSELF. REBELLION IS IN YOUR BLOOD.
WILL YOU STAY? TO HELP US REBUILD?
NO. MY DESTINY LIES ELSEWHERE. THOUGH I PROMISE TO RETURN, ONE DAY.
WE ARE FOREVER IN YOUR DEBT.
GOODBYE, HUGE EYE.
CONSIDER IT PAID IN FULL.
HEY, IRA!
GIVE ME THAT THING!
YOU CAN DO SOME SERIOUS DAMAGE WITH IT.
WOW. I THOUGHT YOU'D BE AMPED 'CAUSE I MADE THIS SWEET PORTAL.
WAY TO PISS IN MY CORNFLAKES, DUDE.
I'M SORRY IF I WAS CURT WITH YOU.
THIS SITUATION IS MENTALLY DRAINING.
IT'S COOL. BUT WHO'S KURT?
AHEM
WHAT HAS TWO THUMBS, A BIG ASS SWORD, AND IS GOING TO KILL YOU?
THIS GUY!

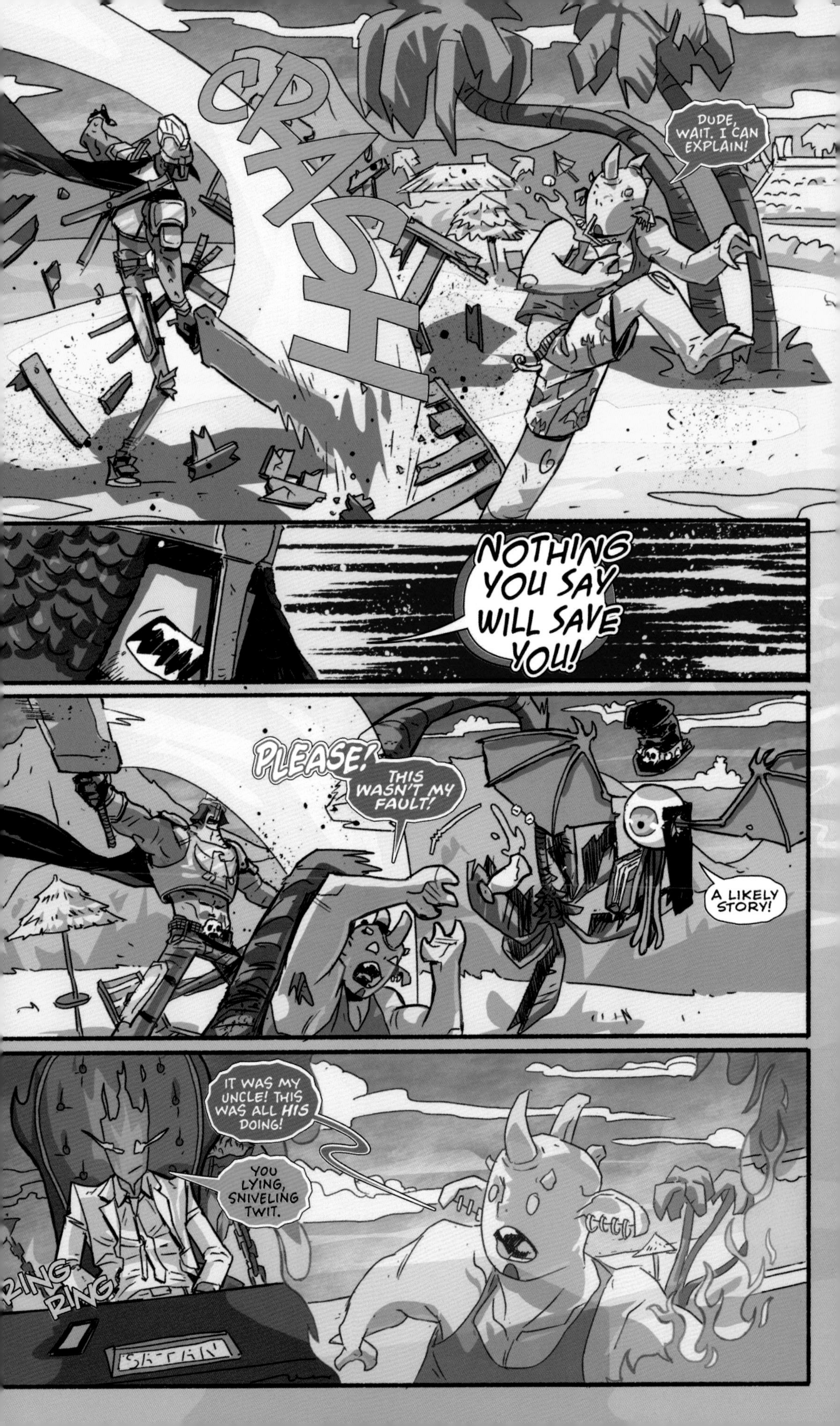
CRASH
DUDE, WAIT. I CAN EXPLAIN!
NOTHING YOU SAY WILL SAVE YOU!
PLEASE!
THIS WASN'T MY FAULT!
A LIKELY STORY!
IT WAS MY UNCLE! THIS WAS ALL HIS DOING!
YOU LYING, SNIVELING TWIT.
RING RING
SATAN

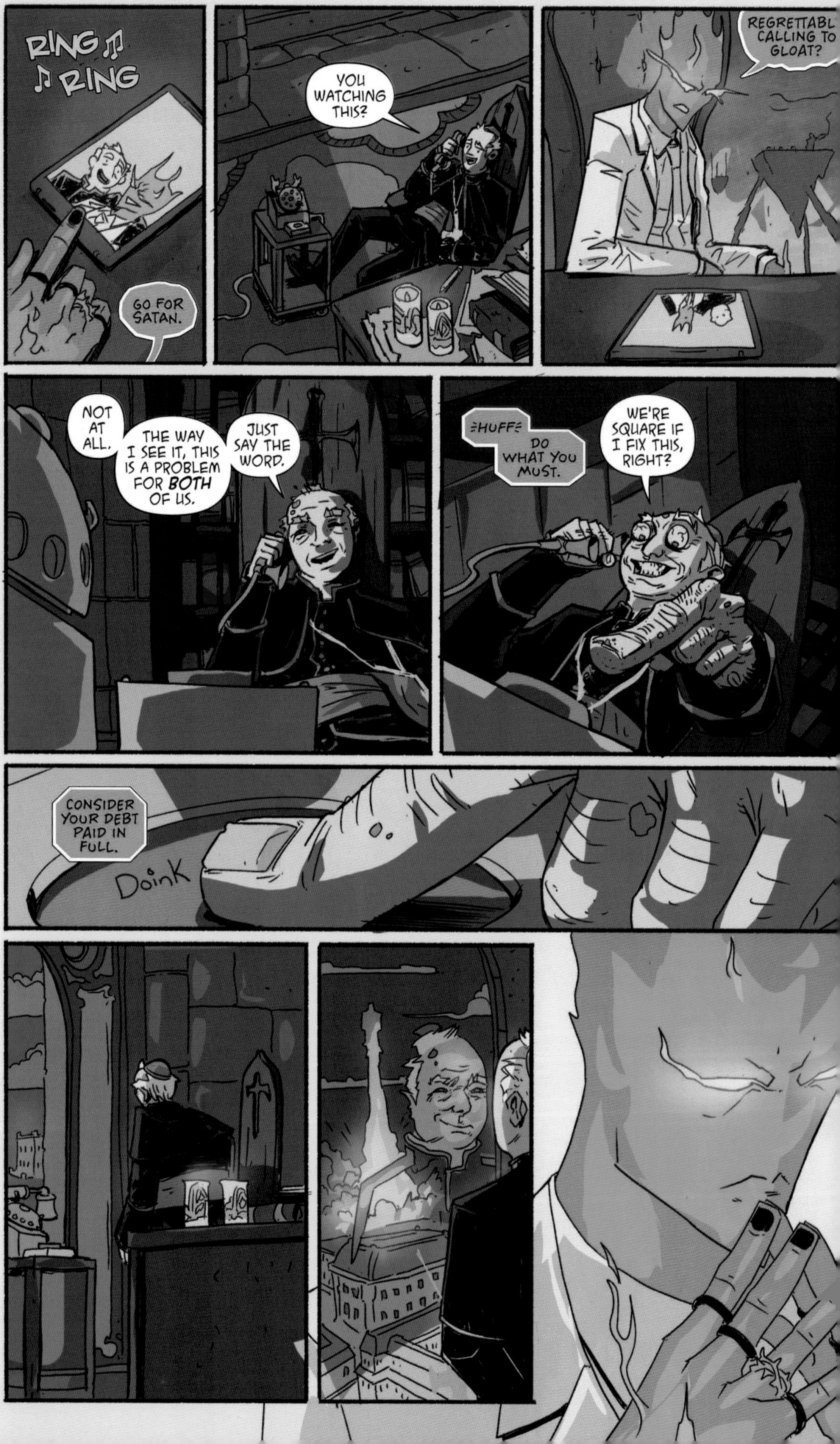
RING ♫ ♪ RING
GO FOR SATAN.
YOU WATCHING THIS?
REGRETTABL CALLING TO GLOAT?
NOT AT ALL.
THE WAY I SEE IT, THIS IS A PROBLEM FOR BOTH OF US.
JUST SAY THE WORD.
HUFF
DO WHAT YOU MUST.
WE'RE SQUARE IF I FIX THIS, RIGHT?
CONSIDER YOUR DEBT PAID IN FULL.
DoinK

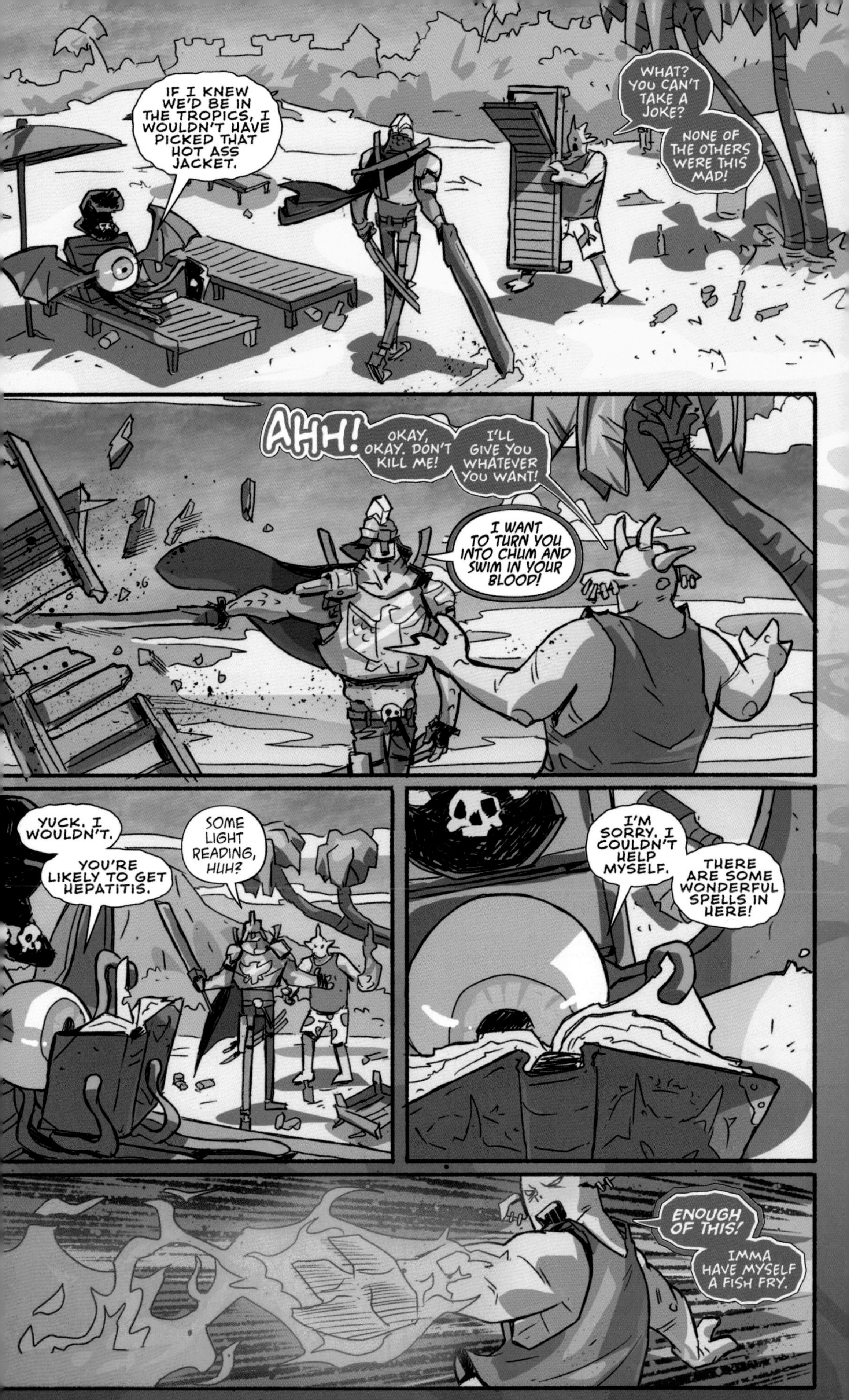

IF I KNEW WE'D BE IN THE TROPICS, I WOULDN'T HAVE PICKED THAT HOT ASS JACKET.
WHAT? YOU CAN'T TAKE A JOKE?
NONE OF THE OTHERS WERE THIS MAD!
AHH!
OKAY, OKAY. DON'T KILL ME!
I'LL GIVE YOU WHATEVER YOU WANT!
I WANT TO TURN YOU INTO CHUM AND SWIM IN YOUR BLOOD!
YUCK. I WOULDN'T.
YOU'RE LIKELY TO GET HEPATITIS.
SOME LIGHT READING, HUH?
I'M SORRY. I COULDN'T HELP MYSELF.
THERE ARE SOME WONDERFUL SPELLS IN HERE!
ENOUGH OF THIS!
IMMA HAVE MYSELF A FISH FRY.

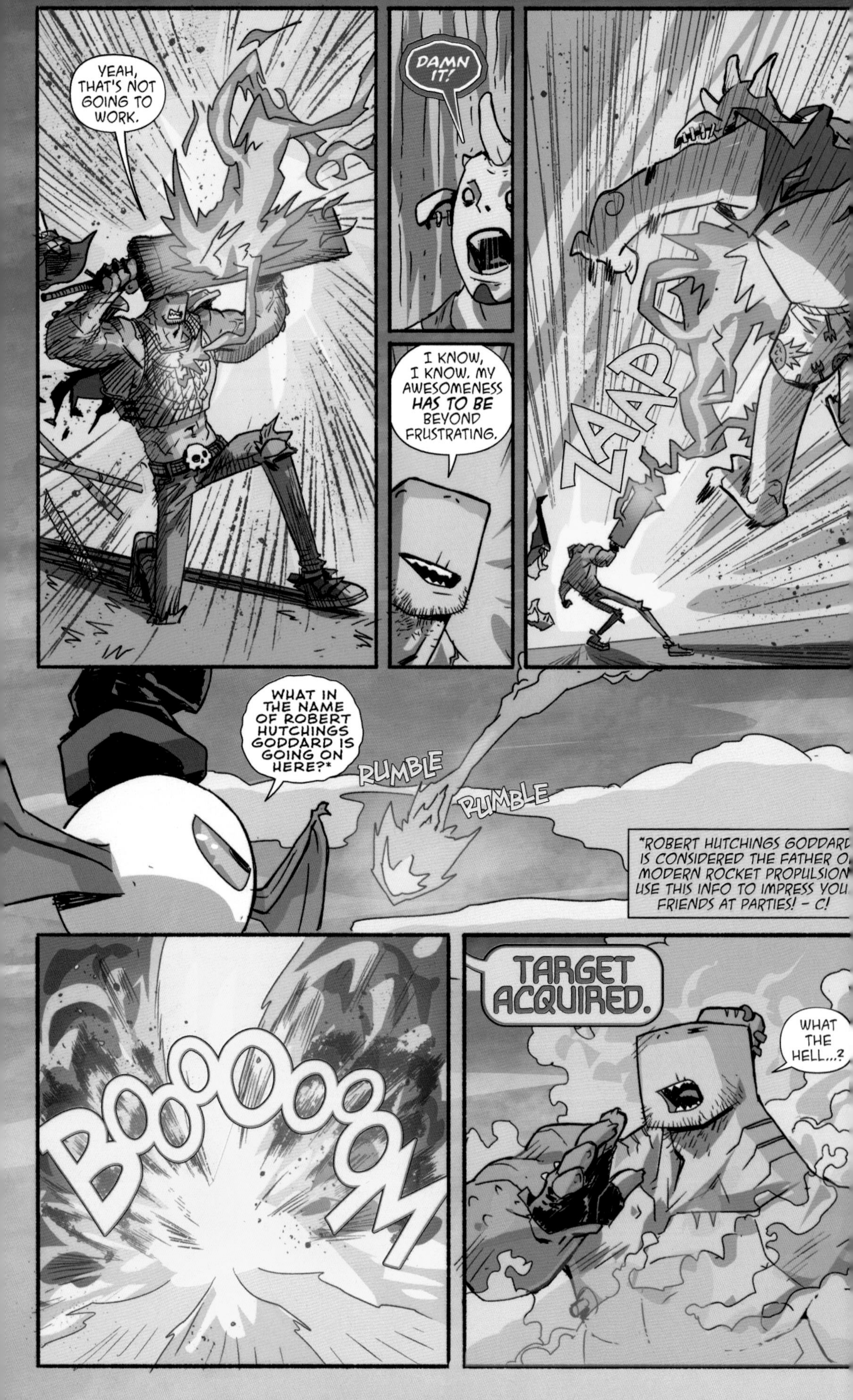
YEAH, THAT'S NOT GOING TO WORK.
DAMN IT!
I KNOW, I KNOW. MY AWESOMENESS HAS TO BE BEYOND FRUSTRATING.
ZAAP
WHAT IN THE NAME OF ROBERT HUTCHINGS GODDARD IS GOING ON HERE?*
RUMBLE
RUMBLE
*ROBERT HUTCHINGS GODDARD IS CONSIDERED THE FATHER OF MODERN ROCKET PROPULSION. USE THIS INFO TO IMPRESS YOUR FRIENDS AT PARTIES! - C!
BOOOOOOOM
TARGET ACQUIRED.
WHAT THE HELL...?

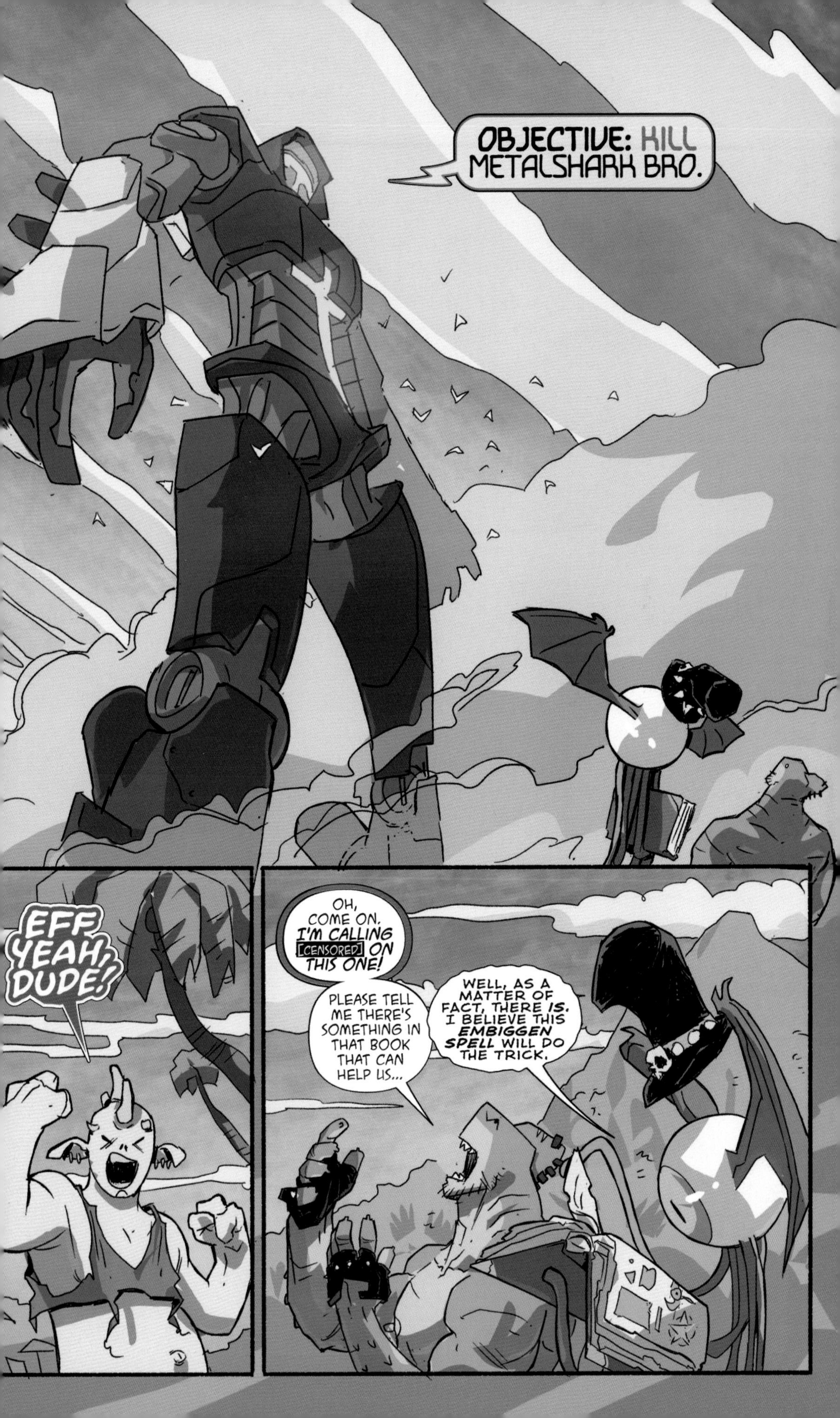
OBJECTIVE: KILL METALSHARK BRO.
EFF YEAH, DUDE!
OH, COME ON. I'M CALLING [CENSORED] ON THIS ONE!
PLEASE TELL ME THERE'S SOMETHING IN THAT BOOK THAT CAN HELP US...
WELL, AS A MATTER OF FACT, THERE IS. I BELIEVE THIS EMBIGGEN SPELL WILL DO THE TRICK.

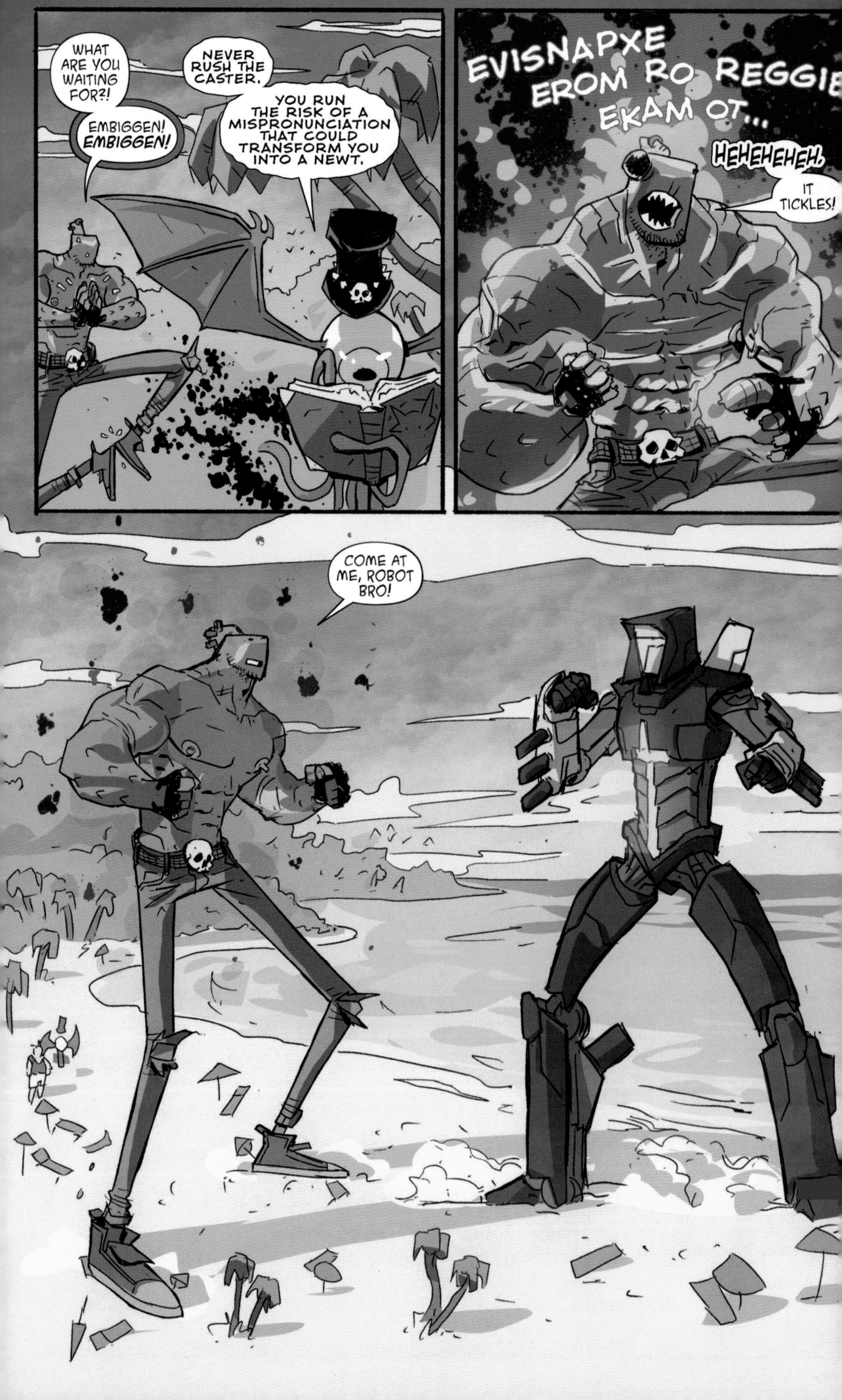
WHAT ARE YOU WAITING FOR?!
EMBIGGEN! EMBIGGEN!
NEVER RUSH THE CASTER.
YOU RUN THE RISK OF A MISPRONUNCIATION THAT COULD TRANSFORM YOU INTO A NEWT.
EVISNAPXE EROM RO REGGIE EKAM OT...
HEHEHEHEH.
IT TICKLES!
COME AT ME, ROBOT BRO!

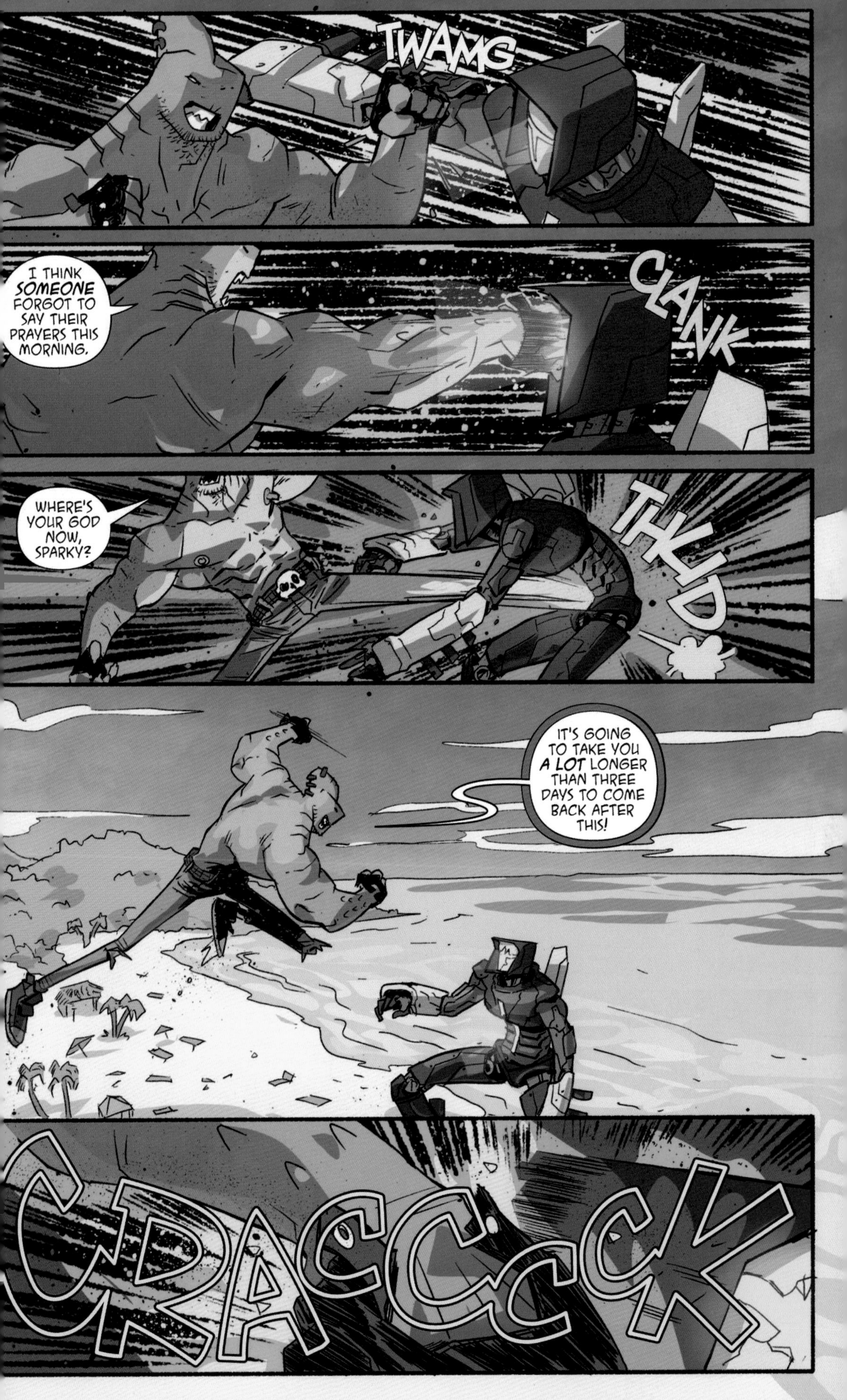
TWAMG
I THINK SOMEONE FORGOT TO SAY THEIR PRAYERS THIS MORNING.
CLANK
WHERE'S YOUR GOD NOW, SPARKY?
THUD
IT'S GOING TO TAKE YOU A LOT LONGER THAN THREE DAYS TO COME BACK AFTER THIS!
CRACCCK

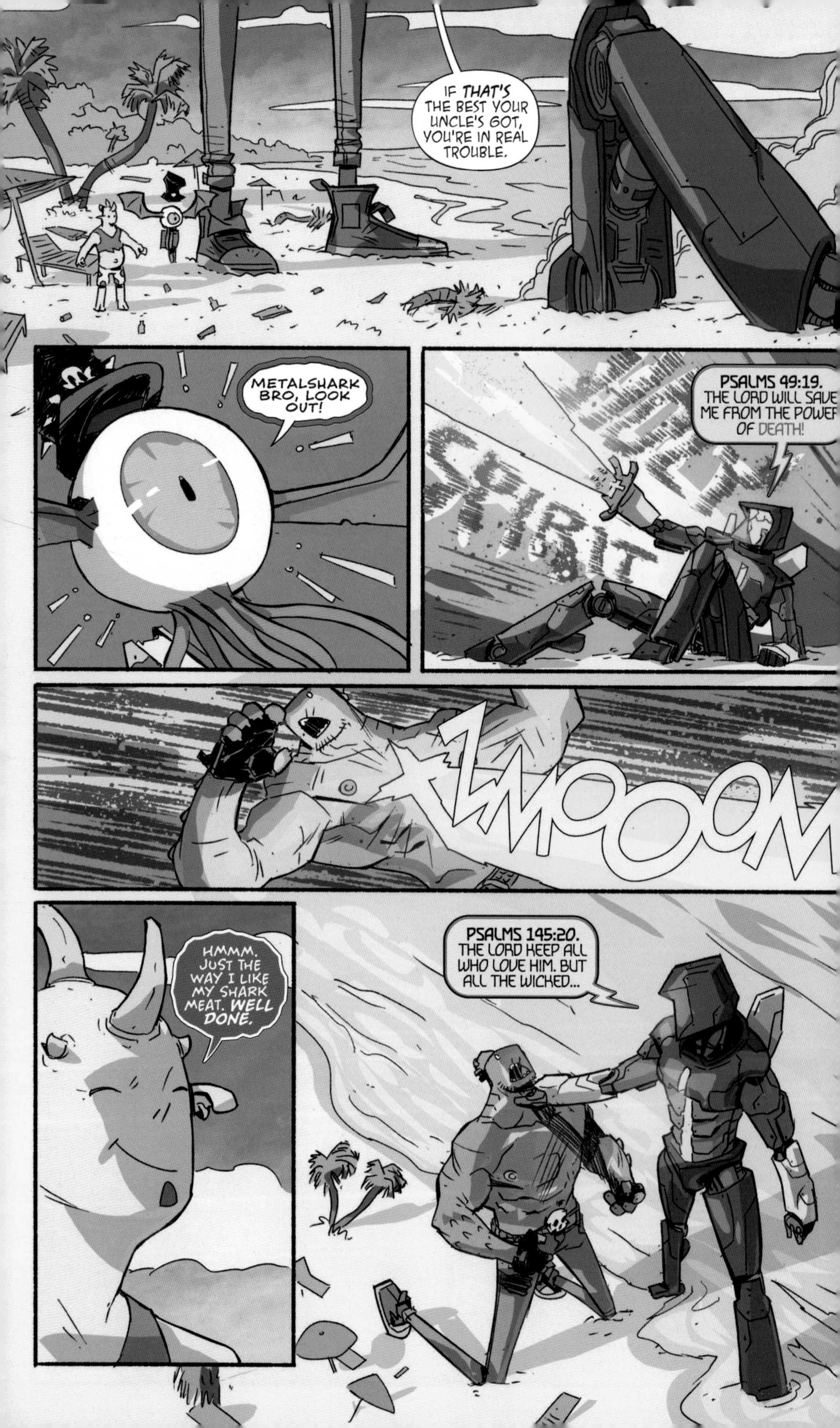
IF THAT'S THE BEST YOUR UNCLE'S GOT, YOU'RE IN REAL TROUBLE.
METALSHARK BRO, LOOK OUT!
PSALMS 49:19. THE LORD WILL SAVE ME FROM THE POWER OF DEATH!
SPIRIT
ZMOOOM
HMMM. JUST THE WAY I LIKE MY SHARK MEAT. WELL DONE.
PSALMS 145:20. THE LORD KEEP ALL WHO LOVE HIM. BUT ALL THE WICKED...

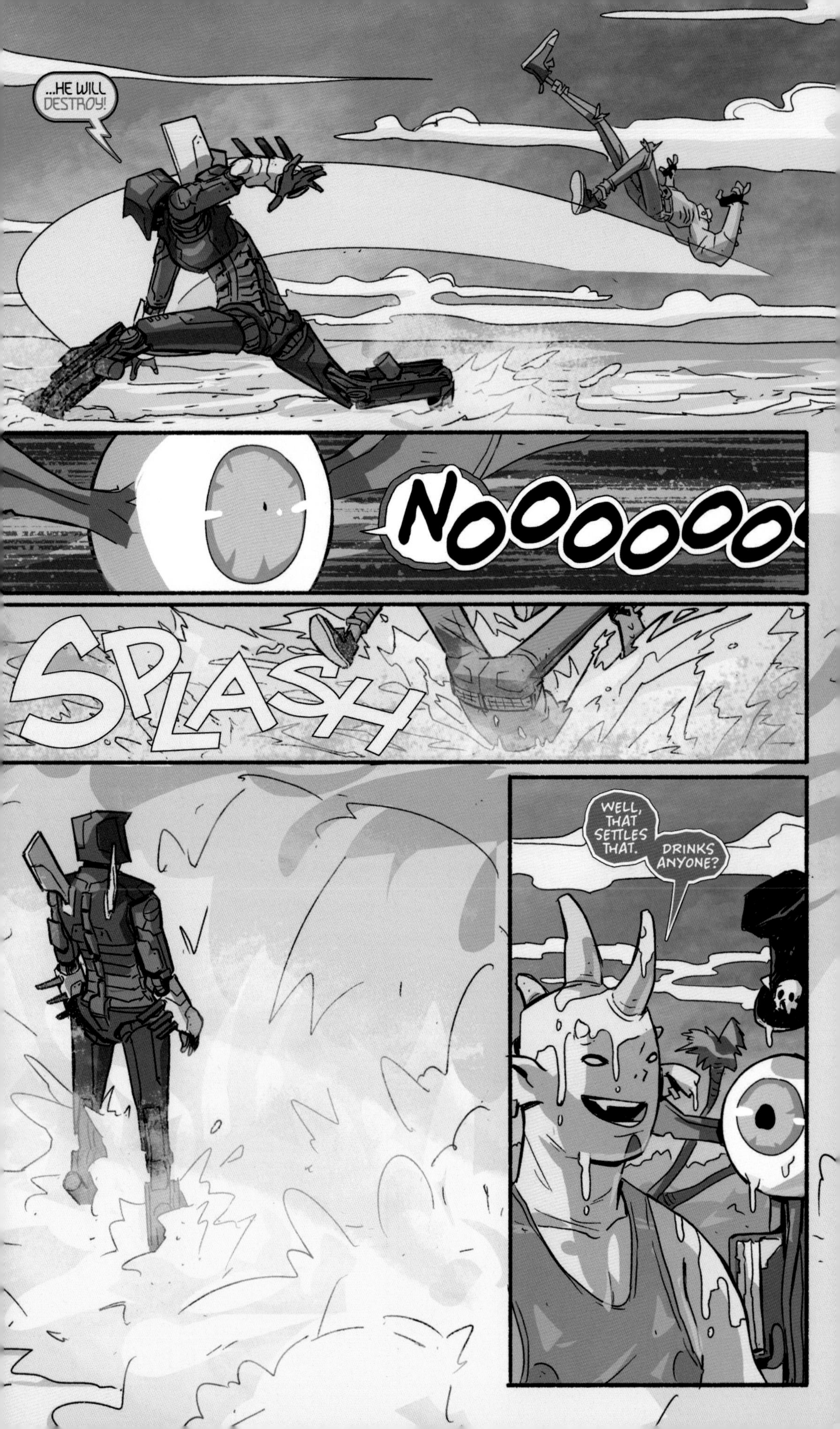
...HE WILL DESTROY!
NOOOOOOO
SPLASH
WELL, THAT SETTLES THAT.
DRINKS ANYONE?

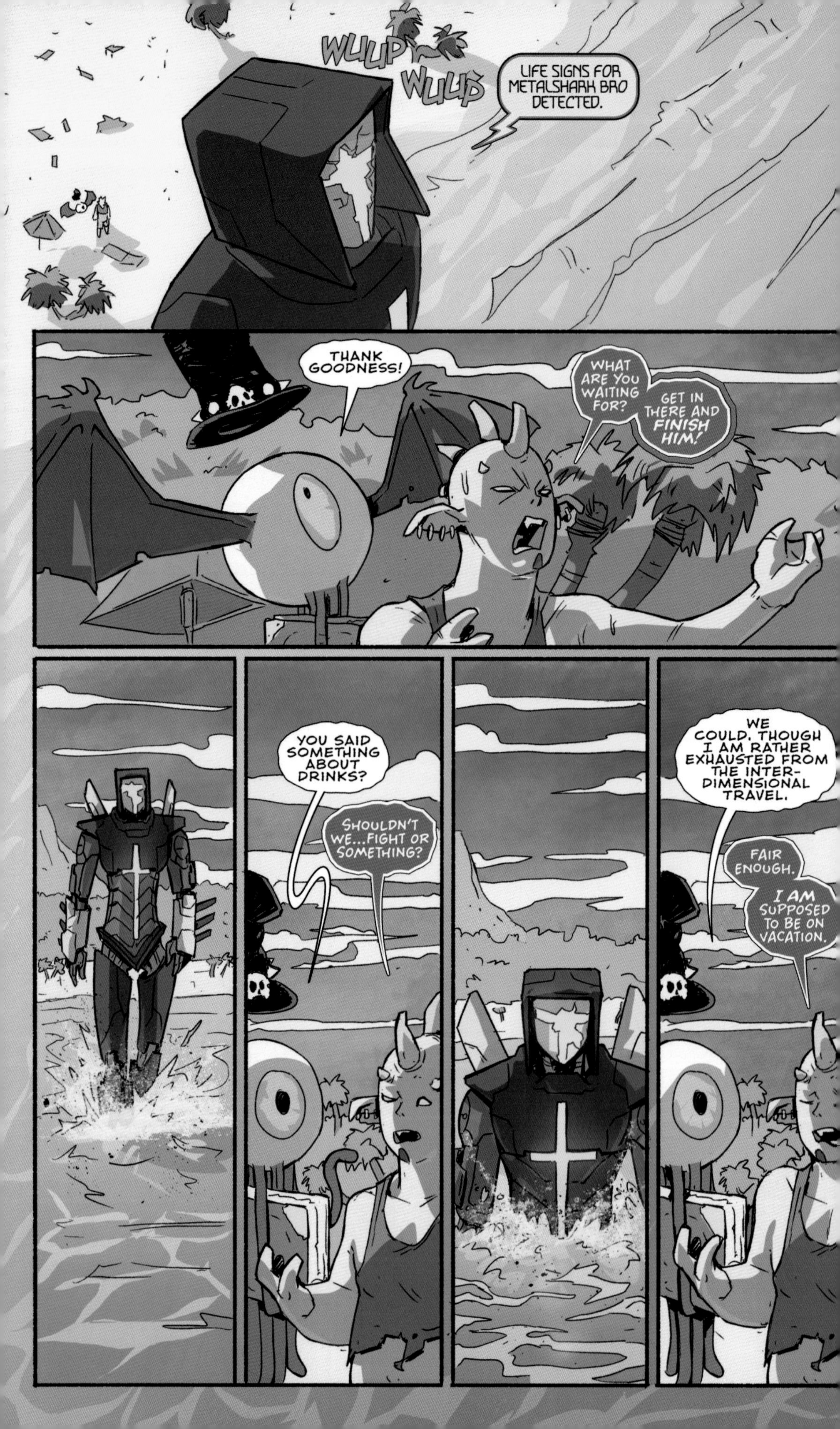
WUUP WUUP
LIFE SIGNS FOR METALSHARK BRO DETECTED.
THANK GOODNESS!
WHAT ARE YOU WAITING FOR?
GET IN THERE AND FINISH HIM!
YOU SAID SOMETHING ABOUT DRINKS?
SHOULDN'T WE...FIGHT OR SOMETHING?
WE COULD, THOUGH I AM RATHER EXHAUSTED FROM THE INTER-DIMENSIONAL TRAVEL.
FAIR ENOUGH.
I AM SUPPOSED TO BE ON VACATION.

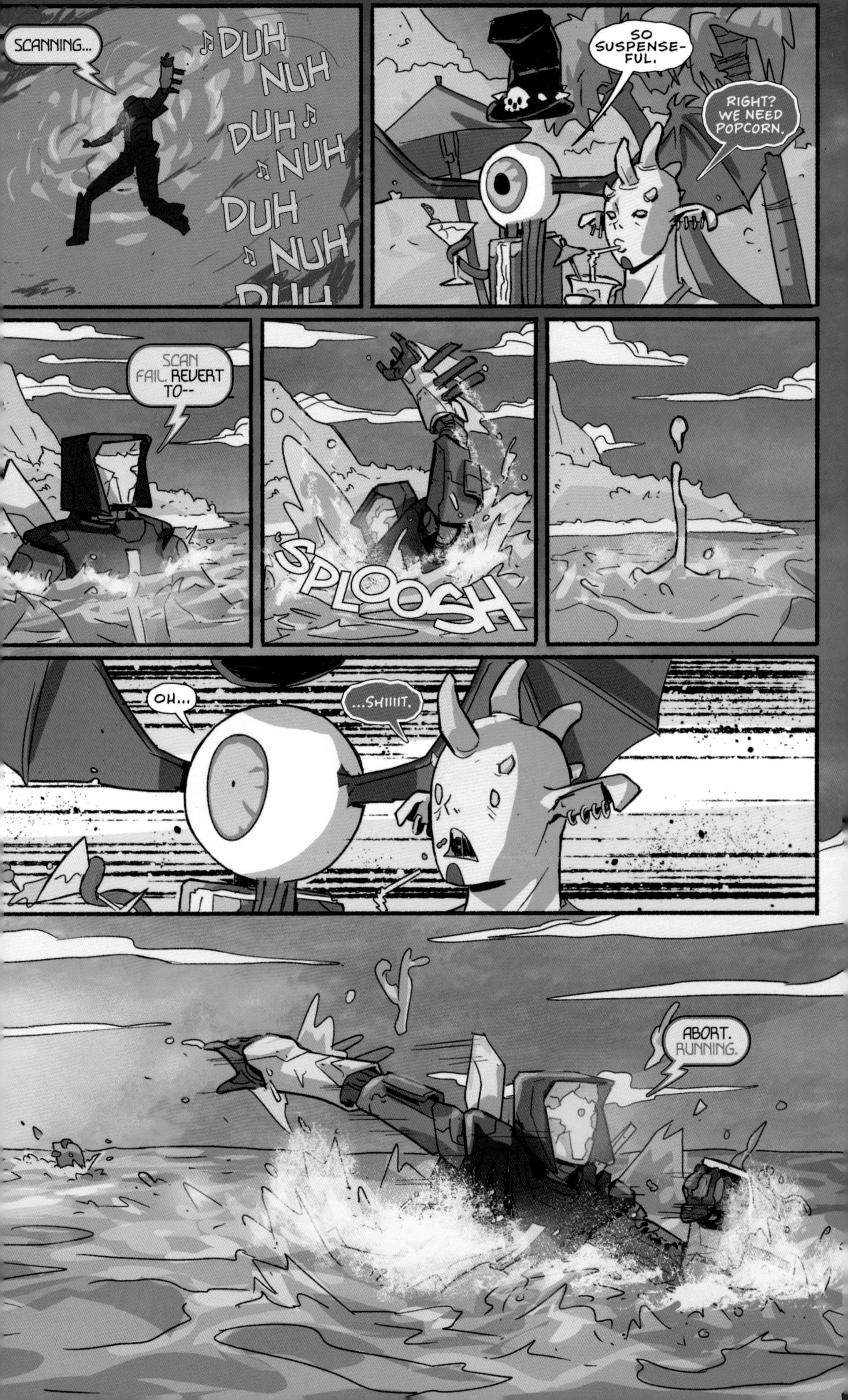

SCANNING...
DUH NUH DUH NUH DUH NUH
SO SUSPENSE-FUL.
RIGHT? WE NEED POPCORN.
SCAN FAIL. REVERT TO--
SPLOOSH
OH...
...SHIIIT.
ABORT. RUNNING.

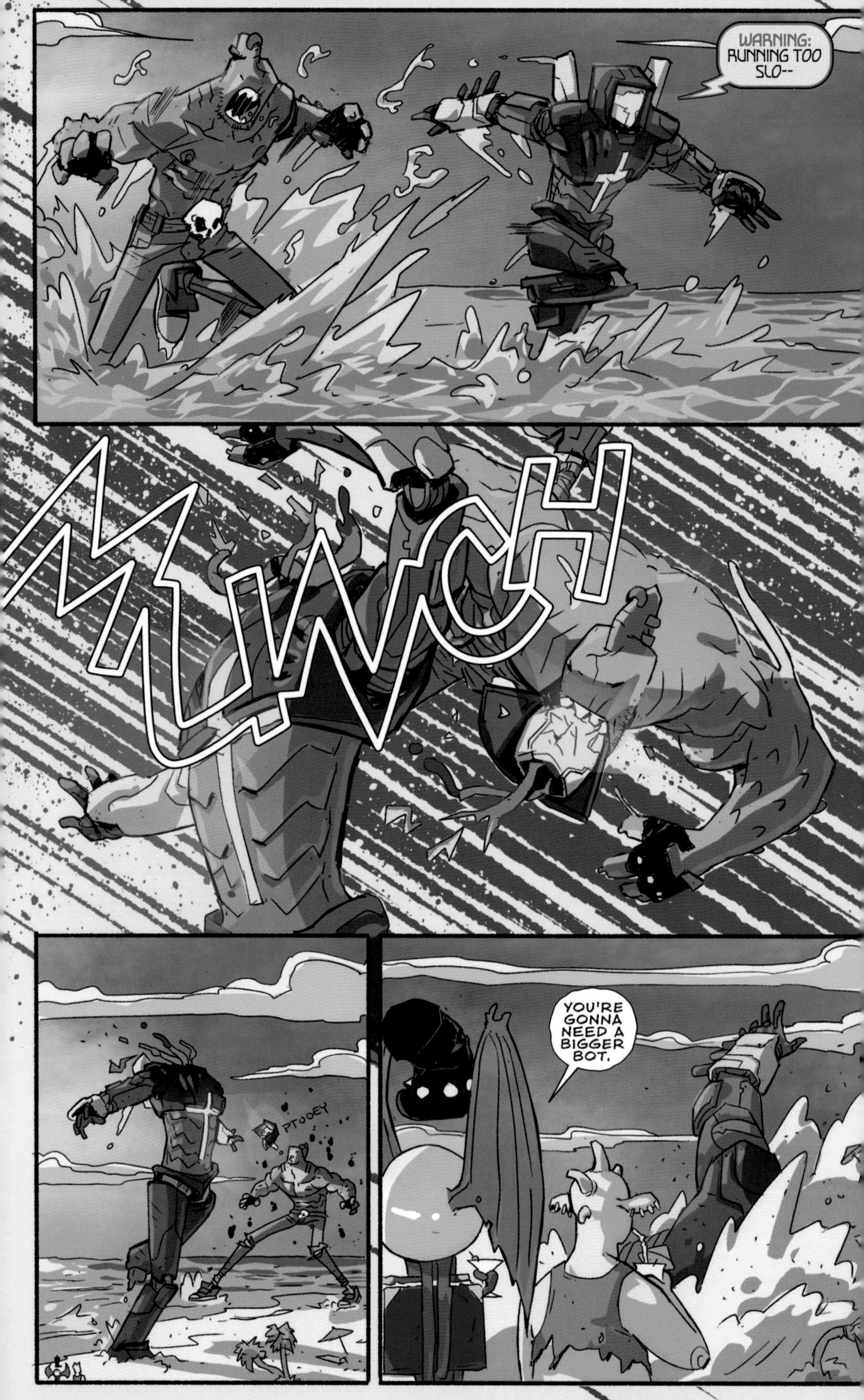
WARNING: RUNNING TOO SLO--
MUNCH
PTOOEY
YOU'RE GONNA NEED A BIGGER BOT.

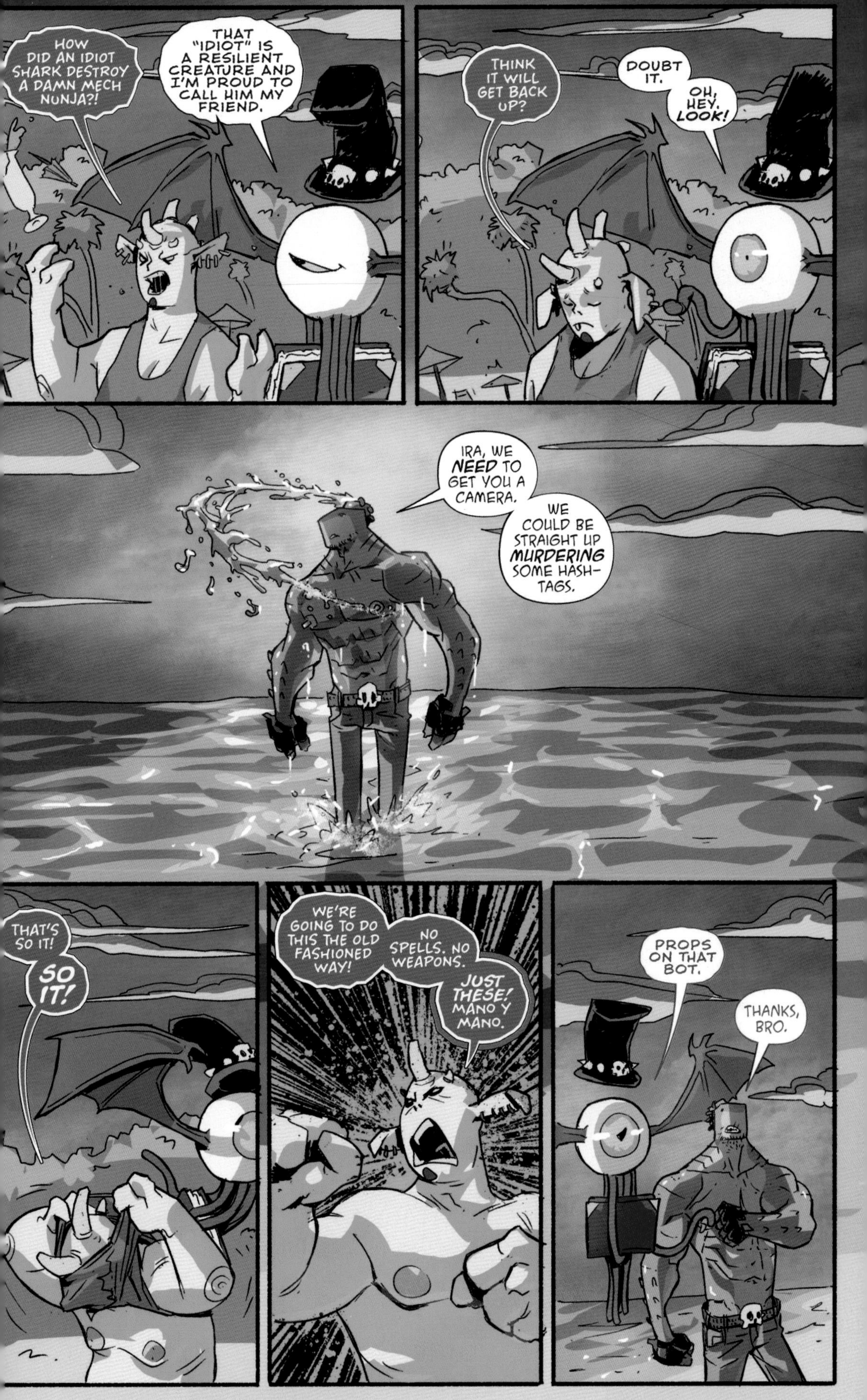

HOW DID AN IDIOT SHARK DESTROY A DAMN MECH NUNJA?!
THAT "IDIOT" IS A RESILIENT CREATURE AND I'M PROUD TO CALL HIM MY FRIEND.
THINK IT WILL GET BACK UP?
DOUBT IT.
OH, HEY. LOOK!
IRA, WE **NEED** TO GET YOU A CAMERA.
WE COULD BE STRAIGHT UP **MURDERING** SOME HASH-TAGS.
THAT'S SO IT!
SO IT!
WE'RE GOING TO DO THIS THE OLD FASHIONED WAY!
NO SPELLS. NO WEAPONS.
JUST THESE! MANO Y MANO.
PROPS ON THAT BOT.
THANKS, BRO.

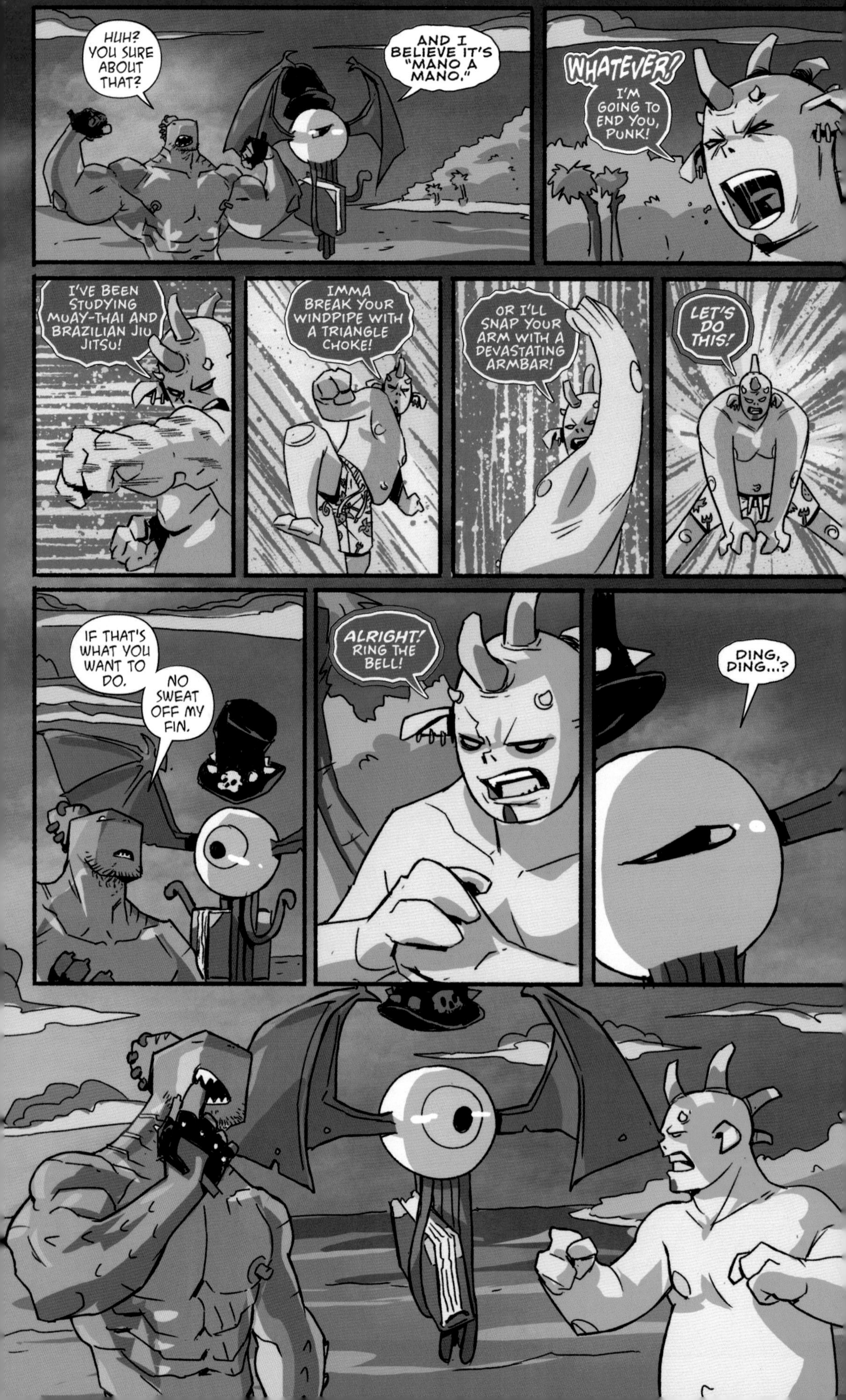
HUH? YOU SURE ABOUT THAT?
AND I BELIEVE IT'S "MANO A MANO."
WHATEVER!
I'M GOING TO END YOU, PUNK!
I'VE BEEN STUDYING MUAY-THAI AND BRAZILIAN JIU JITSU!
IMMA BREAK YOUR WINDPIPE WITH A TRIANGLE CHOKE!
OR I'LL SNAP YOUR ARM WITH A DEVASTATING ARMBAR!
LET'S DO THIS!
IF THAT'S WHAT YOU WANT TO DO.
NO SWEAT OFF MY FIN.
ALRIGHT! RING THE BELL!
DING, DING...?

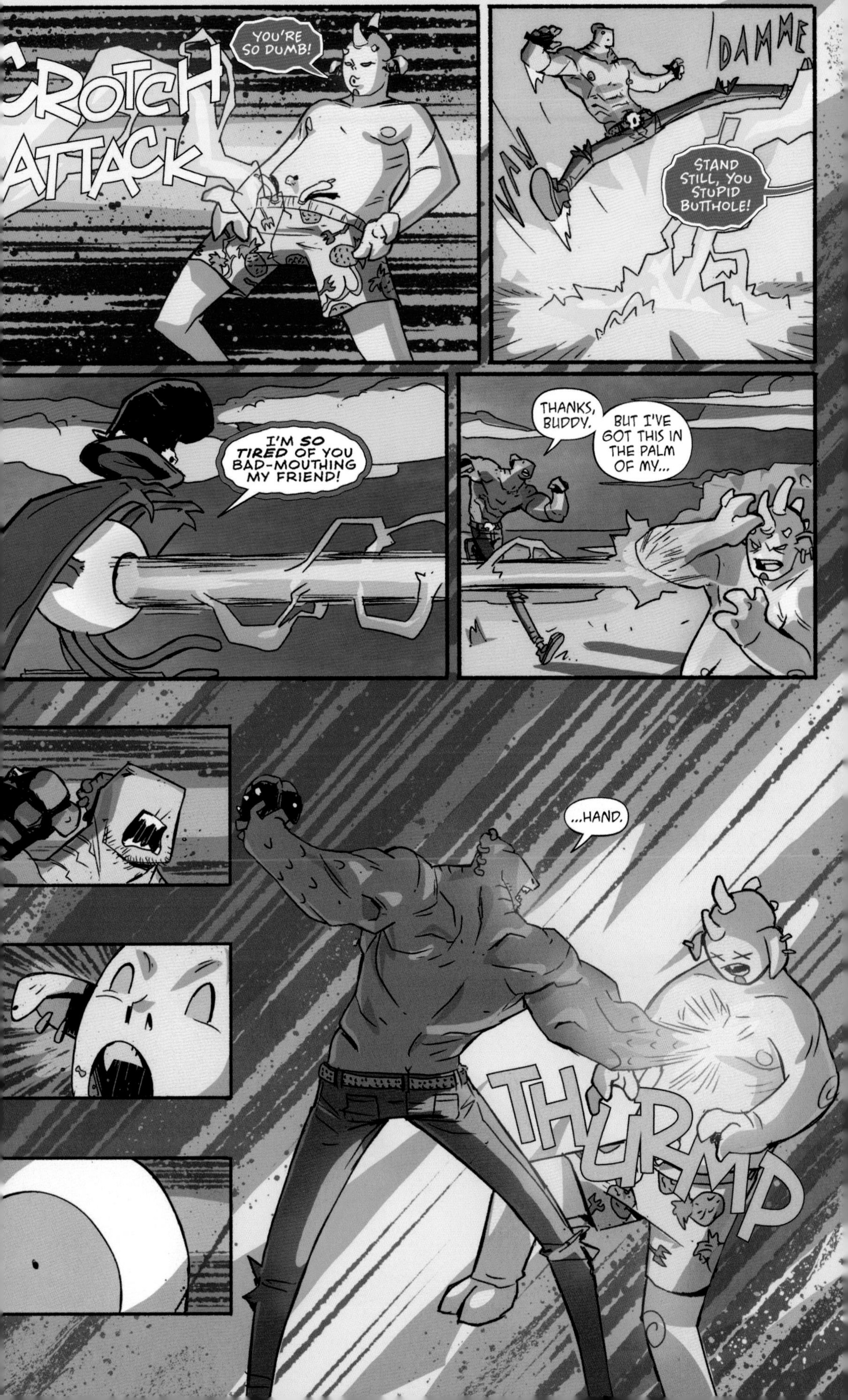
CROTCH ATTACK
YOU'RE SO DUMB!
VAN DAMME
STAND STILL, YOU STUPID BUTTHOLE!
I'M SO TIRED OF YOU BAD-MOUTHING MY FRIEND!
THANKS, BUDDY.
BUT I'VE GOT THIS IN THE PALM OF MY...
...HAND.
THUMP

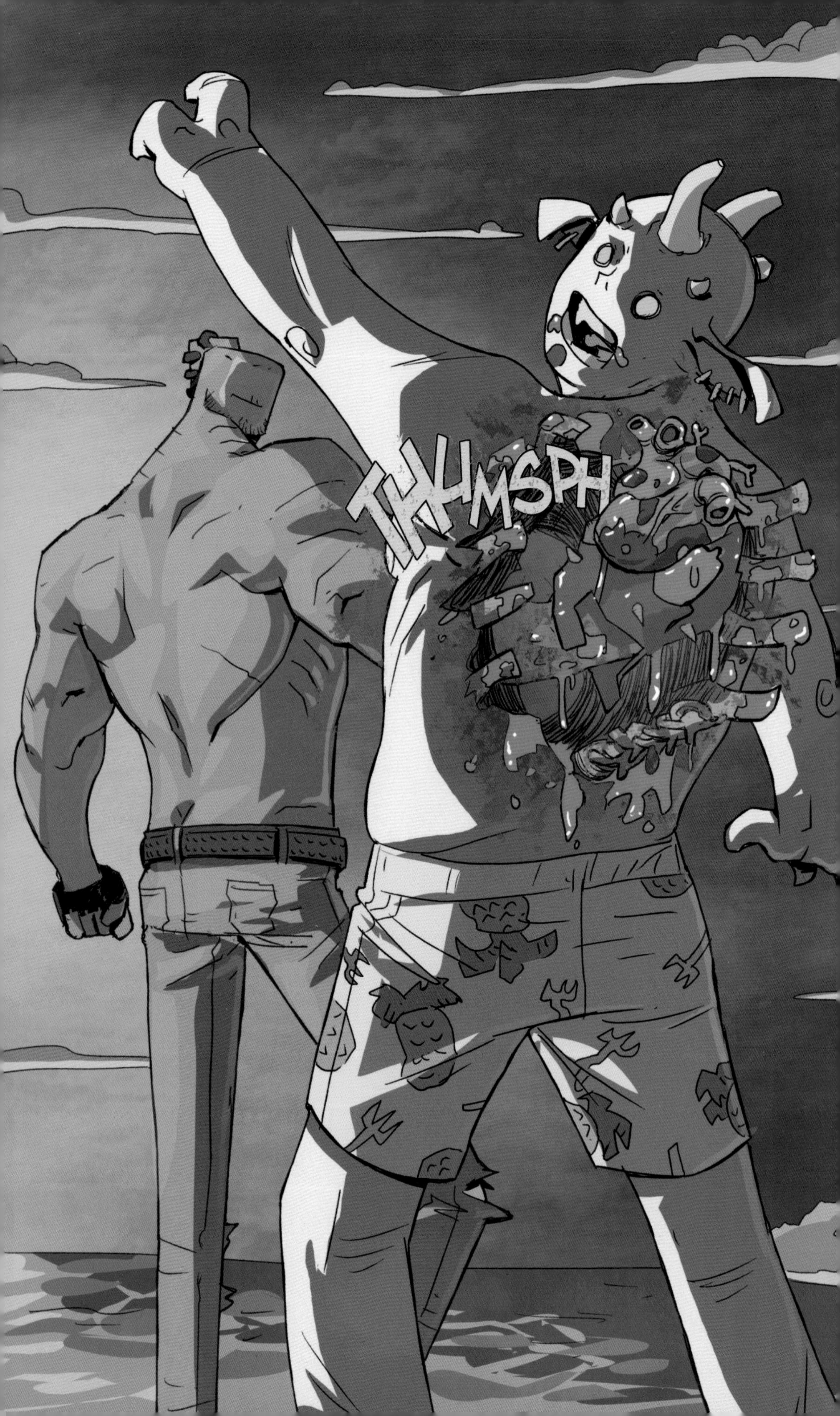
THUMSPH

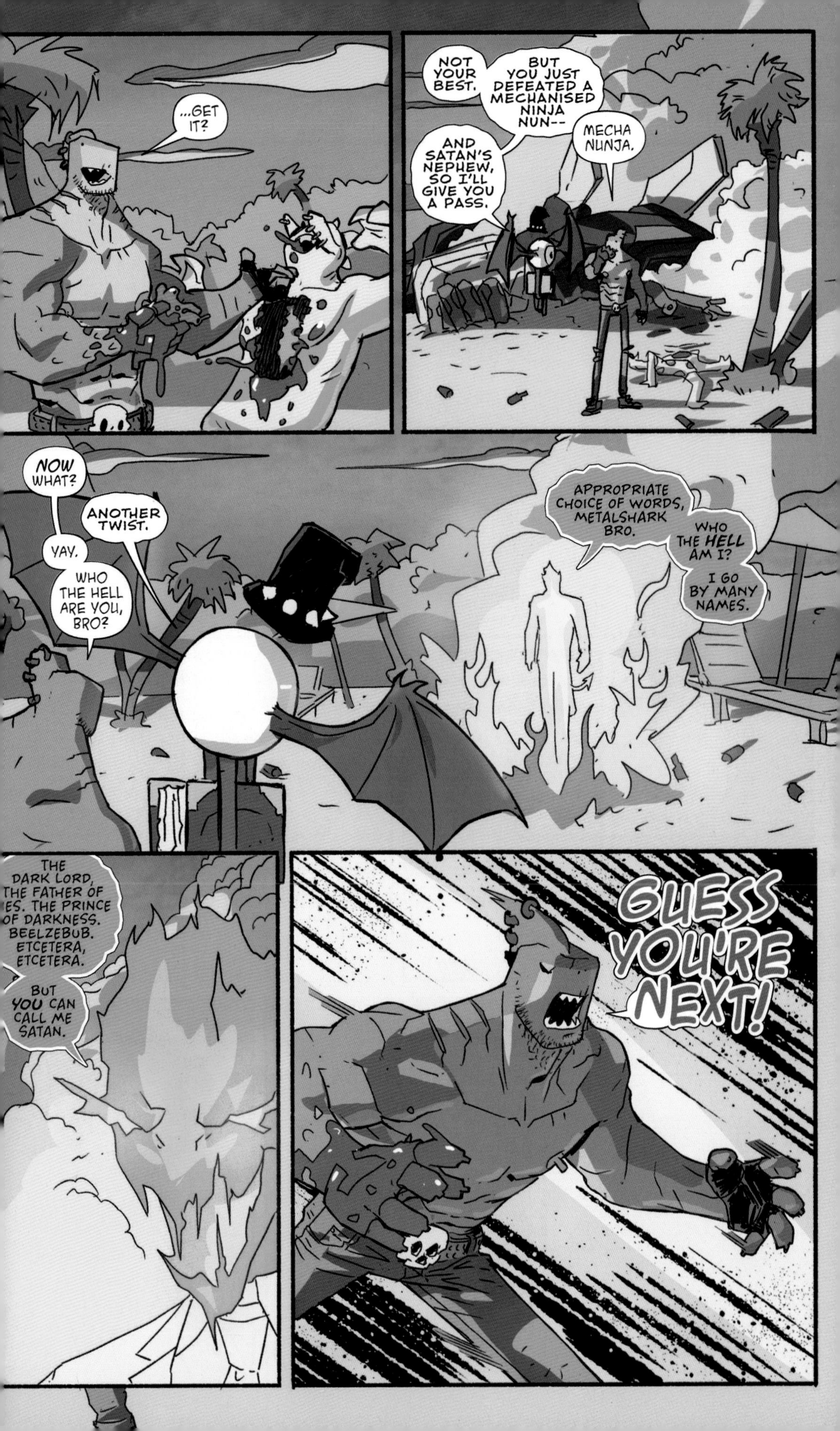
...GET IT?
NOT YOUR BEST.
BUT YOU JUST DEFEATED A MECHANISED NINJA NUN--
AND SATAN'S NEPHEW, SO I'LL GIVE YOU A PASS.
MECHA NUNJA.
NOW WHAT?
ANOTHER TWIST.
YAY.
WHO THE HELL ARE YOU, BRO?
APPROPRIATE CHOICE OF WORDS, METALSHARK BRO.
WHO THE HELL AM I?
I GO BY MANY NAMES.
THE DARK LORD, THE FATHER OF ES. THE PRINCE OF DARKNESS. BEELZEBUB. ETCETERA, ETCETERA.
BUT YOU CAN CALL ME SATAN.
GUESS YOU'RE NEXT!

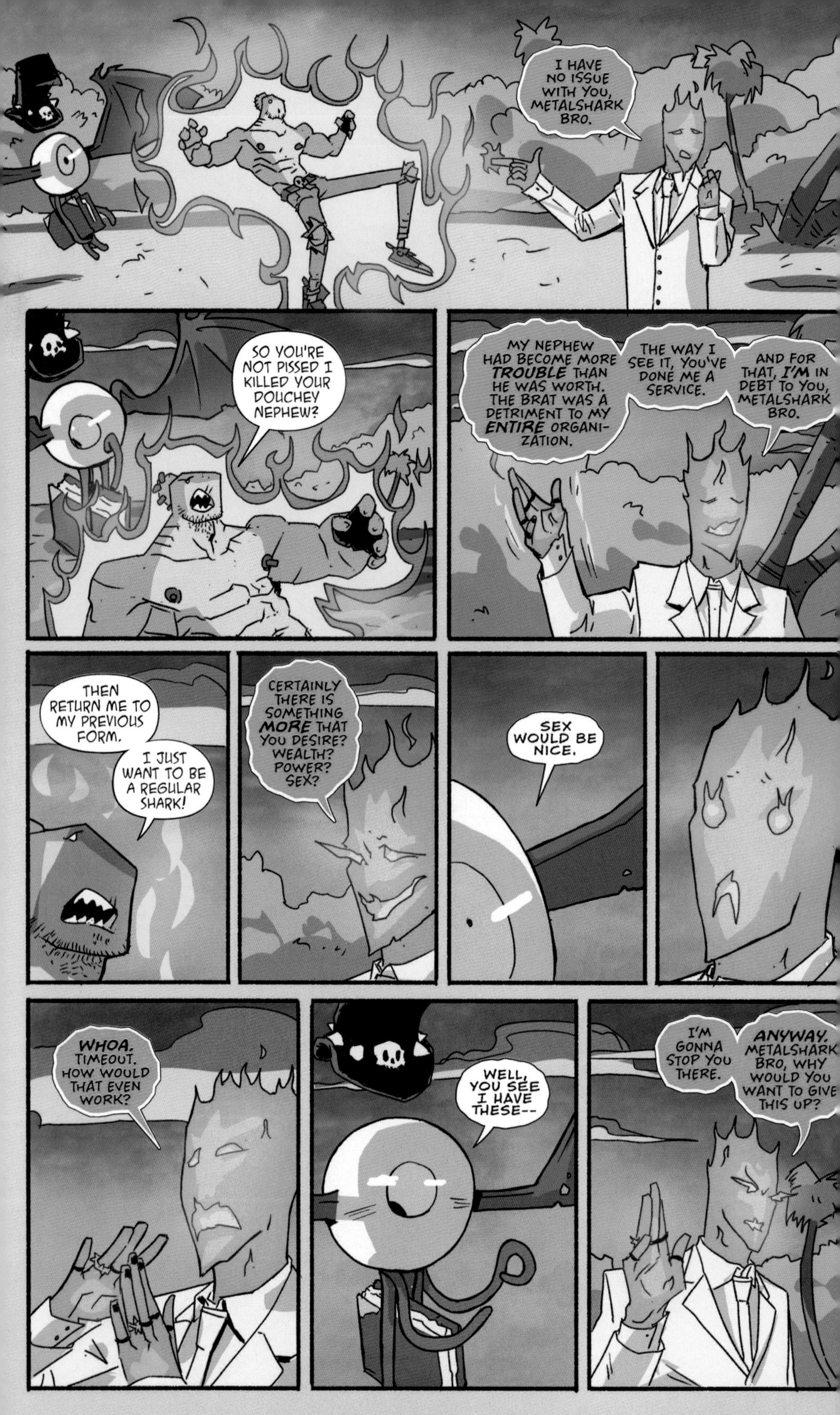

I HAVE NO ISSUE WITH YOU, METALSHARK BRO.
SO YOU'RE NOT PISSED I KILLED YOUR DOUCHEY NEPHEW?
MY NEPHEW HAD BECOME MORE **TROUBLE** THAN HE WAS WORTH. THE BRAT WAS A DETRIMENT TO MY **ENTIRE** ORGANIZATION.
THE WAY I SEE IT, YOU'VE DONE ME A SERVICE.
AND FOR THAT, ***I'M*** IN DEBT TO YOU, METALSHARK BRO.
THEN RETURN ME TO MY PREVIOUS FORM.
I JUST WANT TO BE A REGULAR SHARK!
CERTAINLY THERE IS SOMETHING ***MORE*** THAT YOU DESIRE? WEALTH? POWER? SEX?
SEX WOULD BE NICE.
WHOA. TIMEOUT. HOW WOULD THAT EVEN WORK?
WELL, YOU SEE I HAVE THESE--
I'M GONNA STOP YOU THERE.
ANYWAY. METALSHARK BRO, WHY WOULD YOU WANT TO GIVE THIS UP?

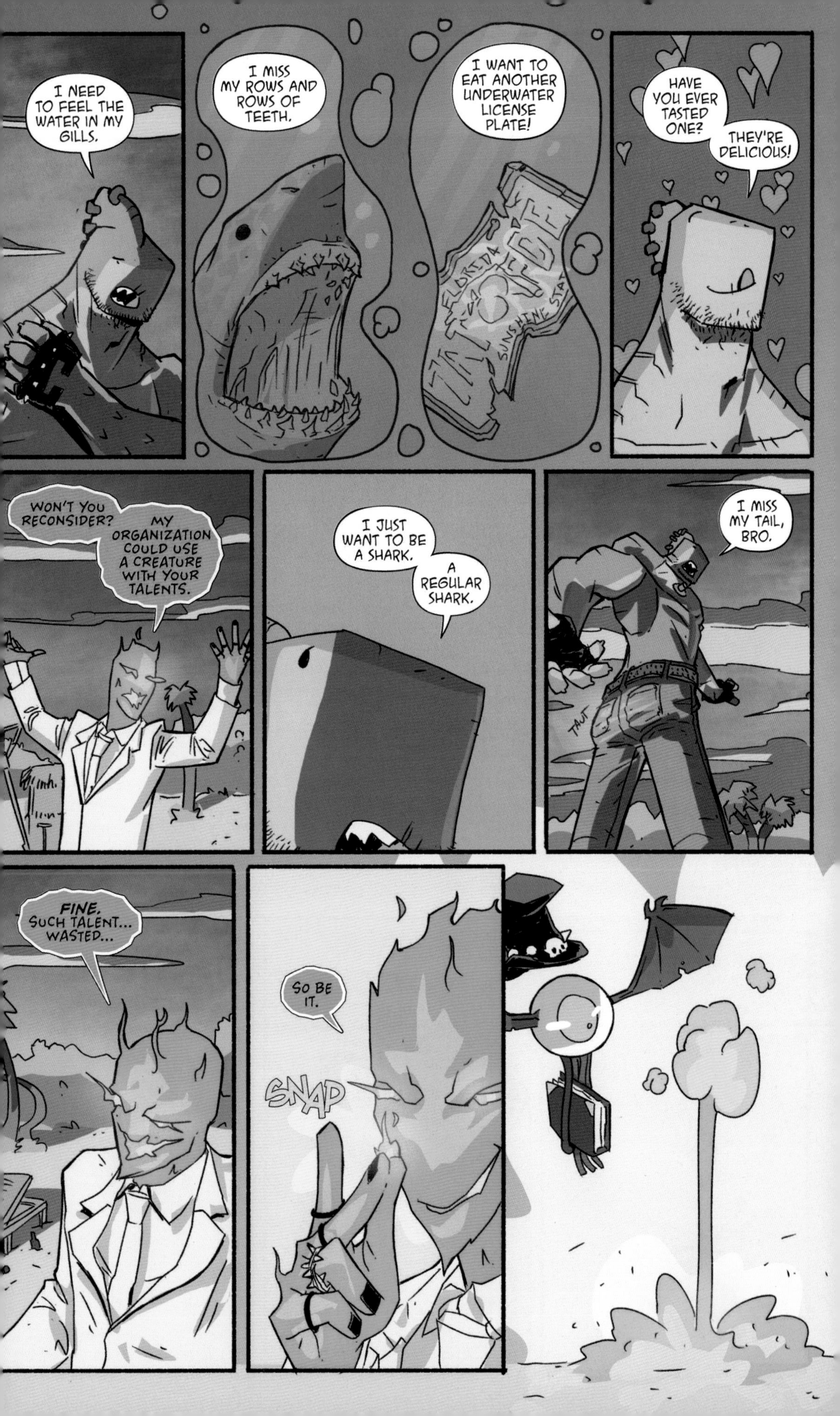
I NEED TO FEEL THE WATER IN MY GILLS.
I MISS MY ROWS AND ROWS OF TEETH.
I WANT TO EAT ANOTHER UNDERWATER LICENSE PLATE!
FLORIDA
SUNSHINE STA
HAVE YOU EVER TASTED ONE?
THEY'RE DELICIOUS!
WON'T YOU RECONSIDER?
MY ORGANIZATION COULD USE A CREATURE WITH YOUR TALENTS.
I JUST WANT TO BE A SHARK.
A REGULAR SHARK.
I MISS MY TAIL, BRO.
TAUT
FINE. SUCH TALENT... WASTED...
SO BE IT.
SNAP

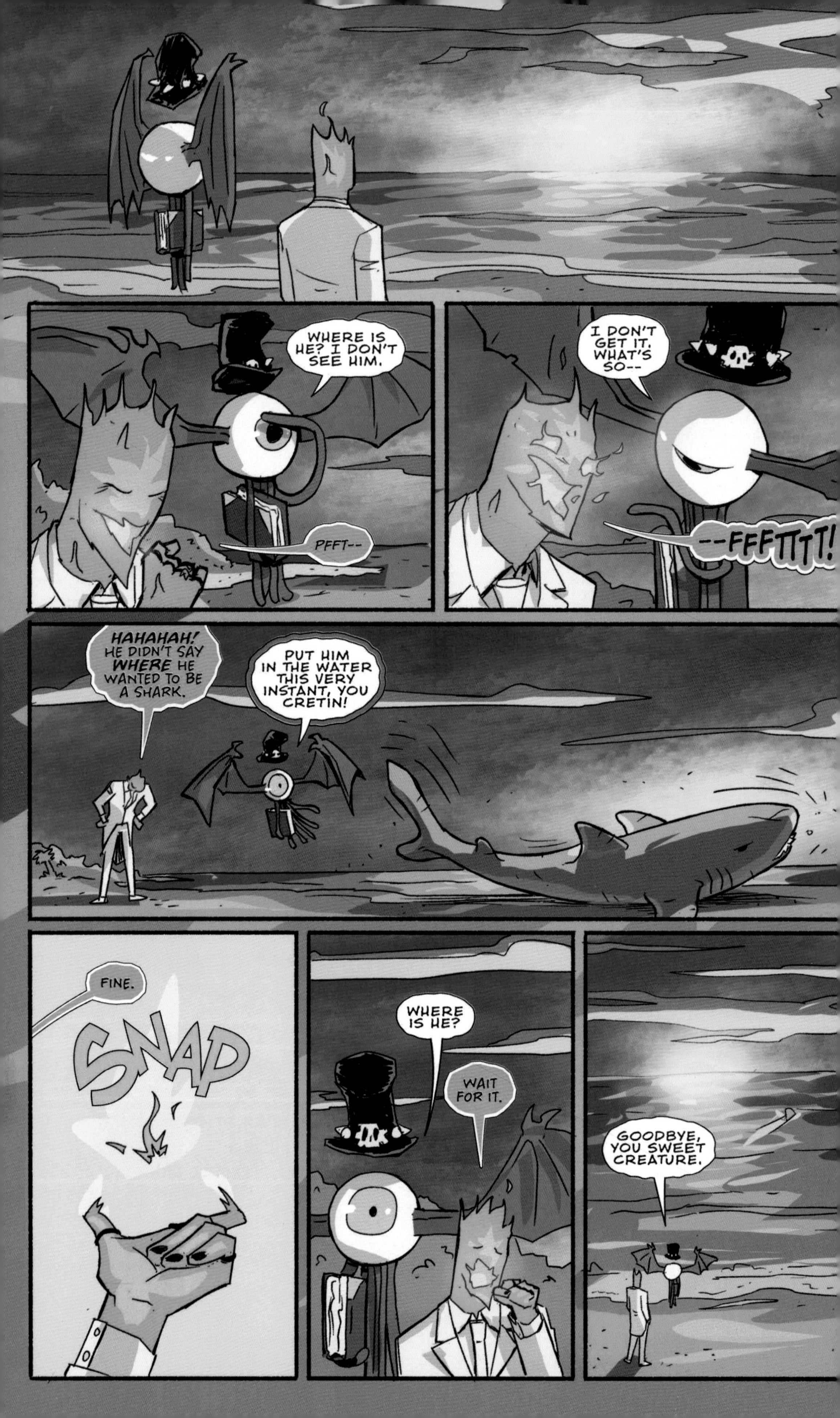
WHERE IS HE? I DON'T SEE HIM.
PFFT--
I DON'T GET IT. WHAT'S SO--
--FFFTTTT!
HAHAHAH! HE DIDN'T SAY WHERE HE WANTED TO BE A SHARK.
PUT HIM IN THE WATER THIS VERY INSTANT, YOU CRETIN!
FINE.
SNAP
WHERE IS HE?
WAIT FOR IT.
GOODBYE, YOU SWEET CREATURE.

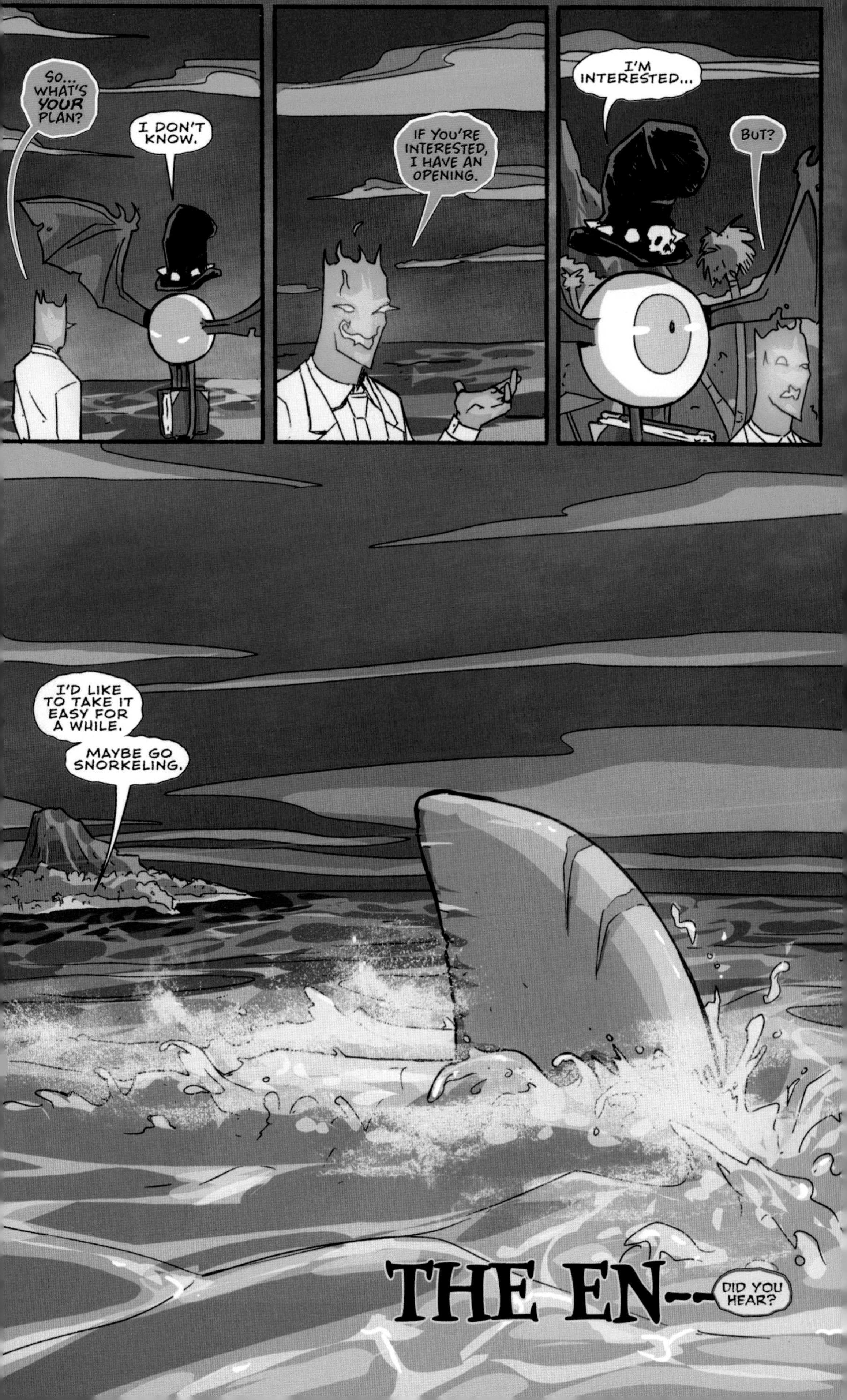

SO... WHAT'S YOUR PLAN?
I DON'T KNOW.
IF YOU'RE INTERESTED, I HAVE AN OPENING.
I'M INTERESTED...
BUT?
I'D LIKE TO TAKE IT EASY FOR A WHILE.
MAYBE GO SNORKELING.
THE EN--
DID YOU HEAR?

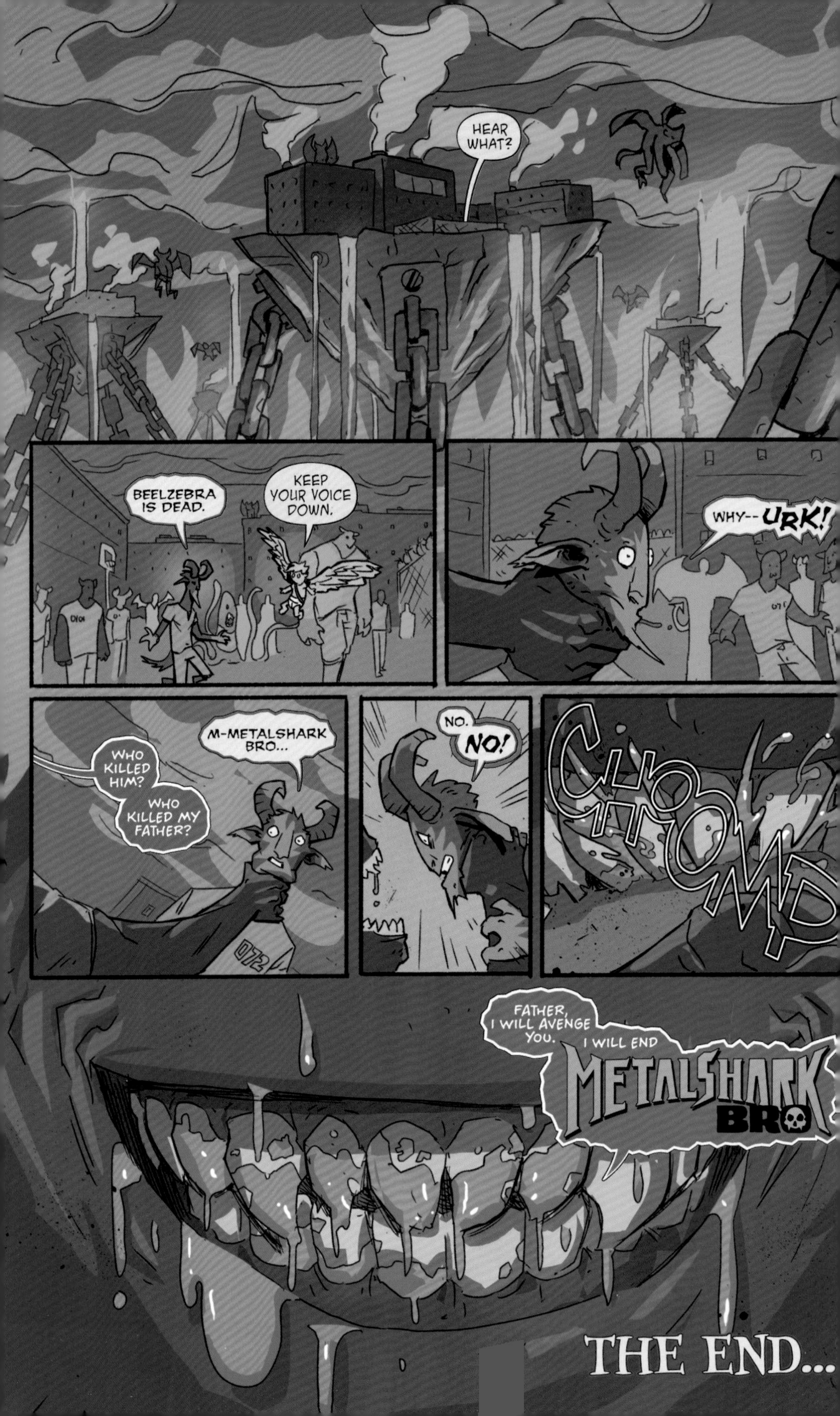
HEAR WHAT?
BEELZEBRA IS DEAD.
KEEP YOUR VOICE DOWN.
WHY-- URK!
M-METALSHARK BRO...
WHO KILLED HIM?
WHO KILLED MY FATHER?
NO.
NO!
CHOMP
FATHER, I WILL AVENGE YOU.
I WILL END METALSHARK BRO
THE END...

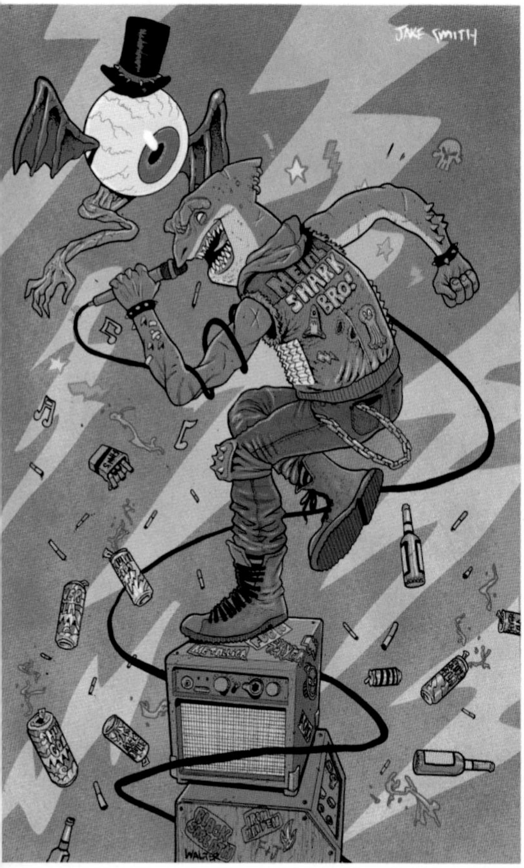
JAKE SMITH
METAL SHARK BRO!

JAKE SMITH

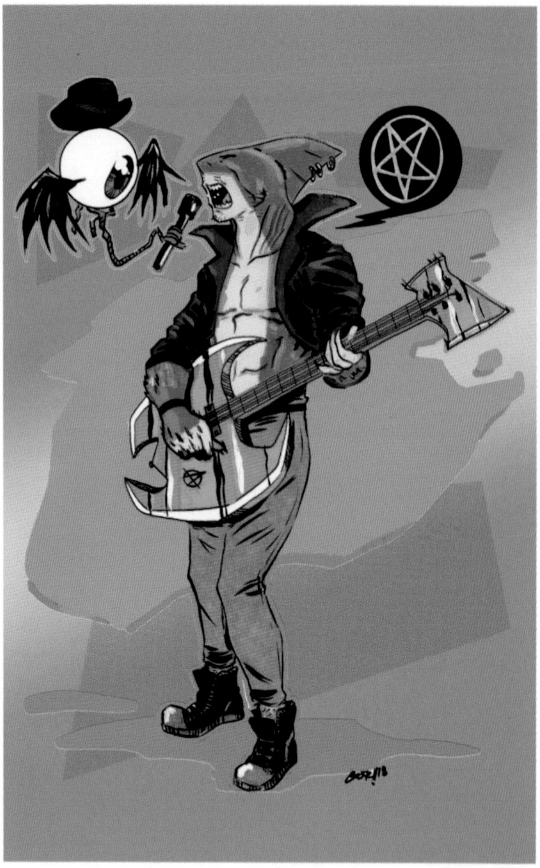

PAUL GORI

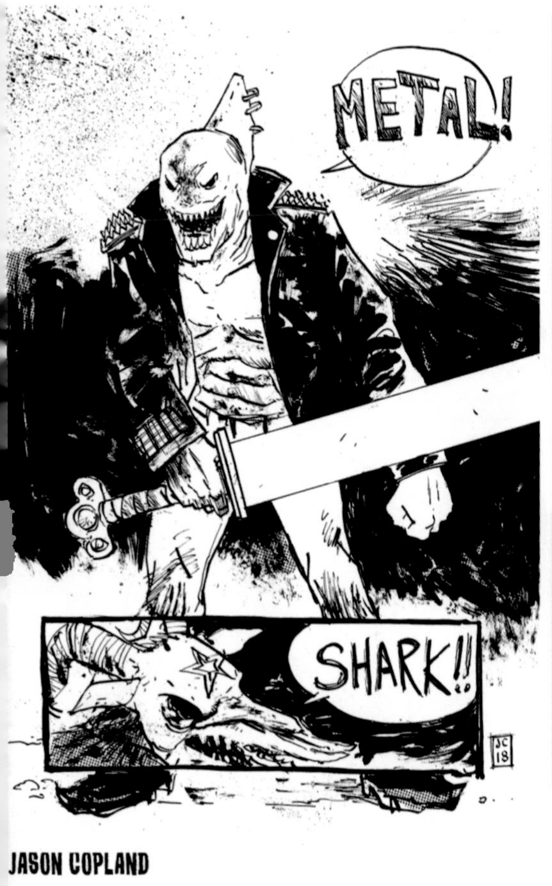
METAL!
SHARK!!
JC 18

JASON COPLAND

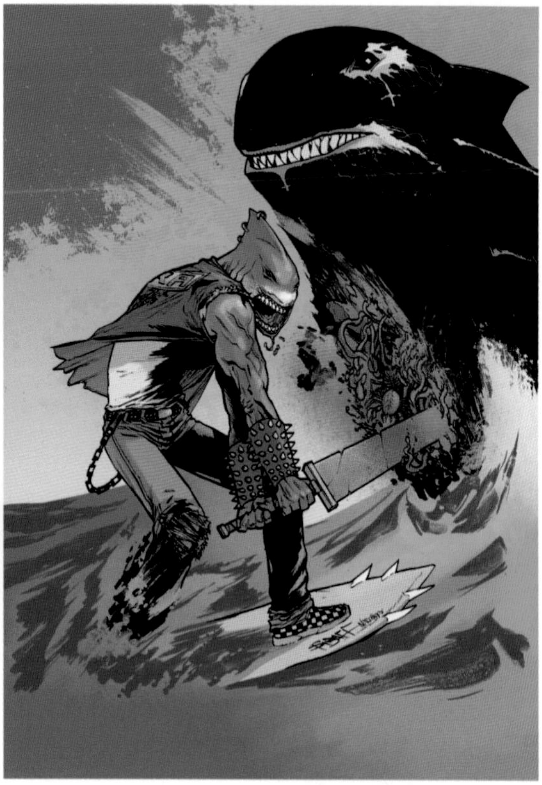

LINES - CHRISTIAN DIBARI
COLORS - CHRIS NORTHROP

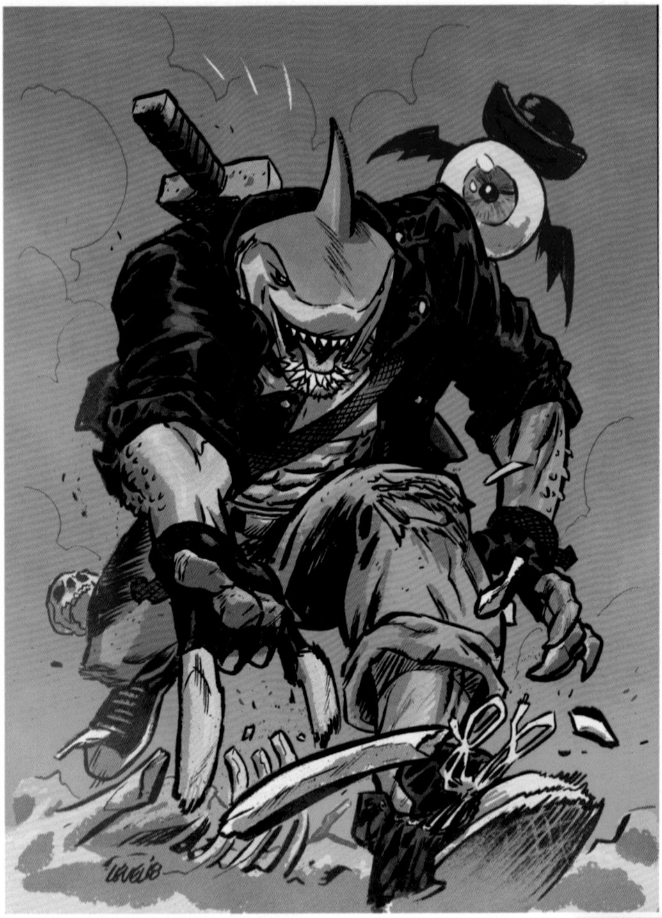

BRIAN LEVEL

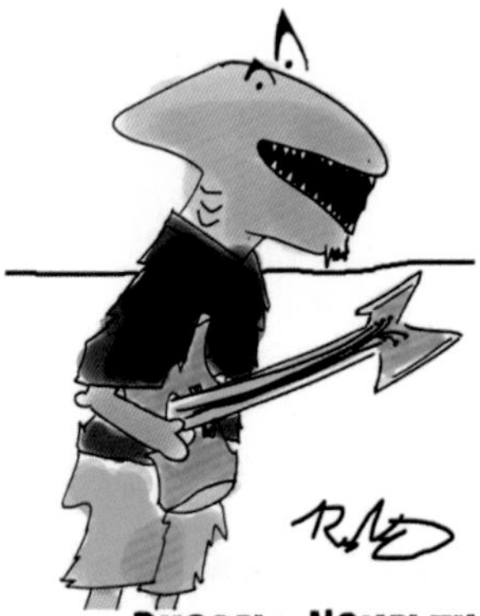

RUSSELL NOHELTY

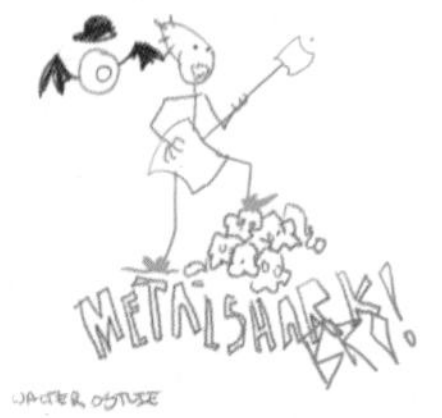
METALSHARK!
WALTER OSTLIE

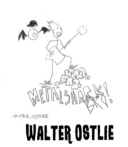

WALTER OSTLIE

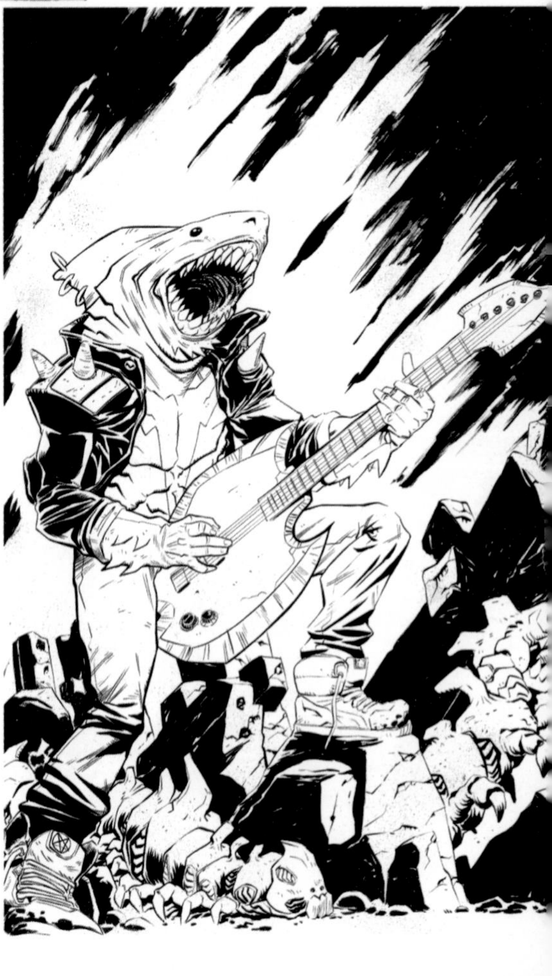

DREW MOSS

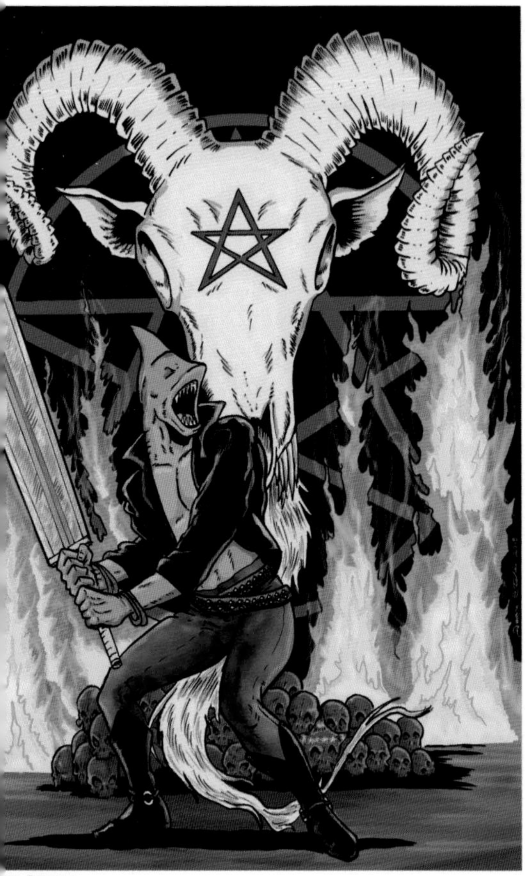

N STAHL

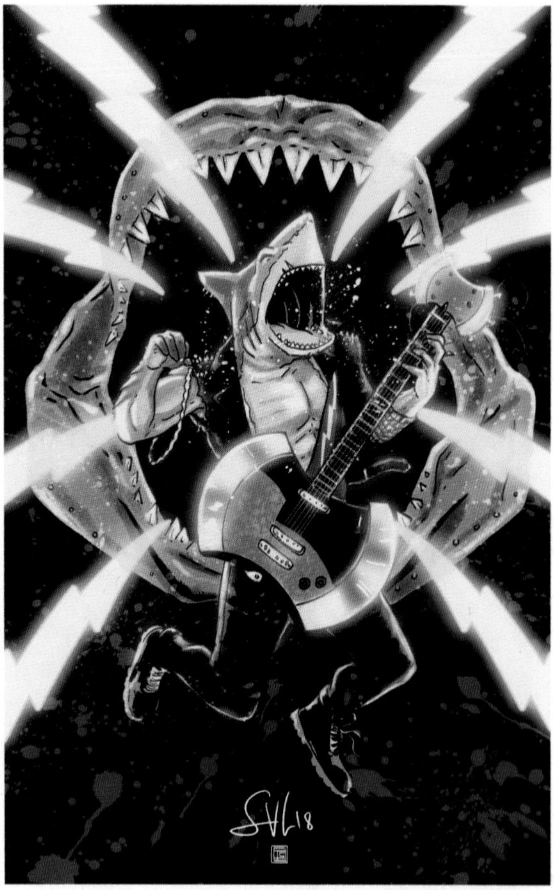

SEAN VAN GORMAN & TIM SHINN

MATT HARDING

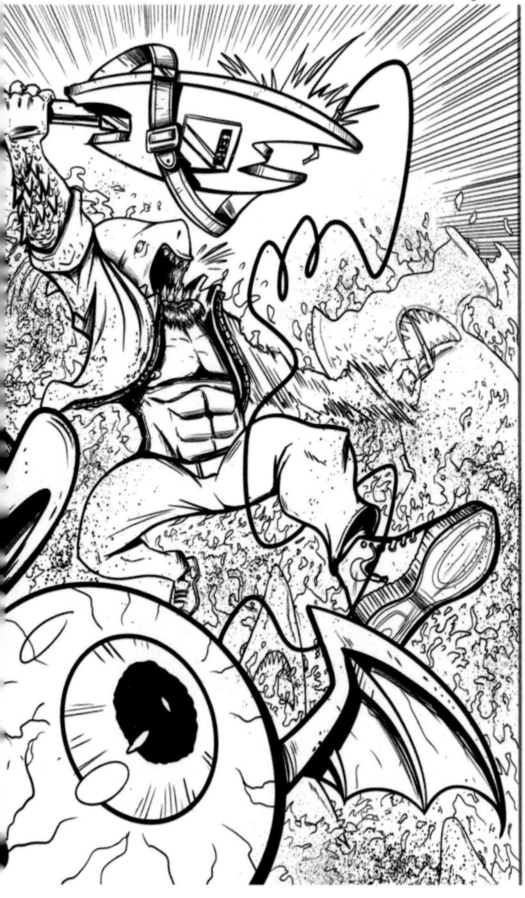

CHRISSYTOR

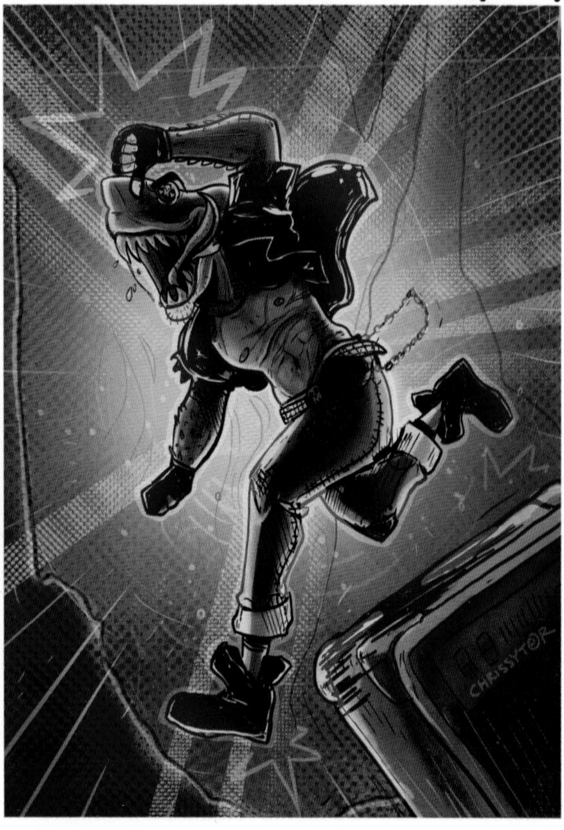
CHRISSYTOR

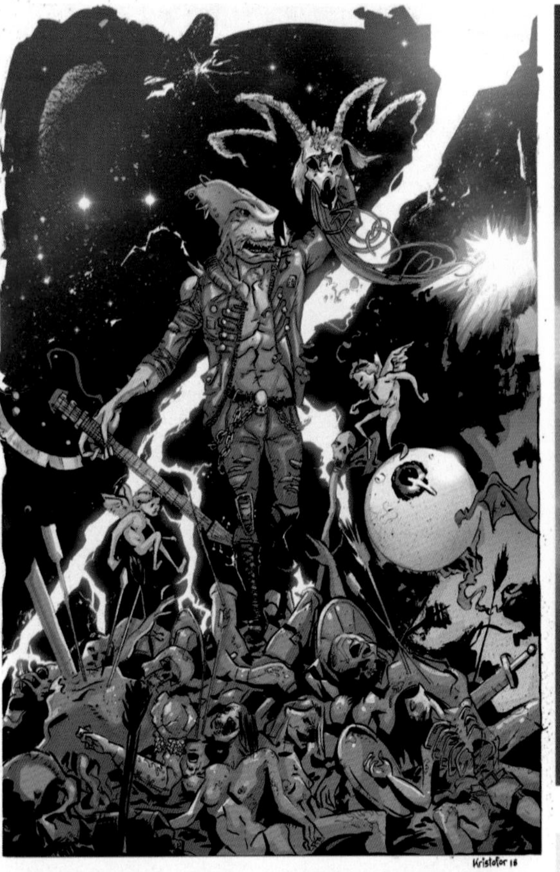

KRISTOFOR HARRIS   COLORS - JUAN MANUEL RODRIGUEZ

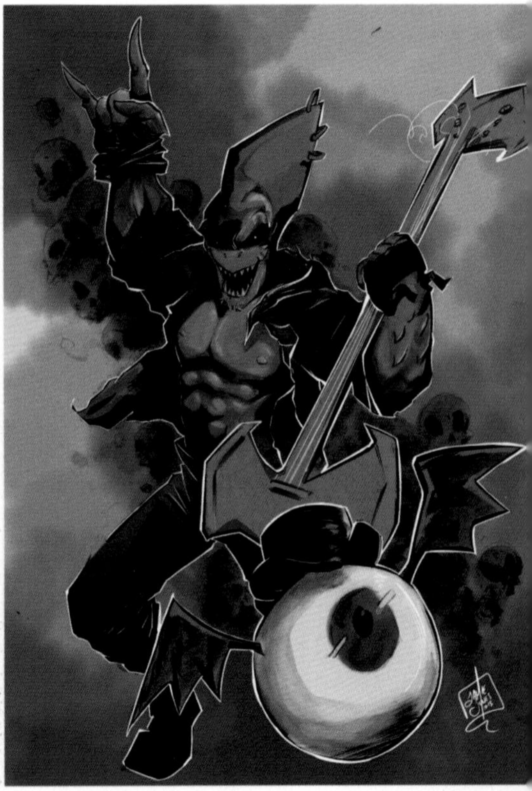

JAMIE JO

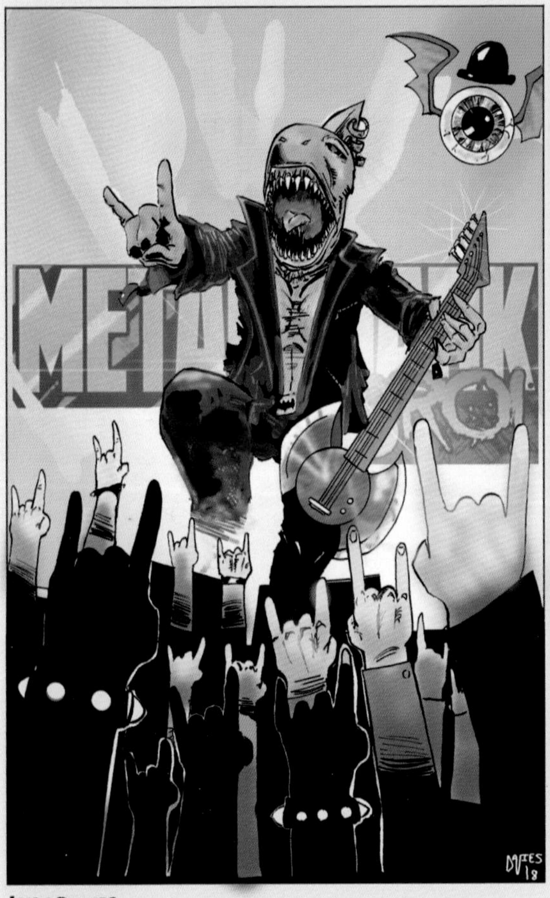

JOHN DAVIES

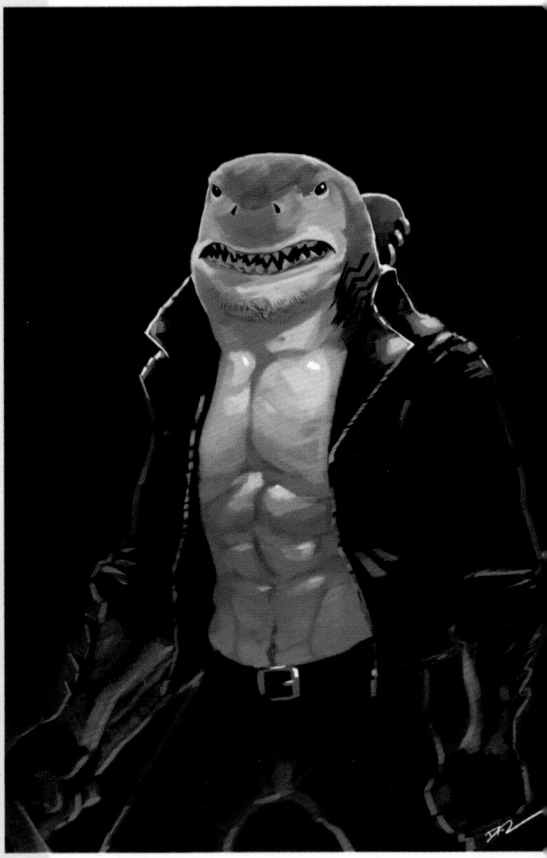

DARYL T

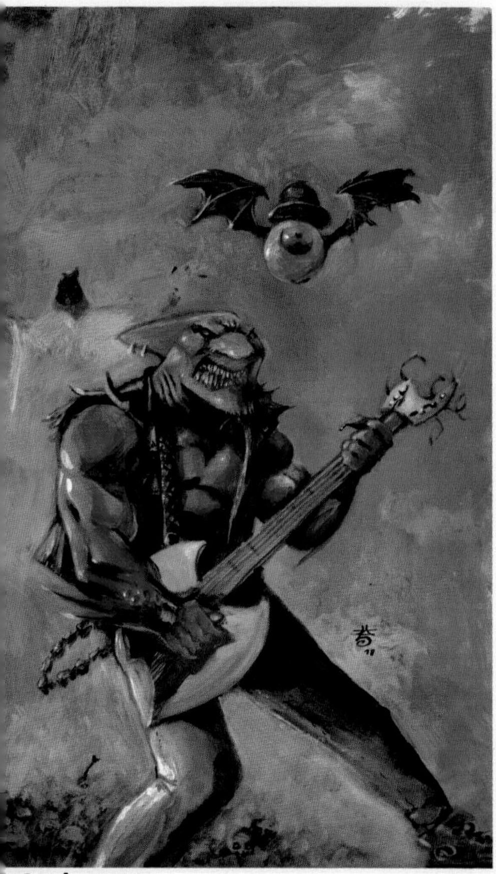

CESCO LAQUINTA

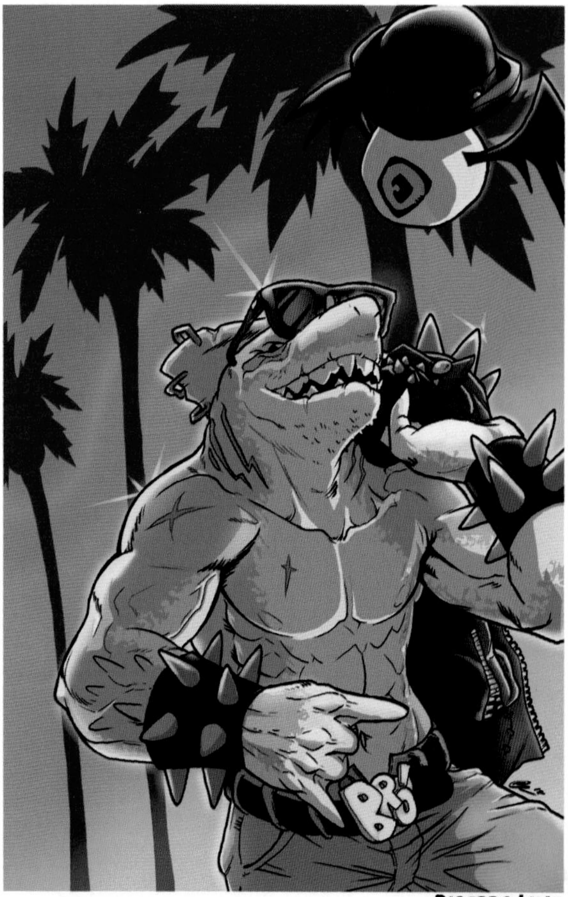
BB

RICARDO LIMA

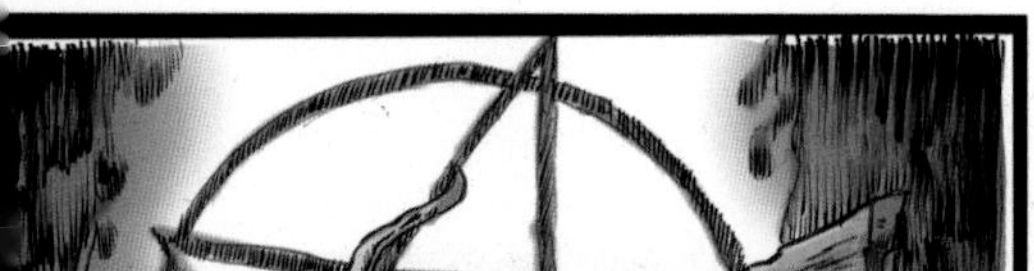

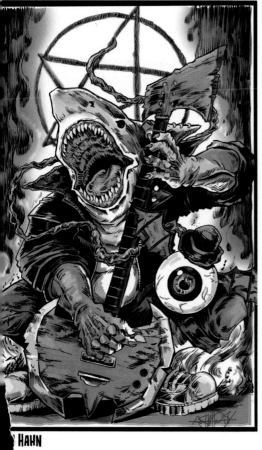

HAHN

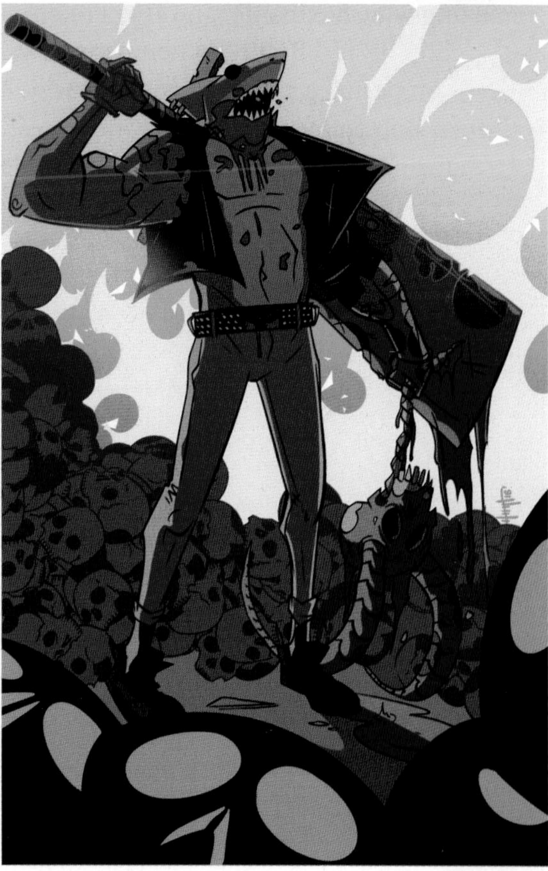

HOYT SILVA

METALSHARK BRO

ASSAULT ON HAMZIG ISLAND

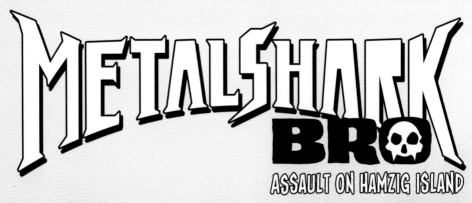

CREATIVE TEAM

Walter Ostlie

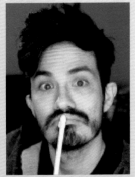

Walter Ostlie is a Florida-based writer and artist who has loved telling stories since he was a kid. He is the creator and artist of *Haxor, Shiver Bureau,Cubicles,* and co-creator of *Metalshark Bro*. Walter is also sharing his comic knowledge and experience on YouTube.

Bob Frantz is a writer who resides in Cincinnati, Ohio with his amazing wife, Stephanie, and two Pokemon-obsessed children, Sophie and Bobby. When he isn't writing funny books or preparing a snack for his kids who haven't touched their dinner, Bob enjoys coffee, fancy neckwear, and swearing at the TV during Machester City matches or New York Mets games. *Pic by Walter Ostlie.

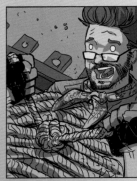

Bob Frantz

Kevin Cuffe

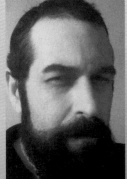

Kevin Cuffe is a father, a sorcerer, and sometimes a comic book author. When not podcasting with Bob Frantz or protecting the universe from malicious extra-dimensional entities, he is usually writing or watching AEW. You can find him on Twitter @Kevin_Cuffe or Instagram @The_right_cuffe.

Chas! Pangburn puts words in balloons. (That's his all-encompassing and cheesy way of saying that he's a writer, editor, and letterer.) He lives in Northern Kentucky with a chubby corgi and two stinky ferrets. Whether you're wanting to swap pet pictures or to talk shop, he can be reached at @chasexclamation on Twitter.

Chas! Pangb

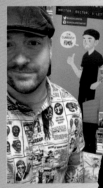